LIBERTY UNDER LAW

American Constitutionalism, Yesterday, Today and Tomorrow

Edited by

Kenneth L. Grasso
Cecilia Rodriguez Castillo

Project on American Constitutionalism
Southwest Texas State University
and
University Press of America, Inc.
Lanham • New York • Oxford

University Press of America,® Inc.
4720 Boston Way
Lanham, Maryland 20706

12 Hid's Copse Rd.
Cummor Hill, Oxford OX2 9JJ

Printed in the United States of America
British Library Cataloguing in Publication Information Available

Copublished by arrangement with
Project on American Constitutionalism
Southwest Texas State University

ISBN 0-7618-0691-1 (cloth: alk. ppr.)
ISBN 0-7618-0692-X (pbk: alk. ppr.)

™ The paper used in this publication meets the minimum requirements of American National Standard for information Sciences—Permanence of Paper for Printed Library Materials, ANSI Z39.48—1984

Contents

Part II: Constitutional Interpretation: Originalism and Its Critics

Part III: Contemporary Issues in American Constitutionalism

Preface

This volume is an outgrowth of the work of the Project on American Constitutionalism. Inaugurated in the Fall of 1992 by the Department of Political Science at Southwest Texas State University, the Project's mission is to promote scholarly inquiry regarding the nature and intellectual and cultural foundations of the American constitutional system, and the major controversies confronting the system today; and to promote informed public discussion of these topics.

The Project's very first initiative was the establishment of an ongoing "Lecture Series on American Constitutionalism." The essays contained in this volume are revised versions of selected lectures from the series: they are collected here in order to make them accessible to a wider audience.

As the project's current Director, I would be remiss if I didn't take this occasion to express my gratitude to those whose hard work made the lecture series–and hence this volume–possible. I particularly wish to thank my close friend and, until his recent retirement, colleague, Dr. Randall W. Bland. The founder and Director of the Project during its first year of existence, he deserves much of the credit for whatever we have accomplished over the past five years. Special thanks should also be extended to the graduate students who have assisted Randy and I in the administration of the lecture series at various points during the course of its existence: Roger Dunlop, Michael Ritterhouse, David Putz, and Robert Coker. Their labors–often above and beyond the call of duty–have been indispensable to the success of the series. Likewise, I wish thank all the scholars who have delivered lectures as part of the series, and, in particular, those whose work is included here for taking time out of their busy schedules to revise their talks for publication.

I would also be remiss if I did not take the opportunity to thank all those here at Southwest Texas State University whose support–financial and/or moral–has made the series possible. I particularly wish to thank SWT's University Lectures Committee; Dr. Leonardo Cardenas, Jr., the chair of SWT's Department of Political

Science at the time of the Project's inception, and Dr. Cynthia Opheim, his successor as chair; Dr. G. Jack Gravitt, the Dean of SWT's School of Liberal Arts; and Dr. Robert D. Gratz, SWT's Vice President for Academic Affairs. Finally, I wish to thank the Intercollegiate Studies Institute of Wilmington, Delaware for its generous ongoing financial support of the series.

My co-editor, Dr. Cecilia Rodriguez Castillo and I also wish to thank our families for their patience and support during our time consuming months of work on the book itself, and Valerie Davidson of SWT's Department of Political Science for her invaluable secretarial assistance with the preparation of the manuscript.

Kenneth L. Grasso
San Marcos, Texas
November 1, 1996

INTRODUCTION

Randall W. Bland

In recent decades, a number of intense debates have erupted regarding various aspects of the American constitutional order. These debates have not been restricted to the world of scholars and jurists. On the contrary, we have witnessed the emergence of ongoing public arguments about the intellectual and cultural foundations of our constitutional system; the norms governing constitutional interpretation and the proper role of the judiciary in this system; and the proper interpretation of certain key provisions of our fundamental law. Controversies about the meaning of the Constitution and the conformity of the actions of our political institutions to its provisions, it is true, are nothing new. Indeed, such arguments are as old as the republic itself. It does not follow, however, that they are unimportant. They go to the very heart of the American political experiment.

They do so because the American republic represents not only an experiment in democracy, an experiment in self-government and majority rule. It is also an experiment in constitutionalism, in limited government and the rule of law. Indeed, the idea of a government of laws rather than of men is fundamental to the *novus ordo seclorum* which America has historically seen itself as inaugurating.

Seen in this light, constitutional controversies of the type we are experiencing today threaten to engulf our political system in a crisis of the first magnitude. This system rests on consensual foundations. One of the cornerstones of the American constitutional order is the idea that government rightfully possesses only those powers delegated to it by the people, and may exercise those powers only on the conditions established by the people. "There is no position which depends on clearer principles," as *The Federalist* affirms, "than that every act of a delegated authority, contrary to the tenor of the commission under which it is exercised is void." The right of the government to command is thus contingent on its fidelity to its prior obligation to act in accordance with the procedures and limits established by the Constitution. To the extent that governmental actions are perceived by large numbers of Americans to lack constitutional warrant–to the extent, in particular, that the decisions of the nation's highest court are seen as mere impositions of the personal policy preferences of its members–the result can only be the progressive erosion of the moral authority of our constitutional system. In other words, the constitutional controversies which beset us today threaten our political system with a wholesale crisis of legitimacy.

These controversies are the subject of these essays. The first four essays address in various ways the question of the intellectual foundations and cultural preconditions of the American constitutional commonwealth. Thomas L. Pangle's essay addresses the nature of the American political experiment in the light of the debate between the Federalists and Anti-Federalists over the ratification of the Constitution. Seen against the backdrop of these debates it becomes clear, he argues, that the Constitution embodies a revolutionary and distinctively modern understanding of the nature and goals of politics. Francis Canavan, S.J., on the other hand, examines the theory of constitutional liberty championed by a contemporary of the American founders, Edmund Burke. The political philosophy of this great English statesman and thinker, he contends, contains important lessons for contemporary America about the nature and cultural foundations of constitutional governance.

In a manner reminiscent of Tocqueville, Jean Bethke Elshtain's essay explores the importance of local self-governance and the cultivation of certain habits of the heart to the vitality and ultimately the viability of the American experiment in ordered liberty. This same Tocquevillian spirit is reflected in Robert Booth Fowler's essay. Religion, he maintains, has played a pivotal and frequently overlooked role in creating the cultural capital on which our political system has historically traded.

The ongoing debate between the proponents of an originalist approach to constitutional interpretation and their nonoriginalist critics constitutes the subject matter of the volume's second section. William Gangi explores *The Federalist's* understanding of the role of the judiciary, contending that this understanding is informed by an unequivocally originalist theory of constitutional interpretation. Gerard V. Bradley argues that an originalist approach is indeed compatible with the outcome of many–if not all–of the Warren Court's innovations in the area of criminal procedure. Christopher Wolfe addresses from an originalist perspective the subject of *stare decisis*. More specifically, he explores the question of under what circumstances an originalist jurisprudence demands the overturning of a precedent that is unjustifiable on originalist grounds. Finally, Sanford Levinson offers a spirited critique of originalist jurisprudential philosophies. The originalist approach, he insists, is unsustainable in practice and hence, in the final analysis, operationally irrelevant.

The contributors to the final section examine several contemporary controversies over the meaning of specific constitutional provisions. The first two essays address the powers of the executive branch. Robert Scigliano examines what he sees as a new understanding of the president's war powers that has become dominant over the past fifty years. Robert J. Spitzer explores how our understanding of the presidential veto power has changed in the course of American history. The next three essays focus on the Supreme Court's interpretation of and the First Amendment. Thomas G. West's topic is the Court's reading of the First Amendment guarantee of freedom of speech and press. Contrary to the widely held view that in the course of the past half-century or so the Court has progressively expanded the boundaries of constitutionally permissible speech, West argues that in certain important respects the Court has significantly narrowed these parameters. The essays by George Weigel and David G. Dalin, on the other hand, focus on the First Amendment's religious provisions. Weigel offers a spirited critique of the church-state jurisprudence of the past fifty years, maintaining that the Court has made a "dangerous mess" of this vital area of our public law. Dalin offers an overview of the changing attitudes within the American Jewish community towards this jurisprudence. In the volume's final essay, Herman Belz examines the controversy surrounding affirmative action in the light of civil rights law, the equal protection clause of the Fourteenth Amendment, and the core principles of limited, constitutional government.

These essays, needless to say, will not be the final words on the subjects they address. They do, however, represent serious contributions to a number of critically important scholarly debates. It is hoped, moreover, that they help equip non-specialists to better understand today's ongoing constitutional controversies, and what they mean to our nation's future. These debates are simply far too important to be the concern of only specialists. Although complex and somewhat technical, the outcome of these debates will play an important role in determining the nature of the American polity and the future of our ongoing political experiment for without constitutionalism neither democracy itself, nor ultimately freedom can long endure.

Part I

American Constitutionalism

Theoretical Foundations and Cultural Preconditions

Chapter 1

The Achievement of the Constitution, as Viewed by the Leading Federalists

Thomas L. Pangle

My aim is to clarify what the most thoughtful Founders saw as the major overall achievement of their Constitution. I will proceed by locating the political thought of the Federalists in the tradition of the previous history of political philosophy. For in order to appreciate properly what the Founding Fathers felt to be their key achievement, one must see clearly the major, the awesome, problem they faced and believed they had overcome.

That problem, simply stated, is this: at the time of the Founding, there prevailed an almost universal doubt as to the viability, the very possibility, of a large-scale republic. Those who opposed or looked with skepticism on the new Constitution appealed to or started from the widely held conviction that America had only two possible avenues of future development. Either the nation could (and should) remain a rather loose confederacy of small republican states; or the nation would inevitably evolve into a centralized, authoritarian, and eventually despotic form of government, dominated by a military or economic oligarchy. This opinion was grounded, in the first place, on the universal experience of all known history: never had there existed a stable republic encompassing more than one city or a federation of sovereign cities. There *had* indeed existed aggressively imperialistic republics–Rome being the premier example–but their successful imperialistic expansion had always sounded the knell of doom for their republican institutions. In the second place, this opinion had behind it the unanimous authority of all great political theorists of the past and present: the tradition of political philosophy manifested a firm consensus to the effect that the very nature of free, republican government demanded a small-scale, urban society–a "polis" or "city."

Montesquieu's Articulation of the Consensus

The authoritative, traditional theoretical outlook was formulated with unrivaled depth and precision by the philosopher who was *the* most influential, *the* most frequently cited, of all philosophers among Americans at the time of the Founding: Montesquieu, the author of *The Spirit of the Laws*.[1] Montesquieu begins from the understanding of a republic as the form of government in which the people at large–or some substantial portion of the population–holds in its own hands the reins of power and responsibility. Now if this is to be truly the case, if a substantial portion of the citizenry is to have direct access to the wielding of governmental authority (partly by rotation of high offices) then the society must remain small, the government close to the people. But mere smallness of scale is only one crucial precondition of republicanism. There are other preconditions and conditions which are even more arduous.

A society whose government is in the hands of the people–in the hands of committees and assemblies in which many or most persons participate–requires in its citizens an intense public spirit. Each individual must dedicate himself to the good of the whole, must be willing to sacrifice much time, energy, and material prosperity to political or public service. In other words, republican government requires "virtue" as does no other form of government. Montesquieu calls "virtue" the "principle" or the "spring" of republics. *Virtue* means here patriotism, love of country–but not as an abstraction; virtue means *fraternity*, a sense of brotherhood that unites the citizenry and makes each feel as a part of a more significant whole. Such patriotism or fraternity requires a genuine homogeneity in the way of life of the inhabitants. Only persons who share the *same* religious beliefs, the *same* education, the *same* family habits, the *same* economic status–who have grown up together, sharing the same decisive experiences of joy and sorrow–can look upon one another with an authentic sense of brotherhood. Virtue is therefore the love of equality, meaning the love of like for like, and the love of and for a society that *prevents* sharp distinctions or pronounced diversity.

From all this it follows that a sound republic cannot be "liberal"–permissive or tolerant. The government in the hands of popular assemblies and their directorates must severely restrict luxury, conspicuous consumption, travel abroad, religious and artistic innovation. The personal lives of citizens, especially family life, where the crucial early education of children in habits of public dedication takes place, must be closely supervised by neighbors and fellow citizens. Individualism of all sorts–whether of excellence or of baseness–must be strictly limited and even discouraged. To find successful models of how republics work–in giving their citizenry enormous political liberty and responsibility, at the cost of personal liberty–Montesquieu referred to the great classical republics like Rome, Sparta and Athens, and to the republics that flourished in Northern Italy in the late Middle Ages. For the form of government that, in contrast to a republic, gave its people considerable personal liberty, Montesquieu pointed to monarchy. Monarchy he sharply distinguished from tyranny or despotism. Monarchy is a product of the evolution of feudalism in Europe, whereas despotism has its roots in pre-Christian Asia. Monarchy is the *limited* rule of one man, where power is checked and balanced by rival centers of power: an established church and its clergy; deeply rooted, and geographically diverse, hierarchies of noble families whose authority is based on inheritance; and strong local magistrates in numerous cities who answer to powerful commercial interests in each city. Monarchy, in other words, is a *mixed regime*, where political power is distributed among very distinct, permanent, and competing classes or "estates." Because power is so distributed, monarchies are "moderate" or undespotic, *without* placing much, if any, political power directly in the hands of the mass of the people. Various segments of the populace are subordinated to, and in some measure protected (though also exploited) by the different centers of power.

The stability of the monarchic balance of power and, even more, the vigor and energy of its military and its politics, depends on competition–between classes and estates, but also among individuals within each class or estate. The "principle" or "spring" of monarchy, according to Montesquieu, is *pride*: a sense of honor that is not incompatible with a certain vanity. Monarchy requires, then, very little "virtue." Monarchies can be much more permissive than republics, and can in fact encourage luxury, diversity, the freedom of women, erotic imaginativeness and artistic individuality. Besides, monarchy not only allows but requires a large-scale nation-state; it therefore promotes greater international security for its inhabitants and possesses much greater opportunities for commercial prosperity.

Montesquieu looked above all to England as the model of the kind of promise monarchy held out for human happiness. For England combined the traditional advantages of older European monarchies with radical new openness to commerce, which in turn promised a fast growth in scientific technology and general material well-being for all. Moreover, England combined the traditional, more aristocratic estates with a House of Commons which gave sovereign legislative power to a substantial portion of the people–not directly, but through the very indirect vehicle of "representation."

Montesquieu admired and even extolled the classical republic, with its noble sense of the common good and nigh monastic self-sacrifice; but he ultimately rejected republicanism as placing on men demands that were contrary to human nature–and therefore too fragile to be very practical and too prone to make men unhappy even when they were practicable. Now the conception of human nature to which Montesquieu appealed is one that he took over from his great teacher, John

Locke; and it is to Locke that we must turn in order to see most clearly the deep foundations of Montesquieu's thought.[2]

The Lockean Conception of Human Nature

Locke is the classic, i.e., the rhetorically most successful, exponent of the "state of Nature" doctrine, a doctrine taken over by Montesquieu and generally accepted or endorsed by literate Americans at the time of the Founding.[3] When this doctrine was first introduced by Thomas Hobbes, it seemed to most hearers outlandish or fantastic. But such was the gentle power of Locke's or his followers', sober rhetoric, that it came to be held as a popular article of faith. According to this teaching, man is not–as Aristotle and the great theologians of the Christian tradition had maintained–a "political animal" by nature. Politics of government is not "natural" but an artificial invention created by men to solve or overcome the terrible problems they "naturally" find themselves in. By nature, or before they use their reason to figure out how to "conquer" nature, men are in a chaotic state of anarchy, where no one is secure in life, liberty, or property. Men are by nature not organized in any stable social structure, but are rootless individuals, drifting in and out of various sorts of relations with one another. Men *invent* and enforce contracts and rules–especially the fundamental "social contract" or "social compact"–which set up political structures that give permanence and security to their lives.

While men have all sorts of natural drives and passions, which vary enormously from one individual to another, they have no generally agreed on goals or purposes or conceptions of "fulfillment." The one thing they do or can agree on is negative: a fear of painful death, and hence a goal of a kind–maximizing personal, material security. Each individual cannot help but seek and demand–as his "right," his "natural right"–life, liberty, and an opportunity to live in such a way as to be secure to pursue happiness however he may conceive it. Crucial to life and security are economic possessions or *property*; hence all men necessarily or "by nature" have a "right," to acquire and use property. All men seek these protections not solely for their individual selves, but also for their immediate families–which are stabilized by laws of marriage contracts and laws regulating parental and filial rights and duties.

Government, and political participation or leadership, is not–in this view of men–an end or a necessary, natural avenue for fulfillment. Government and civic virtue is a means, a tool or instrument, for providing more important goods than active involvement in government. The goal of government or the public sphere is the protection of the private sphere–of individual and family life.

The American Innovations

This Montesquieuian-Lockean outlook was shared almost universally by all factions in early America–by Anti-Federalists as well as Federalists, by Canadians and Loyalists as well as revolutionaries, and by most religious sects. To be sure, there were few who were *strict* Lockeans. In almost every mind, the dominant influence of the Enlightenment philosophers was muted and diluted by countervailing influences of both Judeo-Christian and Greco-Roman provenance. And of course some Americans saw more clearly, more perspicaciously, what the full implications and the full problems were in the prevailing outlook.[4]

Among the farseeing were James Madison and Alexander Hamilton, the authors of *The Federalist*. Indeed, this work is without a doubt the most profound and capacious of all the writing in defense and in explanation of the ideas underlying the Constitution.

Like Montesquieu their teacher, the authors of *The Federalist* look back with some veneration to the heroic figures of the ancient republics, brought to life in the pages of Plutarch's monumental biographies. The penname they chose, Publius, is the name of one of Plutarch's heroes–Publius Valerius Publicola–and testifies to their keen sense of being the heirs to a legacy. Yet, while bowing to the classics and the classical republics, the new Publius also expresses severe criticism of the classics and a proud sense of independence and innovation. According to *The Federalist*, the model of the classical republic is, in the final analysis, unnatural and disastrous in itself, as well as being inapplicable to and inappropriate for America:

> It is impossible to read the history of the petty republics of Greece and Italy without feeling sensations of horror and disgust at the distractions with which they were kept in a state of perpetual vibration between the extremes of tyranny and anarchy. If they exhibit occasional calms, these only serve as short-lived contrasts to the furious storms that are to succeed. If now and then intervals of felicity open themselves to view, we hold them with a mixture of regret, arising from the reflection that the pleasing scenes before us are soon to be overwhelmed by the tempestuous waves of sedition and party rage. If momentary rays of glory break forth from the gloom, while they dazzle us with a transient and fleeting brilliance, they at the same time admonish us to lament that the vices of government should pervert the direction and tarnish the luster of those bright talents and exalted endowments for which the favored soils that produced them have been so justly celebrated. . . . If it had been found impracticable to have devised models of a more perfect structure, the enlightened friends to liberty would have been obliged to abandon the cause of that species of government as indefensible.[5]

In *Federalist* Nos. 9 and 10, the authors trace the reasons for the deficiencies, in their view, of the classical republican model: the virtuous republic is necessarily short-lived because it is impossible to repress for very long, without resorting to fear and violence, the natural diversity of mankind. That diversity is one of opinion–religious, moral, and political opinion–but it is above all an economic diversity, an inequality and heterogeneity which inevitably arises from mankind's "different and unequal faculties of acquiring property." The natural distinctions of men lead necessarily to the development of factions and sects, or parties; and the small republic becomes very soon the scene of fierce partisan conflict. Witness the turbulent histories of Rome, Florence, Venice, and Athens. The dynamic of civil strife in popularly ruled assemblies is in the direction of mob rule and tyranny of the majority, by which minorities are oppressed and out of which demagogues and military despots regularly arise. Pericles in Athens is the example of the demagogue at his best; but usually the type is far, far less meritorious than was Pericles. The shifting whims of the mob or the militant majority render the rights and liberties of every individual insecure, constantly interrupt commerce and trade, discourage prudent management, both private and public, and lead to virtue being replaced by hypocrisy and fanaticism.

Yet in America the liberal or "moderate" mixed regime which Montesquieu favors as an alternative is not possible. Americans will not submit to an established religion or church; the nation lacks both a landed, hereditary aristocracy and a royal family with hereditary title to the executive power; besides, America is infused with a democratic spirit that reflects the essentially egalitarian character of its frontier society. America must, therefore, have a wholly republican form of government–but of a new, unprecedented sort. American must have a liberal republic or democracy, a political system that embodies Montesquieu's ideas in a new form, and with a somewhat altered spirit.

It is this, the Federalists insist, that the opponents of the new Constitution fail to understand. The Anti-Federalists refuse to confront the real problem, the new problem America faces. They still think in terms of the old categories, the old choices, that simply do not fit the new situation. A clear sign of their disposition is their recurring complaint about the "innovativeness" and "hurry," or sense of emergency, inspiriting the Federalists. The Anti-Federalists are essentially conservatives, who like so many conservatives are trying to preserve what has already passed away, and who therefore are entangled in basic contradictions.[6]

On the one hand, the Anti-Federalists evoke nostalgia for the virtuous republics of old. But at the same time they are avid promoters of commercial growth, and of the natural rights and liberties of individuals–especially in the private sphere. They do not seriously long for the total political commitment of the ancient Greeks and Romans: in fact they want to minimize the role of politics and government. They are zealous in their adherence to the doctrines of the state of nature, the Social Compact, the Rights of Man–doctrines which arise from *modern* political philosophy and which do not reflect either a strictly biblical or a classical conception of human nature.

On the other hand, leading Anti-Federalists like Patrick Henry look to the British constitution as the only model for a strong and free government. Yet they know, and admit, that this model is incompatible with the social conditions and political beliefs of Americans. As a result, they offer no alternative to the new Constitution. They call for simple government kept close to the people, and see the threat of oligarchy or aristocracy looming in every form of government. But they cannot show that the existing *state* governments are or will remain simple and small enough to be close to the people. They do not really want to break up the states into smaller republics, or to try to install classical citizenship with its awesome restraints. They admit the need for some national government supervening over the states– but they fail to show how it can be made *either* strong enough to perform the tasks it must perform *or* balanced enough to insure that it will not become oppressive.

But these unanswered questions and unmet challenges *are* answered and met by the proposed constitution. What are the chief features of the new, unprecedented, *liberal* republic?

The first of the chief features is the competitive, interest-group politics of this large, extended republican society. It is true that a large, diverse society renders impossible the classical goals of direct civic participation, homogeneity, brotherhood, and close mutual surveillance of and by the citizenry. It is equally true that this new larger republic lacks the permanent, clear, and deeply rooted class divisions and competition that moderate and animate Montesquieu's liberal monarchy. But this new republic does allow and foster a vast manifold of more petty and mutable competing interests–religious, geographic, ethnic, and especially economic. The diversity and heterogeneity makes the formation of a uniform majority faction unlikely and creates instead the likelihood of the formation of shifting majority coalitions, promoting compromise and accommodation among the competing factions.

This process can only work, however, if it is facilitated and channeled through appropriate governmental institutions, above all the institutions of representative government. Through elected delegates, the people–or the majority–retains control over the government without having to become directly involved in politics and without the possibility of the mob-atmosphere found in old-fashioned democratic assemblies. Besides, representative government can tend to filter and refine public opinion. The men chosen by a mixture of direct and indirect electoral processes are likely to be more educated, articulate, and farsighted than the average citizen; and the relative rarity of election days will make the public's judgment on these occasions more solemn and thoughtful. In other words, the system does presuppose and elicit some measure of civic spirit, moderation, and enlightened interest in government on the part of many–if not all–citizens. But even if a large number of the elected representatives turn out to be men of narrow vision and mean passions, their vices will be checked, and even channeled for the public good, by the need all will feel to appeal to a broad range of interests among their constituents–to bargain and compromise with other, competing representatives. The extended sphere of the large commercial republic will foment a constant clash of competing groups that will keep all within bounds and induce policy judgements that take into account a very wide spectrum of needs and demands.

Yet this mass of distinct, competing interests filtered through representatives is not sufficient to guarantee general liberty, security, and prosperity unless the representatives are in addition split up into competing institutions governed by regulations which guide the political give and take. The first and most deeply rooted institution is the *federal* system or structure. The Anti-Federalists contend that in the new scheme the states are not strong enough; but the Federalists argue that it is the states which are in need of being supervised. For they are not as extended, not as diverse internally, as the whole nation and are therefore more prone to the ancient republican ills of majority tyranny and oppression of minorities. Moreover, the Federalists insist, the national government must be energetic and powerful in order to accomplish the tasks everyone agrees it needs to do: defense, regulation of interstate and foreign commerce, and so forth. The Federalists contend, therefore, that America should *not* rely mainly on the federal system, on the states' opposition to the national government, to check the national government. Instead, the principal control on the central government should arise from *within*, from its own checks and balances among executive, legislative, and judicial branches. This *separation of powers* (yet another fundamental political principle taken over largely from Montesquieu) is therefore the real mainstay of sound republican guarantees, in the opinion of the Federalists.

In Montesquieu, the divisions and competition between different branches and sub-branches of government–between the House of Lords and House of Commons, between king and Parliament, between courts with popular juries and king's officials–reflect the division and competition between distinct classes. In the American scheme, *this* basis for division of power does not exist, and a substitute must be artificially created. All the branches or sub-branches have *similar* constituencies: all are either elected by popular majority or appointed by officers who are so elected. But each branch is given a *part* of the popular constituency, selected in a different way, and exercising its choice at a different interval or time. The hope is that different segments of the general public, or the same segments acting at different times, will be distinct enough to elect representative who differ, compete, and keep one another honest. Moreover, their roles once in office are so defined as to make their personal interests–ambition, above all, but also economic advantage–necessarily competitive. Two farmers may be close friends back home in Iowa; but if one gets into Congress, and the other gets appointed to a presidential commission, they are likely to come into conflict. The Federalists look with special hope to the Senate, whose members are selected from a large enough constituency, and for a long enough time period, to promote in them a longer-range view of their ambitions and of the broad, national reputations they might win. The fears about the Senate expressed by some of the Anti-Federalists (namely, that the senators would become a kind of nobility or aristocracy) miss the point: a senator does not derive his prestige and power from any hereditary position of family history he represents or brings to his position as senator, but solely from the institution of government to which he is elected. Hence his interest and ambition are necessarily tied to, and regulated by, that institution, its rules, and its limited, competitive situation *vis-à-vis* the other major branches of government.

As Herbert Storing has suggested, the one branch of government in the American constitutional system which was and is most open to the sorts of doubts or fears the Anti-Federalists voice is the judiciary. The federal court system under the

Constitution–and especially the Supreme Court–is a very undemocratic institution in its tenure, mode of selection, and largely secret mode of deliberation; what is more, the Supreme Court exercises an aristocratic, supervisory check on the more democratic legislative and executive branches as well as on the state governments. Yet, Storing pointed out, the irony is that the greatest success of the Anti-Federalists actually enhanced the role of this most aristocratic branch created by the new Constitution. For it was the agitations and complaints of the Anti-Federalists–seconded by Jefferson–which compelled the addition to the Constitution of the Bill of Rights; and these amendments in the long run gave to the federal courts enormous additional scope for the exercise of their powers.[7]

Indeed, one may say that the Anti-Federalists' struggle for the inclusion of a Bill of Rights, while it did lead to genuine and substantial improvement in the Constitution, reveals starkly the Anti-Federalists' limited understanding of the issues at stake in the great debate over ratification. The need for a *national* Bill of Rights in addition to the existing state bills of rights presupposes a strong national government which can only be checked by a strong national judiciary and a strong national public opinion.

By the same token, the Federalists' argument *against* a Bill of Rights are rather weak, intrinsically, and often verge on self-contradiction. Sometimes the Federalists go so far as to contend that a Bill of Rights is unnecessary because the Constitution they have proposed leaves the greatest power and therefore the protection of rights, to the state governments! But in addition to this bizarre states-rights argument, the Federalists make the more telling point that the enumeration of certain rights in a set of written amendments may have the effect of disestablishing unmentioned but important rights. After all, *can* all the rights of man be neatly specified? Yet this argument would seem to be met, in part at least, by the exercise of great care in drawing up, in wording, the amendments: the eventual Ninth Amendment is obviously a response to the concern expressed here. Generally speaking, the Federalists tend not to appreciate sufficiently what is perhaps the deepest or most significant Anti-Federalist argument for a Bill of Rights: the argument that such a Bill will have a profound *educational* effect, reminding citizens of the ultimate moral principles and limits or goals of the regime founded on the rights of man.

This reflection leads us to the most far-reaching Anti-Federalist criticism of the new Constitution and the spirit or thought behind it. This criticism the Anti-Federalists advance often and in manifold forms–but without complete coherence. Put simply it is as follows: is there sufficient cultivation of civic virtue, sufficient attention to the moral education and formation of the citizenry, in the regime being proposed? Is the populace at large adequately guided toward patriotism, toward a vigorous watchfulness, pride, and manly capacity to fight and make sacrifices to protect the rights of all individuals? One could add the allied question: Is there adequate provision for encouraging and fostering men of unusual, rare political gifts–statesmen of vision and sublime ambition, leaders who will chastise democracy and the democratic spirit, who will stand against the inevitable tide toward exaggerated egalitarianism? Characteristically, the Anti-Federalists focus much less on this latter question or doubt. That is to say, they do not bespeak the classical or traditional republican spirit, with its focus on the superior political man within a republican setting. Similarly, the Anti-Federalists do not generally view politics as man's highest or noblest vocation.

In this key respect, the Federalists–especially Hamilton, in his great *Federalist* on the presidency–are closer to the spirit of classical republicanism. The Federalists respond to the Anti-Federalists' worry over the lack of provisions for education in popular virtue by arguing that love of country and willingness to become actively engaged in self-government are promoted above all by the spectacle of a vigorous and efficient national government, a government that earns the respect and gratitude of its citizens and arouses in some the vision of glorious and challenging national careers.[8]

One must admit, however, in favor of the Anti-Federalists and their animadversions that some of those worries would have been shared by the great political philosophers of antiquity and even (perhaps) by Montesquieu. The philosophers' expressions of concern would indeed have taken a different form and been characterized by a different emphasis. The ancient philosophers would no doubt have been troubled by the absence of any strong restraint on commercialism, avarice, and acquisitiveness in the new regime; they would have deplored the unleashing, the all-out promotion, of economic competition for limitless private property accumulation and the attendant liberation of the selfish desire for gain. They would have regretted the absence of encouragement of some sort of collective religious sentiments or beliefs that would elevate somewhat the hopes, and restrain the hedonistic passions, of the citizenry. They would have looked askance at the fact that virtue, although it remains a genuine concern, is honored predominantly as a means, a necessary instrument for freedom and prosperity, rather than as a noble end in itself or source of intrinsic dignity. In the same vein, they would have been sorry to see the extent to which rare or outstanding statesmen, when they do arise, are viewed by the Federalists and their spiritual heirs as "*servants* of the people" rather than as the goals, the purposes, of the regime and people.[9]

Such criticisms, however, come from and express a way of thinking and living that lies largely outside the horizon of the debate between Federalists and Anti-Federalists. It is important that we remember that there exists such a radically un-American or pre-American republican tradition, so that we do not commit the vulgar but prevalent error of identifying the alternatives available to us as human beings with the alternatives History or Fate have imposed upon us. To be good citizens, i.e. thoughtful, critical, *free* citizens, we need to study with some reverence the great debates that attended our Founding and learn the intellectual and spiritual power of the protagonists; but we also need to try to see those protagonists as they saw themselves–as the initiators and the critics of something radically new, of a great "experiment," which opposed and must be seen in opposition to a previous, great republican as well as monarchic tradition.

Notes

1. Alexander Hamilton, James Madison, and John Jay, *The Federalist Papers*, with an introduction by Clinton Rossiter (New York: The New American Library, 1961).

2. For a more complete presentation of Montesquieu's political thought see Thomas L. Pangle, *Montesquieu's Philosophy of Liberalism: A Commentary of the Spirit of the Laws"* (Chicago: University of Chicago Press, 1973).

3. See John Locke, *Two Treatise of Government*, ed. Peter Laslett (New York: Cambridge University Press, 1988).

4. For a more complete discussion of the influence of John Locke on the American Founders see Thomas L. Pangle, *The Spirit of Modern Republicanism: The Moral Vision of the American Founders and the Philosophy of John Locke* (Chicago: University of Chicago Press, 1988).

5. Hamilton, Madison, and Jay, *The Federalist Papers*, 71-72.

6. See Herbert J. Storing, *The Complete Antifederalist*, 7 vols. (Chicago: University of Chicago Press, 1981).

7. See Herbert J. Storing, "The Constitution And the Bill of Rights" in *Taking The Constitution Seriously: Essays on the Constitution and Constitutional Law*, ed. Gary L. McDowell (Dubuque, IA: Kendall/Hunt Publishing Co., 1981).

8. For a more complete evaluation of education in the United States see Thomas L. Pangle, *The Ennobling of Democracy: The Challenges of the Postmodern Age* (Baltimore, MD: The John Hopkins Press, 1992).

9. For a comprehensive discussion of the natural law tradition see Leo Strauss, *Natural Right and History* (Chicago: University of Chicago Press, 1953).

Chapter 2

Burke and the Problem of Constitutional Liberty

Francis Canavan, S. J.

Edmund Burke died nearly two hundred years ago, in 1797. He was not an American but an Irishman who was a member of the British House of Commons. The late Alfred Cobban wrote of him: "As a school of statesmanship, Burke's constitutional theory remains of permanent value; as a working system it was dead almost before it was expounded."[1] We may wonder, then, what he has to tell Americans that is relevant to our problem of constitutional liberty. The answer is that he was an exponent of the Whig tradition of limited, constitutional government that Americans inherited from Great Britain.

We must agree with Cobban at least to this extent, that the aristocratic political system that Burke loved was beginning to die even as he defended it. I should perhaps explain that, descended as I am from a long line of Irish peasants, I have no nostalgia for the days when a British aristocracy not only ruled but owned the land on which my ancestors lived. My feelings about that matter, however, are irrelevant to our present subject. I will only attempt here to present Burke's idea of liberty as accurately as I can within the brief compass of this essay.

Let us begin with the words of Walker King, one of Burke's disciples and in later life a co-editor of the first set of Burke's collected *Works*: "The assumption of arbitrary power, in whatever shape it appeared, . . . was the sure object of his detestation and hostility."[2] Liberty, for Burke, was essentially freedom from the exercise of arbitrary power. It was not freedom from all authority, or Everyman's right to do his own will.

Burke's most famous work, *Reflections on the Revolution in France*, was provoked by a speech that the Dissenting minister, Richard Price, gave in 1789, in praise of the French Revolution. But years earlier Dr. Price had similarly provoked Burke to controversy[3] with his *Observations on the Nature of Civil Liberty*.[4] In that work, having listed the several kinds of liberty, Price said: "In all these cases there is a force which stands opposed to the agent's *own* will; and which, as far as it operates, produces *Servitude*."[5] Burke, on the contrary, did not think of liberty as the supremacy of will, but as supremacy of reason governing mere will.

He agreed that "the distinguishing part of our [British] constitution is its liberty." But, he added, "the liberty, the only liberty I mean, is a liberty connected with order, that not only exists along with order and virtue, but which cannot exist at all without them. It inheres in good and steady government, as in its substance and vital principle."[6] On a later occasion he asked: "What is liberty without wisdom, and without virtue? It is the greatest of all possible evils; for it is folly, vice, and madness, without tuition or restraint." Giving people freedom in that sense is all too easy; "It only requires to let go the rein." To combine liberty with order, however, is a demanding task. "To form a *free government*; that is, to temper together these opposite elements of liberty and restraint in one consistent work, requires much thought, deep reflection, a sagacious, powerful, and combining mind."[7] Liberty, for Burke, is ordered liberty.

Civil society, he maintained, is a consequence of man's nature as a social and political being. Yet civil society and its authority, in Burke's mind, were at once a requirement of man's nature and an artificial construct of human minds and wills, which could therefore vary from one civil society to another. "Although Government certainly is an institution of Divine authority [because implicit in God's creation of human nature], Burke explained, "yet its forms, and the persons who administer it, all originate from the people."[8]

Burke therefore preferred to appeal to historically-evolved liberties rather than to liberty in the abstract. "Abstract liberty, like other mere abstractions," he said in his great *Speech on Conciliation with the Colonies*, "is not to be found. Liberty inheres in some sensible object; and every nation has formed to itself some favorite point, which by way of eminence becomes the criterion of their happiness." In the long struggles for liberty in England, this point was the people's right not to be taxed by the king without their own consent, and so also in America.[9]

Speaking in more general terms, Burke refers in his *Reflections* to the famous Petition of Right which listed historic rights of Englishmen, and which Parliament enacted into law in the reign of Charles I. The authors of that law, says Burke, were as fully acquainted with all the general theories about "the rights of men" as Dr. Price or the Abbé Sieyès. "But for reasons worthy of that practical wisdom which superseded their theoretick science, they preferred this positive, recorded, *hereditary* title to all which can be dear to the man and the citizen, to that vague speculative right, which exposed their wild litigious spirit."[10] Burke preferred rights given legal definition in the course of historical experience to rights derived by deduction from abstract ideas.

Human reason, he insisted, should not function in politics and law in the way it does in geometry. Throughout his career Burke detested the kind of rationalism that spins out all the implications of an abstract principle, without regard to circumstances or consequences. He fought it whether the principle was the sovereignty of the British Parliament over the American colonies or the French Revolution's "the rights of men." For him, political reason was largely prudential reason that, without forsaking principles, adapted them to concrete situations.

He did not deny that human life must be governed by moral principles which man does not create but must obey. Quite the contrary. For example, when he received a letter in November 1791 from a papal nuncio praising him for his efforts against the French Revolution, he felt obliged to remark in his reply, "Had the power you serve continued What some centuries ago it had been a more bitter Enemy to it could not be found than the person who now has the honor to address you." But he went on to explain:

> I have ever hated Tyranny under all the forms, it may assume, and there is none which it cannot take. It is Equally odious to me whether it be Regal or ecclesiastical, or Military or Judicial or popular. . . . My Abhorrence to the perversion of Authority arises from my Zealous attachment to it whilst it continues in its proper Course. I love order so far as I am able to understand it, for the universe is order.[11]

Burke's devotion to liberty and his hatred of tyranny are rooted in his conviction that man lives in an ordered universe created by an intelligent and personal God. He therefore believed in a natural moral law grounded in God's creative act. Natural law is the highest and ultimate limit on political power. Thus, when the House of Commons impeached Warren Hastings, the East India Company's Governor-General of Bengal, Burke and the other managers of the impeachment argued for the conviction of Hastings in terms of natural law. Partly they did this because they did not think they could convict Hastings of violations of English law for crimes committed in India, where the Company held power by grant from the Mogul Empire, not from the British Crown. But, whatever other managers may have thought, Burke at least really believed in the natural moral law, and appealed to it in dramatic terms in his opening speech before the Lords.

Hastings had argued that when the Company accepted sovereignty over Indian states, it gained despotic and arbitrary power, for such power was the accepted constitution of Asia and the only means of governing an Asian society. Burke replied that "Arbitrary power is a thing, which neither any man can hold nor any man can give." For "we are all born in subjection . . . to one great immutable, pre-existent law, . . . by which we are knit and connected in the eternal frame of the

Universe." All dominion of man over man is given by God and "is bound by the eternal laws of Him, that gave it, with which no human authority can dispense."[12]

But it was not only the tyranny of an individual that natural law prohibited: "Neither the few nor the many have a right to act merely by their own will, in any matter connected with duty, trust, engagement, or obligation."[13] This applies with particular force to a majoritarian democracy: "A perfect [i.e., unalloyed] democracy is . . . the most shameless thing in the world" and "is also the most fearless."

For a whole people should never be punished because "as all punishments are for example towards the conservation of the people at large, the people at large can never become the subject of punishment by any human hand." It follows, however, that it is "of infinite importance that they should never be suffered to imagine that their will, any more than that of kings, is the standard of right and wrong. They ought to be persuaded that they are full as little entitled, and far less qualified, with safety to themselves, to use any arbitrary power whatsoever."[14]

If the people are to exercise power, they must do it with a strong and humble sense of their responsibility:

> When the people have emptied themselves of all the lust of selfish will, which without religion it is utterly impossible they ever should, when they are conscious that they exercise, and exercise perhaps in a higher link of the order of delegation, the power, which to be legitimate must be according to that eternal immutable law, in which will and reason are the same, they will be more careful how they place power in base and incapable hands.[15]

In this passage we see that, for Burke, reason and will are the same in God, but not in man. God's will is always rational and good, and so also is God's eternal and immutable law. Human law must also be rational and aim at what is good for human beings: "We may bite our chains if we will, but we shall be made to know ourselves, and he taught, that man is born to be governed by law; and he, that will substitute *will* in the place of it, is an enemy to GOD."[16]

Even the power of the people, therefore, must always be in accordance with that law if it is to be legitimate. No human agency, not even the whole community, is entitled to exercise arbitrary power, because will must ever be subordinate to reason. It follows that a theory of freedom, though it necessarily takes men as having free wills, cannot make the essence of freedom lie in the unfettered human will. Liberty is freedom from arbitrary will, not the right to act on arbitrary will.

Burke believed in natural law and in natural rights. He also thought that the liberties of Englishmen were the product of centuries of historical experience, and objected strenuously to appealing directly to the rights of men in a pre-political state of nature. He did not set nature and convention against each other, but saw human nature as realizing itself through conventions. Society and culture for him were historically-evolved networks of conventions which, when shaped in conformity with the common nature of humanity, provided man with his truly natural environment:

> The state of civil society . . . is a state of nature; and much more truly so than a savage and incoherent mode of life. For man is by nature reasonable; and he is never perfectly in his natural state, but when he is placed where reason may be best cultivated, and most predominates. Art is man's nature.[17]

Society, then, is an artificially constructed order meant to serve the needs of human nature: "If civil society be made for the advantage of man, all the advantages for which it is made become his right."[18] But society is not designed to translate every individual's right to govern himself in the pre-political state of nature into a right to vote in the government of civil society: "As to the share of power, authority, and direction which each individual ought to have in management of the state, that I must deny to be amongst the direct original rights of man in civil society; . . . It is a thing to be settled by convention."[19]

Burke's view clearly is not democratic but aristocratic and paternalistic. It insists that the purpose of government is the good of the whole people. "All political power which is set over men, . . . being wholly artificial, and for so much a derogation from the natural equality of mankind at large, ought to be some way or other exercised ultimately for their benefit."[20] The primary question, for Burke, is which form of government, in a particular country with its particular culture and history, best serves the welfare of the people, in which welfare he included their liberty as well as their lives and property.

Government, therefore, is a trust held for the good of the people. Burke went so far as to say: "The King is the representative of the people; so are the Lords; so are the Judges." But what he meant was only this: "They are all trustees for the people, as well as the Commons, because no power is given for the sole sake of the holder."[21] He did not mean, however, that the people can confer this trust only by electing the men who exercise the trust.

Commenting on the penal laws against Catholics in Ireland (who were three quarters of the population of that country) he explained the necessity of the people's consent to law in these terms:

> Now, as a Law directed against the mass of the Nation has not the nature of a reasonable institution, so neither has it the authority: for in all forms of Government the people is the true Legislator; and whether the immediate and instrumental cause of the Law be a single person, or many, the remote and efficient cause is the consent of the people, either actual or implied; and such consent is absolutely essential to its validity.

Normally, in Burke's mind, the consent of the people to the constitution and laws of the country was implied by the fact that they had lived and flourished under them for generations, so that the government had acquired a prescriptive title to authority. He therefore said:

> The people are presumed to consent to whatever the Legislature ordains for their

> benefit; and they are to acquiesce in it, though they do not clearly see into the propriety of the means, by which they are conducted to that desirable end. This they owe as an act of homage and just deference to a reason, which the necessity of Government has made superior to their own.

It does not follow, however, that the people may be presumed to consent to blatant acts of injustice such as the Irish penal laws:

> But though the means, and indeed the nature of a publick advantage, may not always be evident to the understanding of the subject, no one is so gross and stupid as not to distinguish between a benefit and an injury. No one can imagine, then, an exclusion of a great body of men, not from favours, privileges and trusts, but from the common advantages of society, can ever be a thing intended for their good, or can ever be ratified by any implied consent of theirs. If, therefore, at least an implied consent is necessary to the existence of a Law, such a Constitution cannot in propriety be a Law at all.[22]

The order in which men can be considered to be free must be an order constituted by reasonable and substantially just laws, to which the people may fairly be presumed to consent.

Such an order is one that protects due and ordered liberty by maintaining a government of limited and balanced powers. That was the ideal that Burke held up in November 1789 to a young Frenchman who had written to him asking his assurance that the French were worthy of being free; that they would be able to distinguish liberty from license and a legitimate government from a despotic one; and that the revolution now begun in France would succeed.[23] In his reply, Burke first defined liberty:

> Permit me . . . to tell You what the freedom is that I love and that to which I think all men intitled. It is not solitary, unconnected, individual, selfish Liberty. As if every Man was to regulate the whole of his Conduct by his own will. The Liberty I mean is *social* freedom. It is that state of things in which Liberty is secured by the equality of Restraint; a Constitution of things in which the liberty of no one Man, and no body of Men and no Number of men can find Means to trespass on the liberty of any Person or any description of Persons in the Society. This kind of liberty is indeed but another name for Justice, ascertained by wise Laws, and secured by well constructed institutions.

Burke then gave a cautious answer to the questions his young French friend had posed:

> When therefore I shall learn, that in France, the Citizen, by whatever description he is qualified, is in a perfect state of legal security, with regard to his life, to his property, to the uncontrolled disposal of his Person, to the free use of his Industry and his faculties;–When I hear that he is protected in the beneficial Enjoyment of the Estates, to which, by the course of settled Law, he was born, or is provided with a fair

> compensation for them;–that he is maintain'd in the full fruition of the advantages belonging to the state and condition of life, in which he had lawfully engaged himself, or is supplied with a substantial, equitable Equivalent;–When I am assured, that a simple Citizen may decently express his sentiments upon Publick Affairs, without hazard to his life or safety, even tho' against a predominant and fashionable opinion; When I know all this of France, I shall be as well pleased as everyone must be, who has not forgot the general communion of Mankind, nor lost his natural sympathy in local and accidental connexions.[24]

Such was the liberty that Burke thought that the Whig Revolution of 1688 had preserved for the English, and which he sincerely wished for other nations. In the Whig view of history to which he subscribed, English liberty had largely been achieved by struggle against the efforts of the Crown to make itself independent of Parliament. Freedom from arbitrary power, therefore, for Burke, in the early and greater part of his political life, depended primarily on checking the efforts of the young King George III to regain the personal power that his Hanoverian ancestors had allowed to slip into the hands of parliamentary leaders. It was only the advent of the French Revolution that fully awakened Burke to the possibility that a political class without property or inherited rank and social standing could take over a government and turn it into a radical dictatorship.

Whether George III or the French revolutionaries really were as dangerous as Burke thought is a question I shall leave to the historians, who anyhow are not of one mind on it. For the present purpose, which is to explain Burke's idea of liberty, it is enough that he thought they were dangerous.

His main objects in regard to George III were, first, to limit his power to choose his ministers of state and, next to reduce his political influence in the House of Commons. In his first great political pamphlet, *Thoughts on the Cause of the Present Discontents* (1770), Burke proposed that the king, whose right to choose his own ministers was undeniable, should appoint them, as it were, in a bloc, under a First Lord of the Treasury (or Prime Minister), who would take office at the head of a group of minsters committed to a party program. Political parties had hitherto been regarded merely as factions, and therefore disreputable. Burke legitimized them: "Party is a body of men united, for promoting by their joint endeavors the national interest, upon some particular principle in which they are all agreed."[25] The result of accepting this definition would have been to make a ministry responsible to Parliament as well as, and even more than, to the king. Burke was ahead of his time on this point, but he foreshadowed the cabinet government of the following century and the severe limitation on royal power it involved.

Burke made two proposals for reducing royal influence in the House of Commons in his *Speech on Economical Reform* in 1780. He proposed to limit the King's ability to use the money voted for his personal support as a political slush fund; and he advocated eliminating many of the sinecure offices in the royal household to which the king could appoint members of the Commons. He largely failed to get what he wanted and, even in 1782 when his party, the Rockingham

Whigs, enjoyed one of its brief periods of power, he did not achieve all that he had proposed in 1780. But his intention was clear. It was not to abolish the monarchy, but to make it part of a limited and balanced constitution.

In the government of the British Empire, Burke did not wish to limit the power of Great Britain's Parliament.[26] He was an imperialist, but an enlightened one who urged Parliament to use its power wisely and justly. Imperial power, like all power, was a trust held ultimately from God.

Burke never wanted American independence, but neither did he want America to be subdued by force. When independence came, he accepted it graciously and without rancor. Ireland, in Burke's lifetime, was a separate kingdom under the British Crown, but in fact a British colony ruled by a clique that in the 1790's began to call itself "the Protestant Ascendancy." Burke called this governing clique "the curse, scourge, and bane of the Irish nation,"[27] and stated this opinion of it, in varied words, many times in the course of his life. Since India was even more remote from Britain than Ireland was, not only geographically but religiously and culturally, Burke said in his *Speech on Fox's East-India Bill* in 1783, "All these circumstances are not, I confess, very favourable to the idea of our attempting to govern India at all. But there we are; there we are placed by our situation."[28] So far, he said, we have been doing a bad job of it: "Our Indian government is in best state a grievance."[29] In all of these areas, America, Ireland, and India, the policy that Burke advocated was not independence for the colonies but reform of the government in the interest of the natives.

The last great area of Burke's political concern was France after the outbreak of the French Revolution. It led to a painful break with the Whig party to which he had belonged, and which was now led, after the death of the Marquis of Rockingham, by Burke's former associate and friend, Charles James Fox. Fox and other Whig leaders saw in the Revolution the advent of British liberty in France, and they rejoiced in it. Burke saw in it an attack on the whole social, political, cultural religious, and property order of Christendom, and he dedicated the rest of his life to trying to arouse the governments of Europe to crush it before it crushed them.

He had been uneasy about it from its beginning. As time went by, the questions and doubts he had expressed to his young French correspondent in 1789 hardened into a certainty that the Revolution was a total one. More and more he identified the revolutionaries with their most radical wing, the Jacobins. Even after the fall of Robespierre and the suppression of the Jacobin clubs, he continued to call the revolutionary leaders Jacobins because they were still committed to the principles of the Revolution.

The Revolution had concentrated all power in the National Assembly. By confiscating the property of the Church and legalizing the seizure of the property of the landowners, it had rendered private property ineffective as a check on the power of the state. It leveled all ranks and classes in society, and produced a governing class "merely political, and wholly unconnected with birth or property,"[30] a class therefore whose avenue to wealth and social importance lay in gaining political power. The Revolution thus eliminated the intermediate orders that stood between individuals and the state. In so doing, it weakened the monarchy and eventually abolished it altogether.

Finally, it sought to drive from men's minds the Christian religion which was the inspirational source and unifying bond of European civilization, and to substitute for it a purely secular enlightenment. "What is Jacobinism?" Burke asked in 1795, and answered:

> It is an attempt . . . to eradicate prejudice out of the minds of men, for the purpose of putting all power and authority into the hands of the persons capable of occasionally enlightening the minds of the people. For this purpose the Jacobins have resolved to destroy the whole frame and fabrick of the old societies of the world, and to regenerate them after their fashion. To obtain an army for this purpose, they every where engage the poor, by holding out to them as a bribe the spoils of the rich . . . As the grand prejudice, and that, which holds all the other prejudices together, the first, last, and middle object of their hostility is Religion.[31]

By depriving the people of their religion, said Burke, the Jacobins also weaken their morals and destroy their liberty:

> Society cannot exist unless a controlling power upon will and appetite be placed somewhere, and the less of it there is within, the more there must be without. It is ordained in the eternal constitution of things, that men of intemperate minds cannot be free. Their passions forge their fetters.[32]

The Jacobins, he said, are a minority in France. They pretend to be democratic, but in fact are an oligarchic dictatorship who have gained and exercise power by "unity in design, and perseverance, and boldness in pursuit." Against such men the Old aristocratic order has been helpless. "We have not considered as we ought the dreadful energy of a state in which property has nothing to do with the government." We must therefore "reflect again and again on a government, in which the property is in complete subjection, and where nothing rules but the mind of desperate men."[33]

Under the government of these desperate men, Revolutionary France, which began in the radical individualism of democratic ideology, ends in sheer statism:

> In that country, entirely to cut off a branch of commerce, to extinguish a manufacture, to destroy the circulation of money, to violate credit, to suspend the course of agriculture, even to burn a city, or to lay waste a province of their own, does not cost them a moment's anxiety. To them the will, the wish, the want, the liberty, the toil the blood of individuals is as nothing. Individuality is left out of their scheme of government. The state is all in all.[34]

Burke's basic objection to the Revolution was not that it abolished monarchy. Even while the Revolution still left Louis XVI on his throne, he commented: "I believe that most thinking men would prefer infinitely some sober and sensible form of a republick, in which there was no mention at all of a king, but which held some reasonable security to property, life, and personal freedom."[35]

His comments on the American republic show that he was sincere in that remark. Even in 1789, before he had fully made up his mind about the French Revolution, he wrote to a friend, "I should doubt, whether in the end France is susceptible of the Democracy that is the Spirit, and in good measure too, the form, of the constitution they have in hand. It is except the idea of the Crowns being hereditary much more truly democratical than that of North America."[36] The *Parliamentary History* reports him as saying in 1791, "The people of America had, he believed, formed a constitution as well adapted to their circumstances as they could." It was, of course, a republican constitution, because it had to be one: "They had not the materials of monarchy or aristocracy among them." But they had "formed their constitution, as nearly as they could according to the model of the British constitution."[37]

Burke believed that the surest safeguard of constitutional liberty was aristocratic government. He did not mean, however that a kingdom was best off under aristocratic domination. In Great Britain at least, he said that it has not been so:

> If in our own history, there is any one circumstance to which, under God, are to be attributed the steady resistance, the fortunate issue, and sober settlement, of all our struggles for liberty, it is, that while the landed interest, instead of forming a separate body, as in other countries, has, at all times, been in close connection and union with the other great interests of the country, it has been spontaneously allowed to lead and direct, and moderate all the rest.[38]

The aristocracy, then, fitted into a composite constitution in which no one branch of government ruled absolutely. This was the model Burke held up to the French revolutionaries. "Have they never heard," he asked in his *Reflections*, "of a monarchy directed by laws, controlled and balanced by the great hereditary wealth and hereditary dignity of a nation; and both again controlled by a judicious check from the reason and feeling of the people at large acting by a suitable and permanent organ?"[39] Twenty years earlier, in his *Thoughts on the Cause of the Present Discontents*, he had described that organ as the House of Commons, which "was not instituted to be a controul *upon* the people" but "a controul *for* the people."[40]

Burke's constitution of balanced Crown, Lords, and Commons is obviously out of date in Great Britain (but is nearer to being alive in these United States). Yet his constitutionalism has features that are permanently valid. The principal ones seem to be the following.

Liberty must be thought of as freedom from arbitrary power, not as the individual's right to do his will since his will can be just as irrational and unreasonable as the abuse of power. A rational and ordered liberty can exist only under the rule of law. We must therefore think of law, not as the imposition of some wills on other wills, but as being in principle the rule of reason, despite what we know about the grimy reality of the way in which in fact laws are made.

The rule of reason rests on the willingness of the people at large to accept principles of justice and civic virtue as objectively valid and binding upon themselves. It is not enough that they agree on a form of government and a set of procedural rules. For their political system depends on a cultural complex of customs, manners, morals, and religious beliefs that came into being in the course of history and can disappear in the course of history. One of the deepest problems now confronting the United States, I suggest, is whether our democracy can stand the cultural and moral disintegration we are now going through.

I am not suggesting, however, that we need a new and better political ideology. On the contrary, we need today, as much as in Burke's time, to come to the end of ideology and of what Michael Oakeshott called rationalism in politics. Burke rejected it in favor of another use of reason, namely, the prudent application of basic principles to concrete political problems. Hence he favored learning from experience and relying on historically-evolved rights and liberties.

While he certainly had little faith in democracy, he insisted that government is a trust held for the good of the whole people. Even a democracy (or especially a democracy) therefore needs a government of limited and balanced powers. More importantly, the power of government must be checked and kept within proper limits by private property, strong intermediary institutions, and the moral consensus of the people. Only so can we prevent domination by a political class whose power and prestige depend on its control of the government.

Burke is surely not the only writer from whom we can learn these lessons. But we can still learn from him today, with profit to ourselves and to our country.

Notes

1. Alfred Cobban, *Edmund Burke and the Revolt against the Eighteenth Century* (London: Allen & Unwin; New York: Macmillan, 1929), 71.

2. Edmund Burke, *The Works of the Right Honorable Edmund Burke* (London: F.C. & J. Rivington, 1808-1827), 13:viii.

3. Edmund Burke, *The Correspondence of Edmund Burke*, ed. Thomas W. Copeland (Cambridge: University Press; Chicago: University of Chicago Press, 1958-1878), 3:254, n. 4.

4. Richard Price, *Observations on the Nature of Civil Liberty*, 3rd ed. (London: T. Cadell, 1776).

5. Ibid, 3.

6. Burke, *Works*, 3:8.

7. Burke, *Works*, 5:433, 434.

8. Burke, *Works,* 2:288.

9. Burke, *Works*, 3:49-51.

10. Burke, *Works*, 5:76-77.

11. Burke, *Correspondence*, 6:459-460.

12. Burke, *Works*, 13:165-166.

13. Burke, *Works*, 6:201.

14. Burke, *Works, 5:179.*
15. Burke, *Works*, 5:180.
16. Burke, *Works,* 13:169.
17. Burke, *Works*, 6:218.
18. Burke, *Works,* 5:120.
19. Burke, *Works*, 5:121.
20. Burke, *Works*, 4:11,
21. Burke, *Works*, 2:288.
22. Burke, *Works*, 9:348-349.
23. Burke, *Correspondence*, 6:32.
24. Burke, *Correspondence*, 6:42-43.
25. Burke, *Works*, 2:335.
26. Burke, *Works,* 3:69-71.
27. Edmund Burke, *Correspondence of the Right Honourable Edmund Burke*, ed. Charles William, Earl Fitzwilliam, and Sir Richard Bourke (London: Francis & John Rivington, 1844), 4:66.
28. Burke, *Works*, 4:44.
29. Burke, *Works*, 4:42.
30. Burke, *Works*, 7:52.
31. Burke, *Works*, 9:402 and *Correspondence*, 8:129-130.
32. Burke, *Works*, 6:64.
33. Burke, *Works*, 8:255.
34. Burke, *Works*, 8:253.
35. Burke, *Works*, 8:130.
36. Burke, Correspondence, 6:25.
37. *Parliamentary History of England from the Earliest Period to the Year 1803*, ed. William Cobbett (London: Printed by Thomas Hansard for Longmans, Hurst, Rees, etc. 1806-1820), 29:365-366.
38. Burke, *Works*, 8:400.
39. Burke, *Works*, 5:229.
40. Burke, *Works*, 2:288.

Chapter 3

The City, the Law and the Civic Philosopher

Jean Bethke Elshtain

Why is so much political theory so abstract, so removed from any concrete recognition of the lives people live? Why are political theorists so often driven to create blueprints for civic life that resemble grand empty hotels, places in which no embodied creature of the human sort could possibly feel at home? As I put it in *Public Man, Private Woman*:

> A person, after all, is not merely or exclusively . . . an objectified role-player or abstracted object of inexorable laws, but a thinking acting being engaged in particular relations with others within a specific historic time and place. To assimilate public and private into universal laws and abstracted structures requires Abstract Man, Abstract Woman, and Abstract Child in turn. Within this rarified, undifferentiated realm one searches in vain for a recognizable person and a redeemable politics.[1]

We lose a recognition in our theorizing of a reality of all our lives–that we are encumbered beings and persons located in a place. But we are in danger of losing, if indeed we have not already altogether lost, civic and public spaces.

I am less concerned with whether the academy is the burying ground of the intellect or its only safe harbor than I am with the possibility that a non-institutionalized social site for the intellectual is increasingly difficult to locate in American public life.

Perhaps, it is worth musing on how, at a previous time in our history, the American *city* was a real public space, a place where public freedom could be struggled for and even partially realized. Forces have long been at work to denude the city as self-governing social and political location reality: cities are more and more creatures of the state. With the loss of the city, goes one vital spatial location of a public life and the public intellectual as one who speaks to and from a particular concrete site rather than from an abstract set of disembodied assumptions.

One recalls the lives and work of such progressive intellectuals as John Dewey and Jane Addams. Both city-constituted persons, they sought and found real vitality in the concepts of neighborhood and precincts culminating in the city itself–Chicago. Yet the problems being generated by relentless industrialization, social dislocation, tides of immigration and constitutional rulings that rendered the status of the city ambiguous at best–these and more prompted Dewey and Addams and other progressives to leap over the city, conceptually and finally politically, and to embrace the state as meta-city that might (or so they hoped) help to solve city-problems without destroying city autonomy. Such, of course, was not to be. But tracing this story might be fruitful in understanding American politics, public intellectual life, our civic philosophies, as well as our current political perils and possibilities.

Here I want to introduce an essay by Gerald Frug, "The City as a Legal Concept."[2] Frug's provocative discussion weaves together history, law, and political thought. Frug argues that the powerlessness of cities "has become so basic to our current way of understanding American society that no modest effort to 'revitalize' the cities by decentralizing power can succeed. Real decentralization requires rethinking and, ultimately, restructuring American society itself."[3] Frug is on to something and that something is the possibility that city powerlessness and the loss of an intellectually vital public world may go hand-in-hand.

The argument for city power, Frug insists, rests on the presumption that cities have served historically, and might serve again, as "vehicles to achieve purposes which have been frustrated in modern American life. They could respond to what Hannah Arendt has called the need for 'public freedom'–the ability to participate actively in the basic societal decisions that affect one's life."[4] Now, absolute self-determination, whether for individuals or institutions of civil society in an epoch dominated by state formations is, of course, a fantasy. But perhaps there remains some room to maneuver, places to turn to, in reviving a notion of communal freedom that exists in tension with both individualism and statism. That is a much longer story than I can address in this essay, although I will make several stabs at it.

But the point I want to make at the beginning is that Americans currently exist in a social world in which democratic ideals are professed but democracy is feared.

The powerlessness of our cities is poignant proof of that fear–a fear written into law, embedded in the infrastructure of our political-economy, evident in the tirades of many statist liberals against local initiatives and concerns they find almost invariably and by definition irrational or backward. The argument I will be making is a story about democracy and its possibility, about the nature of "the civic" and philosophizing about it, about how we might go about creating active citizens rather than dependent clients or cynical anti-citizens.

Consider, then, the city. Has it served as a locus of public autonomy, of communal freedom, historically? Book III of Aristotle's *Politics* opens with the questions, "whatever is the city?," in some translations, "what is the nature of the polis?" Aristotle offers throughout the *Politics* a strongly teleological appreciation of the city as the supremely authoritative association, as well as a caution against speaking of "the city" in the abstract, for there are many constitutions, many cities, many ways to create this public entity. The root for the words "city" and "citizen" derive from the Latin '*civltas*' but the ideas of the city and citizen go back to the "polis" of ancient Greece. Classical western political thought arose out of this particular form of city-thinking and structured forever after our theorizing about the civic. The city was a particular setting. It had to transcend the household–hence the discussion in Book I with which Aristotle opens his *Politics*, distinguishing between the household and the city. Self-sufficiency was also a requirement for city life, including the capacity of the city to defend itself through force of arms. The citizen had both honors and burdens, rights and responsibilities: he deliberated and served and ruled but he might also be called upon to forfeit his life for that of the civic body.

We continue to celebrate the sentiments of civic loyalty we detect among the Greeks, sentiments that have been reinscribed on the political consciousness of the West over and over again. But there is a darker side to the story. The city emerged out of the crushing of earlier familial and tribal loyalties, or at least putting them in their place, and settled into permanence as a fortification, a fortress. The long elaborate story of the sociology of the city often neglects this complex politics of origins. I tag this history "the discourse of armed civic virtue" in my book, *Women and War*.[5] Historic scholars of the ancient city–A. H. M. Jones and Alfred Zimmern, among others, remind us of what I will here call the war version of city politics. The city held complete control over human bodies for purposes of sexual and social reproduction. Celibacy, for example, was forbidden because replenishment of fighting men was required. Slowly, wider civic loyalties, brought into being in part to curb the "bad side of local patriotism, the never-ending internecine wars between cities," led to the imposition of larger political units *against* the will of the cities. The city gave way to the empire and Cicero's lament over the grave of the Roman republic echoes still through the years: "We have lost the *res publica*." The ancient city ended in Empire and crystallized those civic identities that derived from the experience of the war-city that I encapsulated in *Women and War*, into two grand characters: *The Citizen-Warrior* and *The Spartan Mother*.

We've got to add another ingredient to this already rich mulch, the medieval city, an entity quite different from its classical counterpart, forged out of other historic stuff, constituted in and through an amalgam of ideas derived not just from Roman law and, in the high middle ages, Greek thought, but Christianity with its combination of suspicion of any political formulations claiming ultimate or even penultimate loyalty, yet its insistence that communal entities are necessary to sustain some common good and to achieve certain earthly possibilities, including justice.

It is the medieval city that inspires Frug to castigate the powerlessness of our own cities and it is the medieval city Max Weber emphasizes in this classic work, *Die Stadt*, as a particular site of free-dom.[6] This free domain was available to anyone within its boundaries. The serf could flee to the city and, if not seized within a year, join the ranks of the free man. The city, as it developed throughout the medieval period, existed within larger social formulations–the very loosely structured Holy Roman Empire, the interlaced episcopates and bishoprics of the Church–but it forged its own political independence, it was importantly autonomous. To be sure, the city retained its commercial and defensive properties–it was both fortification and market–but to be a real city the feature of at least partially autonomous law, juridical independence, was required.

The city was a fraternal association–citizenship got construed along familiarized lines, or, perhaps better put, dominated by such metaphors. Members were bound to one another by sacred oaths. In matters respecting land ownership, markets, trade, citizens served as jurymen adjudicating cases affecting their own. Such legal establishments, writes Weber, originated or emerged through time either with practice or specific constitutive characters granted by medieval kings who thereby lost much of their right-or writ- to interfere in city affairs. For our purposes, most important is citizenship as a form of empowerment, sharing in political rule; thus the city named a "new basis for justice and stability of a government."

A particular structure of belief is implicated in all of this. The myth of city origins in the medieval period–again Weber is the main but not the only source–is that the city derives its existence from human free will. Citizenship is a "complex relation of rights and duties to a body conceived as a public possession, and a relation to one's fellow citizens as one's own."[7] Let me add that women were more in than out of this picture. The great pioneer of social history, Eileen Power, apprises us of the fact that medieval woman held a "full share...in private rights and duties" and lived a life that "gave her a great deal of scope."[8] Involved in nearly all the trade guilds, women worked, marketed, hunted and tended animals, and went on pilgrimages. Sharp cleavages between civic and private persons did not exist–these categories in their modern form congealed over time with the rise of nation-states and the construction of whole peoples as mobilizable populations. Women were not the warriors–although a few sneaked in even here. But women did benefit from, and shared in, the autonomy of the city.

The medieval town was a complex economic political and communal association. Towns established their own communal rules and their power to do so was part of a cluster of shared recognitions in the medieval period. Patriotism was local. All inhabitants shared in the peace of the city. One finds a group identity–visible in the writings of such early modern figures as Machiavelli who is, above all, a citizen of Florence, a city-man. Over time, with the evolution of free-flowing capital, hence the notion of markets as not town-bound, and the emergence of what I have called "the political theology of the Protestant nation-state," this city-autonomy was eroded as the power of the monistic sovereign state was consolidated.

If you have borne with me in this *grand jeté* across several millennia, perhaps you are ready to emigrate with me–conceptually and historically–to the shores of the New Land, to explore what America, as place and idea, did to and with this complex and by no means simple heritage as American men and women moved to construct their own civic ideals. Carrying with them the idea of, or ideas about, the city from Europe, the men and women of the American Enlightenment intermingled their commitment to universal natural right, a bit of civic republicanism, and a lot of the theology of the exclusive covenant. Hence, they wavered between trust and skepticism in their attitudes towards self-governance and, in turn, towards what sort of governance was appropriate to what sort of self. The old sinner? The new democratic man? A town? A city? A small Rousseauian republic? A large territorial nation-state?

In a fascinating piece on "The Idea of the City in European Thought," Carl Schorske finds three broad evaluations of the city in the past two hundred years: the city as virtue, the city as vice, the city beyond good and evil. Important intellectuals of the European Enlightenment, Schorske tells us, "formulated the view of the city as civilized virtue" in terms congenial to their respective national cultures.[9] Here is Voltaire on, not Paris, but London: "Rival of Athens, London, blest indeed/That with they tyrants had the wit to chase/The prejudices civil factions breed./Men speak their thoughts and worth can win its place/In London, who has talent, he is great."[10] London is "the fostering mother of social mobility against the fixed hierarchical society" and, interestingly, the urban contrast in the early modern city "between rich and poor, far from holding terrors for the philosophe, provided the very basis of progress."[11]

Not so for our Thomas Jefferson who feared the propertyless, potentially anarchic mobs of the big cities of Europe as much as he detested highly centralized government. The communitarian morality of the city-ideal inherited from the middle ages did not enchant Jefferson; rather, virtue for him reposed in the robust souls of independent, landed yeomen-farmers. These readers of Cicero in their spare time were the only sure and secure basis for a decentralized republic. Suspicion of the city was bred in the bones of our stalwart forebears.

The city got construed as more the site of de-civilization rather than the necessary foundation for civility and citizenship. Citizenship was relocated in the notion of the township, an anti-city civic formulation, a place within which each was, in Tocqueville's turn of phrase, the best judge of his own interest. Acknowledging the "utility of an association with his fellow men," the Tocquevillian citizen

> is a subject to all that concerns the duties of citizens to each other; he is free, and responsible to God alone, for all that concerns himself. Hence arises the maxim, that everyone is the best sole judge of his own private interest, and that society has no right to control a man's actions unless they are prejudicial to the common weal or unless the common weal demands his help. This doctrine is universally admitted in the United States . . . I am now speaking of the municipal bodies.[12]

Extolling the idea of the New England township as a "free and strong community," Tocqueville elides the distance between the township and his own celebration of a peculiarly American brand of civic freedom. Others, I am thinking here of Michael Zuckerman's sobering book, *Peaceable Kingdoms*,[13] apprise us that the New England town was a "totalitarianism of true believers," with a stress on consensus and homogeneity meaning one either had to accommodate or separate. But Tocqueville's reading came to prevail, no doubt in part because it offered such a powerful contrast between the spirit of the free township and the dangers of undifferentiated mass opinion and overly centralized, European style government. It seemed to free us from Jefferson's anomic urban mob and the weighty burden of centralized despotism at one and the same time.

But dangers lurked within the Tocquevillian formulation, a strong fear that even as American democracy freed individuals from the constraints of older, undemocratic structures and obligations, it might also unleash atomism, individualism, and privatization. His fear is not that this invites anarchy; rather, he believes that the atomized individualism of an acquisitive bourgeois society will engender oppressive new forms of social and political domination. Individuals disassociation invites the tyranny of mass opinion and some future overly centralized political authority might be needed to check that tyranny. The lure of private acquisitiveness, a deformation of good self-interest, might spawn political apathy and invite democratic despotism. Isolated and politically impotent, all the social webs that once held persons intact having disintegrated, the individual would find himself exposed and unprotected. Into this power vacuum the organizing force of government, the centralized state, would move, trailing in its wake European style sacral (hence potentially demonic) sovereignty.

The township, it is true, is the crucible of democracy. It also, however, threatens the vitality of democracy. It might not be strong enough to bind the individual to the civic. The associational air might be too thin; the concatenation of combined self-interest as a form of civic virtue too labile for one of democratic inclinations to draw much sustained comfort and easy reassurance in the future of American democracy. But Tocqueville could not and did not turn to the older notion of the city as communal association, an actual social site, a symbolically potent place. Too immersed in the old, pre-Enlightenment world, the medieval city was besmirched with the Enlightenment reading of all pre-Enlightenment social forms–seeming to embody reaction, religion, all that must be overcome and washed away.

To be sure, some American commentators extolled the city as, in Theodore Parker's phrase, "the fireplaces of civilization whence light and heat radiated out into the dark world,"[14] and saw the city as a supreme achievement of the new industrialism of the late nineteenth-early twentieth century. A new brand of urban intellectual and progressive reformer arose, with some finding the city the generating center for social and intellectual progress. In the words of Arthur Schlesinger, Sr., "To dwell in the midst of great affairs is stimulating and broadening; it is the source of a discontent which, if not divine, is at least energizing. In a populous urban community like could find like; the person of ability, starved in his rural isolation, might by going there find sympathy, encouragement and that criticism which often refined talent into genius."[15] And Schlesinger turns empirical to buttress this boast, informing us that, based on Who's Who in America, c. 1908-1909, "towns of eight thousand and more people produced nearly twice as many men of distinction as their numerical importance warranted." And a study of distinguished American men of science "disclosed that a disproportionate number of these were likewise of city birth."[16] City birth may not make you a free citizen but it can get you into Who's Who!

But the Jeffersonian cloud hovered always nearby, always looming, the fear that cities were "ulcers on the body politic," their "civic splendor" offset by squalor, vices, the city of darkness, the city as the dearth of the civic. The city becomes a problem rather than presaging possibility. Even as–remember–the law was construing the city as problematic at best, parasitic at worst, the dependent creature of corporations and the federal government, views of the city as the site of dis-order came to prevail in the minds of many reformers. A unified political system, so held the centralizers, was necessary to deal with the factions of the city as "state control of cities" became "a defense of freedom . . . rather than a restriction of freedom," and got encoded as such. The city could not be allowed to frustrate either the wider interests of the state, nor to restrict the freedom of more and more robust construal of the self as sovereign. Too many sovereign selves, especially if they traffic with one another, seem to invite more disorder. It was this very dis-order, or apparent dis-order, that attracted several generations of artists and intellectuals to the city as Bohemia. One person's purposive social complexity is another's social disarray.

Political philosophy offered up increasingly legal abstractions, "like Individual and State" or economic abstractions "like Capitalist Class or the Proletariat" while life as it was lived concretely got washed away. Lewis Mumford calls this development in the realm of thought, together with the upsurge of the anomic metropolis, a form of "growth by civic depletion" as all organs of communal and civic life other than the state are effectively extirpated or allowed to exist only in clientage and shadowy forms.[17] We wind up with the picture of the city as a place where the private search for wealth predominates and civic possibilities stagnate, prompting Thomas Bender in an essay, "The End of the City?" which appeared in the short-lived journal, *Democracy*, to write: "In current political discourse the city has no legitimate existence prior to or superior to the claims of the market. There is no political justification of the city."[18] In what must surely be seen as a denouement, Irving Kristol twists Jefferson's republican sympathies and fears of the "mob of great cities" into a stated conviction that the urban population is a mob.[19] A hapless and helpless rabble that requires ever more vigilant discipline–this is the cure and too much democracy a disease. Having immunized economic decisions for the political realm, we find ourselves confronting the civic wreckage thereby wrought. And, in light of our long-standing suspicion of cities, and our politically and imaginative incapacity to conceive of real sites of citizenship and power intermediary between the individual and the state, we turn to experts and managers to help us control both our fears and the urban mob.

Two laments, from Mumford and from the writer and historian, Raymond Williams: for Mumford what was once a "simple love of country and home and soil . . . is turned by official apologists of the state into . . . coercive group unanimity, maudlin national egoism . . . a willingness to commit collective atrocities for the sake of national glory."[20] If we can be citizens only with reference to the state, this is the outcome, he insists. Williams fears a subtle but pervasive alteration of consciousness as the contemporary working adult lives in a world in which the dominant mode of production and social relationships impress, teach, and make normal rigid "modes of detached, separated, external perception and action: modes of using and consuming rather than accepting and enjoying people and things."[21]

What gets left out of all the accounts, interestingly enough, is a discussion of the role played by war in the nationalizing of citizenship and the diminution of the civic. The discourse of armed civic virtue in this society was the creation of nationalizing progressives, those who championed universal military training and conscription as an "effective homogenizing agent in what they regarded as a dangerously diverse society"–embodied in the bewildering mix of urban life. Shared military service, one advocate colorfully argued, was the only way to "yank the hyphen" out of Italian-Americans of Polish-Americans or other such imperfectly assimilated immigrants." In 1917, President Wilson committed himself to universal service, not just for defense in case of hostilities but to help mold a new nation. Two years before the war resolution, Wilson launched an attack against hyphenated Americans. "There are citizens of the United States, I blush to admit, born under other flags but welcomed under our generous naturalization laws to the full freedom and opportunity of America, who have poured the poison of disloyalty into the very arteries of our national life . . . Such creatures of passion, disloyalty, and anarchy must be crushed out . . . The hand of our power should close over them at once."[22] Congress responded in kind by passing legislation to check espionage and treason that vested the government with powers to censor the press, punish interference with activities of the armed services, including recruitment and control of the mails to prevent dissemination of allegedly treasonable material.

The Supreme Court endorsed wartime assaults on dissenting opinion, weaving into the nation's legal fabric restrictions in freedom of speech that had been unknown before 1917. America's school systems got mobilized for the duration. America's institutions of higher learning went for the war with relish, using the universities to contribute to the war cause as an embellishment of the "service ideal" that had been part and parcel of the emergence of the modern university in America during the Progressive era. The dream of civic life became that of a national unity through armed civic virtue, the presence of undigested immigrants, the residual power of cities–the base for those immigrants, was an ongoing irritant.

Progressive and liberal opinion proved particularly susceptible to the cry for unity, in part because they already construed the city as a cauldron of problems, in part because the sovereign self seemed to require the centralized sovereign state to achieve the best of all possible worlds: the nation must be bound as one. A body political cannot consist of many parts. Service to society, as compared to the state, seemed too disparate, too locate, too parochial for architects of national unity who sought human mastery over the dangerous drift of affairs. The only way to gain such mastery, it seemed, was to strengthen the powers of the state. What got generated were nationalistic as compared to civic impulses. Sovereignty prevailed. The nationalizing project triumphed.

I do not intend to allow this particular reading to prevail or to triumph, at least not without a fight, as I turn to some closing reflections of whether or not we might redeem a notion of "the city," hence possibilities for politics and civic philosophy that moves away from grandiose abstractions to make contact with the messiness of concrete human realities.

Having offered up such an apparently gloomy set of construals, I am somewhat daunted at the task of presenting alternatives. But here goes. What remains of the city as an idea–an imagined political space? Not the city as contrast to the benighted countryside, so cherished by many American writers, interestingly primarily male writers who were in revolt against the small town, but the city as a real civic space, big enough to allow for diversity and guarantee clashes and difference; small enough to constitute its members as public persons without requiring, as the price of membership, that they diminish the many other things they are.

Recalling the origins of national citizenship in and through the discourse of armed civic virtue, my alternative requires taking a skeptical stance towards the pretenses and homogenizing features of state sovereignty. It requires figuring out how to reanimate civic life throughout the body politic, to chart some course that does not land us yet again in the lap of rule by managers and a public policy elite. How can we come not merely to tolerate but to offer an incitement to genuine involvement in civic entities beneath the state? (You will notice that it is almost impossible not to deploy spatial metaphors as one discusses these matters.) Can we trust ourselves enough to rethink the possibility of a public or civic freedom–a freedom that must exist in tension with the pretensions and claims of the sovereign self and the sovereign state alike.

Many in this audience will no doubt appreciate much more than I what the legal possibilities might be–what cracks in the constitutional edifice could be deployed to this particular end. So I shall concentrate on what I hope it is I do best, following Hannah Arendt's insistence that the vocation of the political theorist is to think what we are doing. To speak of alternatives is to confront the nature of our understanding of power and the way it constitutes contemporary political life in modern statist orders. Interestingly, political power as a characteristic of national strength is a usage dating from the eighteenth century, a relatively "late use," claims the OED, and one preceded by "a celestial or spiritual being having control of influence; a divinity." Before Plato and Aristotle and the self-conscious beginnings of political thought, sacred, mytho-poetic usages predominate wherever the site of power is located. Political meanings in the West got layered upon older, mythic understandings, potent images of ritual, taboo, the demonic, the sacred. "Thine," says the Old Testament, "is the power and the glory."

Power understood as singular, unitary, emanating from an awesome, not to be trifled with, source. I want to offer for your consideration the following possibilities, returning, for a moment, to Latin terms for power. One, *potestas*, means political power, control, supremacy, dominion. Another, *potentia* is a term for power understood as ability, efficacy, potency, especially "unofficial and sinister." Fascinatingly, these contrasting images demarcate roughly the boundaries of male and female forms of power historically. Males have been the official wielders of institutional power and dominion; women the unofficial (hence potentially uncontrollable) repositories of non-legitimate, non-political power. *Potentia* conjures up the threatening, the deviant, occupying a boundary that touches on the polluted, the uncanny, the potentially dis-ordered. Even more fascinatingly, having tracked the story of the city, that city seen as dangerous is also symbolically feminized in several senses. She–this civic mother–gives birth to a possibly uncontrollable mob. And, in American history, the politics of cities in the late nineteenth and early twentieth centuries was specifically "domesticated," seen as civic housekeeping, by men and women alike, but especially the female creators of this particular discourse.

Like the good mother bringing order (*potestas*), she must defeat, sweep clean, her anarchic disordered counterpart (*potentia*). This is quite a stretch admittedly but it is worth thinking about. To give civic birth to Athens, Athena must quell the Furies. To give civic birth to clean cities, Jane Addams must clean up neighborhoods, and re-order unruly kids, and all the rest. The sovereign state, then, becomes both solution to and escape from this domesticated, feminized entity. The state has defining power–we can project it against others, bring them under our sway deploying our awesome instrumentalities of sovereign force. So we have come to our current impasse. Worshiping penultimate power and fantasies of perfect control. We find ourselves dominated by instrumentalities of our own creation.

The reed I am trying to grasp moves us away from the terrible deadlock of awesome *potestas* needed, or so we have come to believe, to check potentially anarchic *potentia*. Power and politics, yes, but what forms of power, what sorts of politics? And what has this to do with revivifying "the civic" and the city as a political space? Here I shall turn to a perhaps unlikely source, the Czech playwright and dissident, lauded Václav Havel, who understands the civic much better, I fear, than many current American commentators. Havel reminds us that to continue to think boringly in the inherited categories of right/left, conservative/radical, progressive/regressive is, in his words, to give one a sense of "emerging from the depth of the last century." He writes: "It seems to me that these thoroughly ideological and many times mystified categories have long since been beside the point."[23] They do not capture the complexity of the best of our civic thinking and they cannot come close to the content of our actual beliefs and actions. While monological statism, Havel continues, "moves towards increased conformity, uniformity and discipline," genuine democracy moves towards plurality, diversity, and independent self-constitution.

What the great movements in Prague and Gdansk and elsewhere offer to my reflections in this essay is an insistence that one must reject categories with which many remain all too comfortable and, as well, in searching for ways to reanimate our civic capacities, we should refuse to privilege the state as the only legitimate political site.

At the conclusion of *Public Man, Private Woman* I articulated the vision of an "ethical polity." I wrote:

> Rather than an ideal citizenship and civic virtue that features a citizenry grimly going about their collective duty, or an elite band of citizens in their public space cut off from a world that includes most of the rest of us, within the ethical polity the active citizen would be one who had affirmed as part of what it meant to be human a devotion to public, moral responsibilities and ends.[24]

I called my ideal one that preserves "a tension between spheres and prompting ideals and purposes." At the conclusion of *Women and War* I gave my citizen a name–the Chastened Patriot–drawing away from the nationalist conception of citizenship that has come to prevail in the twentieth century, to a civic character who is capable of modulating the rhetoric of high patriotic purpose by keeping alive the distancing voice of ironic remembrance, including a recognition of the way patriotism can shade into the excesses of nationalism. The Chastened Patriot constitutes men and women as citizens who share what Hannah Arendt calls "the faculty of action." This citizen is skeptical about the forms and claims of the sovereign state. He or she has come to understand that there are other possibilities within our repertoire, multiple ways to understand and to achieve power and to engage in civic activity. But my chastened patriot needs a place to live–she requires a civic home. The space that might sustain her is the city, not quite the shining city set on a hill, but certainly not the ugly, menacing, unruly city we have come so much to fear. My city as an imagined civic place is a site in which plurality is cherished and commonality is an honored achievement. Is this city a worthy ideal? If so, what historic, legal and political repertoire can be called upon to help call her into being? For only a city such as this seems a worthy civic dream for the Chastened Patriot to be dreaming.

Notes

1. Jean Bethke Elshtain, *Public Man, Private Woman: Women in Social and Political Thought* (Princeton: Princeton University Press, 1981).

2. Gerald Frug, *The City as a Legal Concept*, 93 Harvard Law Review 1057 (1980).

3. Ibid., 1060.

4. Ibid., 1068.

5. Jean Bethke Elshtain, *Women and War* (New York: Basic Books, 1987).

6. Max Weber, *The City*, trans. and ed. D. Martindale and G. Neuwirth (New York: Collier Books, 1958).

7. See Danny L. Schwartz, "Communitarian Citizenship: Marx and Weber on the City," *Polity* 17, no. 3 (winter, 1985): 530-540.

8. Eileen Power, "The Position of Women," in *The Legacy of the Middle Ages*, ed. C. G. Crump and E. F. Jacob (Oxford: Clarendon Press, 1948), 432-33.

9. Carl Schorske, "The Idea of the City in European Thought," in *The Historian and the City*, ed. Oscar Haudlin and John Burchard (Cambridge: MIT and Harvard University Press, 1963), 95-115, 96.

10. Ibid., 96-97.

11. Ibid.

12. Alexis de Tocqueville, *Democracy in America*, vol. 1 ed. Philips Bradley (New York: Vintage Books, 1945), 67.

13. Michael Zuckerman, *Peaceable Kingdoms* (New York: Knopf, 1970).

14. Theodore Parker cited in Arthur Schlesinger Sr., *The Rise of the City* (New York: Macmillan, 1933), 79.

15. Ibid., 80.

16. Ibid., 80-81.

17. Lewis Mumford, *The Culture of Cities* (New York: Harcourt, Brace and Co., 1938), 249.

18. Thomas Bender, "The End of the City?" *Democracy* (winter 1983): 8.

19. Irving Kristol cited in Bender, "The End of the City?," 9-10.

20. Mumford, *The Culture of Cities*, 284.

21. Raymond Williams, *The Country and the City* (New York: Oxford University Press, 1973), 297-295.

22. Quoted in David M. Kennedy, *Over Here: The First World War and American Society* (New York: Oxford University Press, 1980), 24.

23. Václav Havel, "Power and Powerlessness," in *Václav Havel: Living in Truth*, ed. Jan Vladislav (Boston: Faber and Faber, 1987).

24. Elshtain, *Public Man, Private Woman*, 351.

Chapter 4

The Constitution of Religion and American Culture

Robert Booth Fowler

Preface

My interest is in religion and culture–and government–and how they interact in the United States. How they do interact I see as part of the United States constitution. It is not mostly a matter of what is written in the formal Constitution of 1787, but in the constitution that matters a good deal more, the informal constitution of practice in the United States. The pattern of relations between culture and religion is an important aspect of the constitution in that sense, one that affects the operations of government and politics and the lives of almost all American citizens.

My argument is that religion and culture in the United States are what I have termed "unconventional partners," unintentional allies in sustaining our culture as well as a good deal of organized and unorganized religion in this country.[1] Moreover, both partners very much need each other and are, I contend, dependent, perhaps even co-dependent on each other. Theirs is no casual, accidental, or mundane partnership. It looks suspiciously integral to each partner and therefore to understanding this part of the constitution of the contemporary United States.

By religion I mean simply what people in this nation, or any other, consider religion. In the case of the highly pluralistic United States, religion can and does imply and include a great many things, but it usually revolves around concern with the ultimate meaning in life and the universe. By culture I mean what people believe and do as a collective people. While one may argue that we have little shared culture in the Untied States today, I contend that in certain crucial ways a culture does survive.[2]

Culture's Need for Religion

The first half of my argument is that our culture and government need and thus use religion for three reasons: to help provide meaning, morality, and community in the culture that it needs–thus the claim that the contribution of religion is vital. My claim is that every society requires all three–it is hard to conceptualize a culture–or a society–without each. More to the point of this paper, my claim is that meaning, morality, and community are especially needed today in modern liberal American society.

My view is that our society has a great deal of difficulty today generating these sinews of culture. Our cultural watchwords are quite different. The vocabulary of society today is individual desire, pluralism, and skepticism of absolute truth claims. The practice of society is an increasingly faithful reproduction of this vocabulary in action. Individual freedom and subjectivity are more and more the norm, in terms of meaning, ethics, art; the range of what is acceptable has ballooned as have individual and group "rights." There are few general cultural norms beyond disapproval of acts such as murder that flagrantly deny the individual (though there are, perhaps predictably, an enormous number of murders), being sensitive (in tribute to pluralism), and avoiding too strong assertions of Truth (in deference to skepticism and tolerance). Meanwhile, our society is plagued by crime, divorce prone, and has too many homeless and socially unattached people.

Such facts only make the need for generating meaning, morality, and community all the greater, of course, and make the dependence on religion to generate them all the more important. They do not necessarily imply that our culture is somehow a failure. After all, our social openness, considerable personal freedom, and expanding tolerance may be goods that make the costs worth it.[3] Moreover, one might argue that the very ability of modern culture to draw on religion to help provide needed social mortar is admirable. Our culture may demonstrate considerable ability to heal its own wounds.

Another premise is obvious, but worth articulating. Religion plays a real role in assisting the culture by providing some meaning, morality, and community, but it is hardly the only source of each in contemporary America. This is particularly true of community which in senses strong and less strong people sometimes find in their homes, on the job, among their friends, in clubs and organizations, in many settings–and, sometimes, in too few. The same applies in terms of people's values, often diverse today, and frequently products of complicated and confounding lives–and the setting, whether communities or not, in which those lives are lived out. But there is no doubt that religion is, nonetheless, an important factor in these matters for many people.

I also assume in my argument that religion in the United States is a refuge from the culture, not a rejection of it. If religion's leaders, or its laity, pursue the rejection perspective, of course there would be quite different consequences. Refuge means a place of somewhat different values that is respected and sought out for them, but is not a substitute for the dominant culture. So it is with religion in the United States, on the whole. It participates in what I call the unconventional partnership just because it does not fundamentally stand as enemy to society. It follows that religion attracts many Americans into its houses of worship under exactly these terms–and only under them.

Premises aside, the evidence connecting meaning, morality, and community and organized religion especially is strong. Numerous studies suggest that people join religious groups because they seek meaning and morality.[4] It is true enough that church growth does not strictly correlate with the degree to which a religious group offers clear and firm meaning and morality, since matters such as birth rates, geographical location, the pastor, and luck also matter. But people are looking for spiritual meaning and where it is provided with concrete connections to everyday life, growth is predictably present. Moreover, this has long been true in American religious history.[5]

Such students of religious opinion as Gallup and Castelli affirm this picture. People seek out meaning and ethical grounding; they are often happy with religious communities they join and sometimes they are not, but whether they deliver in these terms is crucial to people's judgment.[6] This is only reaffirmed by Wade Clark Roof's recent examination of the religious dispositions of the generation of the 1960s in his fascinating *A Generation of Seekers*.[7]

Roof's interviews found that the middle aged generation of today, with its roots in the 1960s and 1970s, recapitulates the traditional orientation toward religion in terms of meaning, morality, and community. The diversity of paths followed is greater than ever before, of course, as we would expect. And there is some uneasiness over institutionalized religion. But religion is important in this generation–when some predicted it would not be–for the usual reasons. Even where it takes forms that are decidedly unconventional, it is for quite conventional goals, including community.

Of course, in every generation meaning and morality are associated with religion, *but* in the U.S. the belief is that religion must not lead one into fanaticism or social alienation. Meaning and morality must be nice.[8] In public life they must not seem abrasive nor clash too sharply with the culture. This reflects the partnership between religion and culture in the United States. Part of the terms of that partnership is the implicit agreement not to rock the other's boat. Whenever a clash emerges, there will be pressure to conform to these terms of the unconventional partnership, as the Mormons learned in the late nineteenth century and Operation Rescue is learning today. Individualism and pluralism have their limits in this land of partnership between religion and culture and a large part of the limit is that religion has to be nice–nice and quiet.

The issue of community is an especially interesting one. Our culture is struggling to retain the secure communities of home, neighborhood, and private associations that flourished more abundantly at other periods. Perhaps we are simply undergoing an evolution to new forms of old groups, but in the meantime widespread social disorganization and alienation are hardly invisible. It is in this light that there is abundant evidence that people turn to organized religion to find some of the community they judge to be in short supply elsewhere in society.

People seek community in religion in terms of a shared worship of God, a common ethical outlook, and of course, in social terms. By the last, I mean coffees and picnics, but also participation with others in numerous ministries within and without a particular religious community. Whether or not many or even most attenders take advantage of available opportunities to participate is not quite the point. What matters is that people expect to find community in religious organizations. In fact, studies show most of those involved believe they find it there and when they don't that fact is a central reason for their moving on in disillusionment. Religious communities that people perceive to be unfriendly, impersonal, or closed pay a large price.[9]

Recent work on "mainline" Protestantism confirms the well-known linkage–and expectation–people make between community and religion. Mainline Protestantism has suffered because it succeeds less and less well in presenting itself and its denominations in terms of community, as worlds that share something unique and important together. Particular churches succeed in fashioning community, but overall a sense of the distinctiveness in the mainline and in its denominations has faded. Its declining numbers over the past thirty years and its inability to reverse that pattern are undoubtedly directly related to this perceived loss of community and distinctiveness.[10]

At any point some religions and some religious communities will make more progress in providing meaning, morality, and community than others. Such variation is inevitable. But the fact remains that overall religion, especially organized religion, play a major role in furnishing and maintaining these essential pilings of cultural order. In this way, our society depends on religion to supply individuals with what our culture does not always otherwise provide them and through these citizens to strengthen the society as a whole.

Religion's Need for the Culture

My argument is that the other side of the partnership between religion and culture is the need for (and frank use of) the culture and government by religion in the

United States. Religion is far from only a giving partner. It gets a lot back in a partnership from which it benefits deeply.

There are four features in this partnership that particularly redound to the benefit of religion in the United States. The culture (often through the agency of government) guarantees religion substantial freedom, offers widespread support for pluralism, provides advantages from the pervasive presence of religion in the United States, and, through the culture's weaknesses, encourages religion in various ways. All of them make a tremendous difference for the health (as well as the direction) of religion in America.

Consider first religious freedom. There is nothing particularly common about religious freedom in human history nor in our own time. U. S. experience today, however, is dramatically different. We have a tremendous amount of religious freedom, rooted in a First Amendment often sustained by the Supreme Court, but more importantly accepted within the overall culture.

Of course, we have had our ups and downs in terms of the practice of religious liberty throughout our history. But there is no doubt that the degree of religious freedom has expanded until it is now one of the glories of the nation–and one immensely valuable to religion of all varieties. That there are still skirmishes at the margins of religious practice today remains true as does the fact that the Supreme Court or the local neighborhood sometimes choose not to protect religious freedom when the moment to make a painful value choice arrives. Yet by any standard of comparison the range of American religious freedom is striking and its reality for the vast majority is unquestionably secure.

Closely allied is the tremendous advantage religion gains from the pluralism that is present in the United States. Over time our culture has become increasingly diverse and permitted pluralism in religion as well as in much else. The pluralism within the ranks of American religion is truly astounding and it is growing all the time. It has even come to include, as we know, those dedicated to the abolition of religion.

This diversity sometimes depends on government support, often through courts, to maintain itself, but it also encourages diversity in other arenas of life. Diversity feeds on and nourishes diversity. The result is not just that most religious groups are able to carry on their corporate life within surprisingly modest constraints, but also that religion as a whole grows. For there seems little doubt that where there is religious pluralism, there are more outlets for religious needs and concerns, more chances that diverse religious impulses will find an outlet and flourish. This is perhaps the major single reason why religion is so widespread and so strong in the United States. Diversity not only breeds diversity; it can also breed growth.[11]

A more concrete but not always more obvious advantage accrues to religion from government's many particular aids to all religious communities, what is sometimes termed our establishment of religion in general. The facts of this establishment can hardly be avoided. Government help for "nonprofit" religious hospitals, orphanages, old age homes, colleges, child care facilities, among other institutions is palpable. So is government assistance to military and prison chaplaincies and, even more, to thousands of local religious communities who, as nonprofit institutions, do not have to pay property taxes. Consider also government support for religion and its legitimacy through such cultural symbols as "In God We Trust" on the currency, the establishment of Thanksgiving as a holiday, and the incorporation of the phrase "one nation under God" in the Pledge of Allegiance.

Pleasantries about separation of church and state abound in the rhetoric of public life in the United States. Rather than take them too seriously, we might do better to note how much establishment the nation has accepted. Certainly our form of establishment is inclusive; government helps not one church or one religion, but most all of them. Its policy is like our whole culture–unusually inclusive. But we should not ignore this establishment nor the fact that it advantages organized religion in its many forms in the United States.

Lastly, it is clear enough that the very problems that seem to beset our culture in this contemporary era–its struggles with creating community, meaning, and shared values–prove to be of advantage to religion. They create, as I have argued, a considerable need for religion to play a significant role in offering society what it often cannot otherwise create. Thus even the weaknesses of culture and government redound to the benefit of religion in the United States. They make a place for religion, an important place, and this benefit to religion, while intended the least, may be the largest of all. It is yet another reminder of how dependent our religion and culture are on each other–to the benefit of religion as well as the culture.

Discussion

To this argument that I have made there are commonly two lines of counter argument, both worthy of attention and respect. One concentrates on normative objection to my thesis. Its advocates do not necessarily dispute my analysis, but they are concerned that my view does not criticize the "unconventional partnership" I observe. Their unease often comes from several, quite different directions with a shared complaint. Some argue that our culture, and certainly our government, would be well to be rid of religion, or at least public roles and manifestations of religion. For them, the partnership must be broken for the sake of our culture.[12] Others agree that the corrupting bonds between culture and religion must fall, but they do so from their religious perspective. For them, religion is sullied and compromised by its immoral connections with culture and government. Their agenda remains popular in elite religious circles among those who judge themselves faithful to the perspective H. Richard Niebuhr termed "Christ against Culture."[13]

There is no question today that there is a major "separatist lobby" that is strongly committed to the proposition that our culture would be much better off if we took religion out of the public life as well as the culture as a whole. Sometimes this view is articulated by those such as Madalyn Murray O'Hair or Anne Gaylor who are prominent in the crusade against all religion, especially Christianity. Gaylor of the explicitly named Freedom from Religion Foundation makes no bones about her goal. Since religion is a delusion that interferes with freedom and oppresses women, Gaylor and her group seek its extirpation. Getting it out of the public is only, therefore, the first step, though a vital one.

The case can be made that such groups as the Freedom from Religion Foundation, while ardent and persistent, are not terribly significant. Perhaps that is right. What is less debatable, however, is that support for separatism has other stronger bases as well. This is the case in such groups as People for the American Way, founded by the sitcom creator, Norman Lear, or in such Jewish organizations as the American Jewish Committee or the Jewish Anti-Defamation League, all of which are committed to getting religion out of the public square. Again motivations differ. Much of the concern behind the PAW is a disagreement with and fear of the Religious Right; for activist Jewish groups the concern is Christian dominance over the Jewish community in the United States.

None of these groups has anything *per se* against religion, as they frequently protest. Their strict definition and zealous pursuit of separatism suggests that it is the kind of religion that worries them–as well as the kind of politics that may accompany it. For them, the unconventional partnership which I have described is no fantasy. They see it as clearly as anyone does, but they believe it is a threat to their interests and seek to strike it down.

Another expression of a similar disposition, albeit from a very different quarter, is the objection that the relationship I have described sullies religion since it involves religion's compromise with the culture at the expense of religion. This complaint is present in some parts of Protestant fundamentalism in its critique of permissive American culture. The same is true within Orthodox Judaism. It is also common among some liberal leaders of "mainline" Protestantism.

There one may encounter the argument that too much of American religion has become an agent of the principalities and powers of American culture and that the true church must break with this unholy alliance. In this version, the argument is that the church and indeed the entire culture must be brought into line. The lost soul of America must be reclaimed. Not withdrawal, but principled engagement might be the political agenda. If the consequences prove costly for believers or for the church, so be it. A church that is a saving remnant is assumed to be better than a growing, large one compromised by the culture. For this view, such compromises as the unconventional partners arrangement are just the problem and deserve nothing but scorn.[14]

My reaction to such views is not unsympathetic, but I am not arguing the normative questions in this context. However much such groups in the American culture may dislike the partnership, their dislike does not change its existence. And it is to that fact that my analysis speaks. To be sure, the normative objections would become practically relevant if they reached such force that they threatened the existence of the unconventional partnership between culture and religion in the United States. But there is, let us be frank, no serious sign of that.

Perhaps I may add that some caution should be exercised by those who are eager to enjoy what they expect to be the religious benefits of breaking the partnership of religion and culture. After all, the attempt to create a holy remnant might not succeed. Even if it did, the cost would be the alienation of many or perhaps most current religious community members. Forcing people to make such a stark choice is a dangerous business. Forcing them to do so in our culture–changing religion from a temporary refuge to a radical alternative–would likely make most unable to resist selecting secular individualism and pluralism–and private religion.

This choice would have impact not just on church budgets and the vast apparatus of institutional supports for American religion, though such supports are of enormous importance to U.S. religion's health. It would also greatly weaken the culture's–and government's–commitment to help religion in all the ways it now does. That could be disastrous, including damaging for religious freedom in the long run.

While much of the objection to my argument is normative–and I sympathize with it in part–the crucial argument must first be empirical: whether my argument well describes the behavior of religion and culture in our society. Needless to say, there are plenty of empirical objections to my contentions, some of which you may wish to argue. Let me just mention two here.

One is that the unconventional partnership thesis assumes that religion and the culture are somehow different from each other in their values, perhaps especially in religion's communal emphasis as opposed to society's celebration of self-interest, the will, and the individual. But how different are they really? Isn't American religion permeated by the culture and in no way more thoroughly so than in its individualism? Ours is an overwhelmingly Protestant religious culture, one where most Catholics and Jews and others are Protestants. That is, ours is culture where most people self-define their relationship with God and with others; they form their own religion and their own church, so to speak, and anoint themselves its priest; and they insist on the complete propriety of such a "priesthood of all believers." Thus all authority in American religion is suspect unless it is the individual conscience.

There is more than a little truth to this claim, even granting that there are significant pockets of American religion that decidedly are not expressions of individualism. But at least, we have to recognize that community is also present in American religion. That world is neither all one or another, but a complex and mixed world of the culture and its values, as well as a refuge from them. I have already argued that it is not an alternative world, yet there can be no ignoring the evidence that religious Americans find in their religions and their religious institutions more than just individualism; they also find community there and that is a powerful reason why they seek organized religion.

A second objection is that my unconventional partnership argument cannot explain the vigorous action of religious groups challenging the culture. If the partnership is so real, surely we would not expect to see the challenges that abound. This would be a good point if there were plentiful or sweeping challenges or both.

But there are not. Challenges are few and far between and most that are heard are thin. Sometimes, for example, there are declarations from the leaders of the National Council of Churches–for example on the Gulf War–or from Protestant fundamentalists–for example on the evil of America's astounding level of abortions. But these critiques are at best episodic; they are almost never genuinely radical and systemic; they rarely are connected with radical action; often they do not even represent most of the faithful. Challenges just are not particularly present. Does this mean that most American religion has been captured by the culture? Might it not be better to say that it represents an unconventional partnership with the culture, not a copy of it, a refuge rather than an alternative?

Toward the Future

A few thoughts toward the future may be appropriate by way of conclusion. Prediction is a risky business, but that makes it all the more interesting. It is not, perhaps, to be taken terribly seriously, but as long as one winks in the process, there is no harm.

In this mood, it is reasonable to predict that the unconventional partnership of religion and culture and government will continue in a robust form into the foreseeable future. Religion will continue to flourish just as long as it is both different from and yet supported by the culture, now a long, long story in American history. There is plenty of reason to agree with Roger Finke and Rodney Stark that churches and religions that demand either too little or too much sacrifice from their members are those which have always faced trouble in America.[15]

In my terms, if religion is a refuge, a real refuge, it will flourish; when it becomes indistinguishable from the culture around it *or* becomes a full scale challenge to that culture, then it damages its unconventional partnership with the culture. The fact is there are few signs of such a disruption. While some denominations grow and others do not, the pattern is predictable. For example, the numerical decline of the United Church of Christ is no surprise; its denominational elite often challenges the culture, while its laity is highly integrated with the culture, both formulas for trouble. The Assemblies of God, on the other hand, are booming; they offer a refuge but not a radical alternative to the culture around them.

The companion point about the future is that the unconventional partners arrangement is likely to go on as it has if the culture and the government continue their present policies of being supportive of religion without somehow becoming too much so, provoking reaction. Here too, from the limited vision of today, the prospects appear strong for more of the same. All of the features that make for cultural and governmental support for religion are in place and seem securely so–a strong cultural pluralism, a legal system committed to wide free exercise of religion, and plenty of concrete government aid for religions in general. The wars over this or that aspect of each realm of assistance rise and fall in intensity. But a perspective apart from particular battles suggests that little changes that is fundamental.

And the more cries there are that the Supreme Court's policies are confused and confusing in this realm, the more we know that the current situation continues as before. Clear Supreme Court rulings open the door to focused reactions and directed counter-strategies. The unconventional partnership is based on more subtle social relations, strong in fact, but messy and confused in the public eye.

Quite another view might approach the future with the argument that increasing secularization is what lies ahead. From this perspective, religion will be less and less able to maintain its unconventional partnership with the culture. The entire issue of secularization is worth considerable attention in the contemporary United States where the extent of secularization in the population at large is debatable. But even were secularization to advance dramatically, it would not necessarily follow that the unconventional partnership between religion and our culture would end. As likely would be an implicit renegotiation of the terms of the partnership, which is something else again.

The best prediction is that we can expect more of the same. That important element of the United States constitution that is the complex relationship between the culture and religion, wherein each helps the other, will likely continue. Unconventional partnerships have a way of lasting, even when people don't expect them to, and that appears to be the future for the part of our constitution that is an unconventional partnership between religion and politics.

Notes

1. Robert Booth Fowler, *Unconventional Partners: Religion and Liberal Culture in the United States* (Grand Rapids, MI: Eerdmans, 1989).

2. On culture I still find Clifford Geertz the most interesting. See his *The Interpretation of Culture* (New York: Basic Books, 1973).

3. As Peter Clecak, for example, has argued: *American's Quest for the Ideal Self* (New York: Oxford University Press, 1983).

4. See Fowler, *Unconventional Partners* for a detailed discussion of the relevant studies.

5. Roger Finke and Rodney Stark, *The Churching of America: 1776-1990* (New Brunswick, NJ: Rutgers University Press, 1992).

6. George Gallup, Jr. and Jim Castelli, *The People's Religion* (New York: Macmillan, 1989).

7. Wade Clark Roof, *A Generation of Seekers* (San Francisco: Harper, 1993).

8. An interesting discussion of niceness in American is John Murray Cudihy, *No Offense: Civil Religion and Protestant Taste* (New York: Seabury, 1979).

9. See Fowler, *Unconventional Partners*, ch. 3 for a detailed discussion of some of the relevant data.

10. A fascinating set of studies in this regard is in Jackson Carroll and Wade Clark Roof, eds., *Beyond Establishment: Protestant Identity in a Post-Modern Age* (Louisville, KY: Westminster, 1993).

11. See Fowler, *Unconventional Partners* and Finke and Stark, *The Churching of America* for two arguments that religious pluralism has tremendously strengthened religion in the United States.

12. See the next paragraph for some specific examples.

13. Two classic expressions: Franky Schaeffer, *A Time for Anger* (Westchester, IL: Crossway Books, 1982); and Jim Wallis, *Agenda for a Biblical People* (New York: Harper, 1976), the first full length expression of the Sojourners' philosophy. See also Niebuhr, *Christ and Culture* (New York: Harper, 1951).

14. I think the noblest expression of this view that I have seen is by Stanley Hauerwas, *A Community of Character* (Notre Dame, ID: Notre Dame University Press, 1981).

15. Finke and Stark, *The Churching of America, 1776-1990.*

Part II

Constitutional Interpretation

Originalism and Its Critics

Chapter 5

The Judicial Power: A View From *The Federalist Papers*

William Gangi

My essay is about judicial power–more particularly about how the authors of *The Federalist Papers*–James Madison, Alexander Hamilton and John Jay–understood the role the federal judiciary would play in our constitutional system.

I believe their understanding is a very different one than exists today, and I am very concerned about the facet of political science traditionally known as American constitutional law. When you pick up today's newspaper, leaf through the pages and scan the headlines carefully. Almost certainly you'll read somewhere that a judge is instructing legislators about what to do, and how to do it. The public lectures reflected in the headlines often are about important matters such as by what standards police searches or interrogations may be conducted, under what circumstances an abortion may be obtained, whether or not a convicted felon may be executed, and, as the citizens of Texas are well aware, whether the American flag may be burned. And I merely scratch the surface.

The impression the headlines make on a daily basis is very accurate: judges today more often than not have the last word on issues which concern the public most, and the more one explores the subject the more one realizes that legislatures often operate at the sufferance and direction of judges.

I contend that in many instances contemporary judicial decisions are illegitimate because they are inconsistent with the constitutional design understood by those who framed and ratified the Constitution, and that unless that design is formally changed through the amendment process we remain bound to their view of the judicial power. Judges are no more entitled to abuse the powers granted them than would be the Congress or President. I go further. Should a convincing case be made for the modern view of judicial power (that, for example, since *Brown v. Board of Education*, judges have accomplished good and moral things), as a constitutional scholar I would oppose such judicial decisions if convinced that the judges had acted illegitimately, that is, had usurped the legislative role. I take that position because I am convinced that looking the other way undermines the Constitution and the most important right it contains–the right of people to govern themselves. But perhaps I will have time to answer questions on those broader issues later. Now I wish to get to the substance of this brief essay.

One is immediately intrigued by the fact that of eighty-five papers, *Publius* (the common name used by all three authors of *The Federalist Papers*, and the name I shall use throughout this essay when referring to their combined authorship), does not begin a systematic discussion of the judiciary until the much acclaimed but often misinterpreted seventy-eighth paper. I cannot, however, begin my essay with number 78 because before Publius discussed the judiciary he established certain principles when he explored the legislative and executive branches of the government. Permit me to discuss only four of these principles. I will first state these principles and then return to each in turn:

1. A government must possess sufficient power to accomplish the ends assigned to it.
2. You cannot get cold feet once you have decided on the ends sought and the powers necessary to accomplish those ends.
3. All governments tend to tyranny.
4. Republican majorities have a tendency to abuse their power.

Let me now explain each of these principles in greater detail.

1. Of all the tasks assigned to a government the first is national defense. If a nation cannot defend itself little else matters. Publius illustrates the underlying principle when he raises the specific issue of how much power ought to be ceded to the proposed central government for purposes of common defense? He pulls no punches:

> these powers ought to exist without limitation, *because it is impossible to foresee or to define the extent and variety of national exigencies, and the correspondent extent and variety of the means which may be necessary to satisfy them.* The circumstances that endanger the safety of nations are infinite, and for this reason no constitutional shackles can wisely be imposed on the power to which the care of it is committed. This power ought to be coextensive with all the possible combinations of such circumstances; and which are appointed to preside over the common defense.[1]

Publius sums up the applicable principle in the simplest terms: "*the means ought to be proportioned to the end.*"[2]

2. You cannot get cold feet once you have decided on the ends to be sought by the government and the powers necessary to achieve those ends. Publius dismisses any reluctance to grant powers because they might be abused. That approach is unacceptable because any power needed to advance the common good potentially can be used to the common detriment.[3] He instead counsels constitution-makers first to consider "whether such a power be necessary to the public good [and only then to] . . . guard as effectually as possible against a perversion of the power to the public detriment."[4]

Withholding an admittedly needed power because one fears it may be abused, he contends, is as naive as it is foolish. When circumstances arise where that power is needed by the government, only two options exist. Either that government will dissolve for want of that power, or, more likely, that government will exercise the very power officially denied it, and that action of course renders doubtful any other restriction contained in a constitution.[5]

3. All governments tend to tyranny.

Publius defines tyranny as "the accumulation of all powers, legislative, executive, and judicial, in the same hands; whether of one, a few, or many, and whether hereditary, self-appointed, or elective."[6] Tyranny then is the use of governmental power (executive, legislative and judicial) against the governed and it is the greatest threat to a free people. Self-government is the opposite of tyranny and what was won by the American Revolution. Think of self-government as the right to define liberty or what today we might call individual rights. Without the right to govern ourselves, all other individual rights would be meaningless because *someone else* would define them.

In papers 47 through 51 Publius discusses how in the proposed constitution the universal tendency towards the consolidation of legislative, executive and judicial powers (i.e., tyranny) is combated. He calls these protections "auxiliary precautions."[7] They fall into three categories. First, the national government would be ceded only those powers necessary to accomplish the tasks entrusted to it. Beyond that, however, the states would be left independent and competent to otherwise meet the needs of their citizens. Second, with respect to the powers that were ceded to the national government, they would be separated and parceled-out according to their legislative, executive and judicial character. The executive and judicial branches also would be granted sufficient powers to defend themselves from legislative encroachments, the latter branch possessing the most power and therefore the branch most likely to exceed the powers granted to it. [Parenthetically– it is here, as we shall see before long, that Publius certainly envisioned an important role for the judiciary, and that role is included in what today we call judicial review.] Third, and finally, Publius suggests that all three branches be structured in such a fashion that private ambitions could simultaneously serve the public good. He concludes: "hence a double security arises to the rights of the people. The different governments will control each other, at the same time that each will be controlled by itself."[8]

Never, however, from the time Publius begins his discussion of governmental tyranny in paper 47, until two-thirds into paper 51, is the separation of powers ascribed the purpose many contemporary political scientists and legal scholars confer upon it:[9] that the judiciary should check abusive, though not unconstitutional, exercises of majority power.

4. Republican majorities have a tendency to abuse their power.

Publius admits, however, that when governmental powers are more widely distributed as they would be under the proposed constitution, tyranny–the concentration of power–would be less likely to occur. This brings us to our final principle: republican majorities also have a tendency to abuse their power. Republics, Publius warned, in addition to being prone like all governments to the concentration of power were also prone to a related but distinctly republican defect: majority abuses of power. He states that "when a majority is included in a faction, the form of popular government . . . enables it to sacrifice to its ruling passion or interest *both* the public good *and* the rights of other citizens."[10] In this instance, however, it is one faction (the majority of citizens) that uses governmental power against another faction (a minority of citizens), instead of those who possess governmental power using that power against all citizens.

There is little doubt that Publius considered the two issues distinct, and at this very juncture in paper 51, Publius turns from the problem of governmental tyranny, a problem he calls the "*first*" one, to the problem he explicitly labels the *second* one: the problem of majority tyranny. He states: "it is of great importance in a republic not only to guard the society against the oppression of its rulers, but to guard one part of the society against the injustice of the other part."[11] He maintains there are only two means to prevent such injustices. The first is to forge "a will in the community independent of the majority–that is, of the society itself," while the second, depends on "comprehending in the society so many separate descriptions of citizens as will render an unjust combination of a majority of the whole very improbable, if not impractical."[12]

Which solution do you think he selects? Many Americans today are very comfortable with the notion that the framers empowered the Supreme Court to regulate almost every aspect of public conduct and morals. They have come to believe that the Supreme Court ought to prevent a majority of citizens from using the law to do "bad" things; or conversely, should use its power to obtain "good" results, which over the past fifty years, certainly includes reform of race relations, state criminal justice systems and ever expanding perceptions of, for example, privacy and first amendment rights.

Could it be that Publius was referring to the judiciary, when he refers to establishing "a will in the community independent of the majority"? After all, as we shall see shortly, judges probably would serve life terms; they are trained to interpret the law, and by temperament should be (the framers' believed) less likely to make emotional decisions. Would they not be, therefore, particularly well-suited to resist majority pressures? Surely, if Publius opted for such an institutional check the judiciary would be the only conceivable governmental branch that would qualify.

The difficulty modern proponents of judicial power have with the first option put forth by Publius is, that no matter how convincing a case they make for it, he rejected it as *unacceptable* in a republic. Publius thought such a check appropriate only–in his own words–for "all governments possessing a hereditary or self-appointed authority."[13] And why did Publius and the framers reject the first option out of hand? Because they understood that to locate the right to make final public policy choices anywhere other than in the legislature would *change the form of government* from a republican one, to one that was *not* republican.

Publius instead concludes that only the "second method will be exemplified in the federal republic of the united states."[14] He elaborates:

> [I]n a free government the security for civil rights must be the same as that for religious rights. It consists in the one case in the multiplicity of interests, and in the other in the multiplicity of sects. The degree of security in both cases will depend on the number of interests and sects; and this may be presumed to depend on the extent of country and number of people comprehended under the same government.[15]

Interestingly enough, Publius' and the framers' selected the second option, despite their well-known and often misunderstood grave misgivings about popular governments: its tendency toward instability and ineffectiveness because in such governments public passions were habitually and often immediately injected into public policy-making. The proposed constitution, however, Publius argued took as many precautions as were reasonably possible for supporters of a republic, and having taken those precautions the framers never hesitated in recommending the republican form, where elected policy-makers remained directly or indirectly accountable to the people.[16] No other governmental form would have been acceptable to the American people.

So, it should come as no surprise that here, in paper 51, Publius refused the opportunity to embrace an institutional check to prevent the "cool and deliberate sense of the community . . . [from] . . . prevail[ing]," while at the same time he considers the judiciary as one of several "auxiliary" structures essential to prevent governmental power from concentrating.[17] An institutional check would be inconsistent with republican rule, but an independent judiciary would provide a reasonable means to assure that the limits *the people* put on themselves in their constitution would remain in place until future generations abandoned them by using the same extraordinary procedures used to adopt them in the first place–the amending process. Had Publius turned either to the executive or the judicial branches to protect a minority from legitimate (though perhaps abusive) legislative authority, he would have changed the character of the proposed constitution from a republic to a monarchy or to an oligarchy, respectively. And I unhesitatingly contend that contemporary advocates of judicial power lack the framers' confidence in republican government and the American people. They place greater confidence in the judiciary than the republican remedy: the multiplicity of interests.

We will return to these principles at the end of this essay, but now I want to detail what the Constitution says of the judicial power before I examine the views expressed in *The Federalist Papers*. The Constitution states that "the judicial power of the United States, shall be vested in one Supreme Court."[18] However that "judicial power" might be defined the text specifies that it would extend to "all cases in law and equity, arising under this Constitution, the laws of the United States, and treaties made, or which shall be made." It then specifies a more particular list of the cases where this power would apply: e.g., "To all cases affecting ambassadors, other public ministers and consuls."[19] It goes on to state that in a few instances the "supreme court shall have original jurisdiction [meaning that it would be the first court to hear the case, while in] all other cases. . . [it] shall have appellate jurisdiction, both as to law and fact, with such exceptions, and under such regulations as congress shall make."[20]

One might be surprised to learn that nowhere in the third article, or anywhere else in the Constitution, is the Supreme Court explicitly granted the power to declare legislative and executive acts void–what today is commonly referred to as the power of *judicial review*.[21] In *The Federalist Papers*, however, Publius unquestionably advocates and defends judicial review, though he does not specifically call it by that name.[22] And since my views on judicial power are frequently misunderstood or distorted I want to say here, as clearly as I know how, that I share Publius' judgement–I too believe that judicial review is essential to the constitutional schema, that the framers' anticipated its use, and that its use is essential for maintaining the Constitution. But after having said that, I also contend that today the federal judiciary abuses the power granted to it, and in doing so, frequently and illegitimately denies the American people the full extent of their right to govern themselves. In sum, it reserves to itself decisions that legitimately belong to the people and their legislators.

I already noted that not until paper 78 does Publius begin any systematic discussion of the judiciary. In earlier papers he had observed that it was commonly agreed that the absence of a separate and independent judiciary was one of the principal defects of the national government established under the Articles of Confederation.[23] Given such a consensus he claims that only three related issues had to be worked out,[24] and of those three issues only the second directly concerns us: "the tenure by which [judges] are to hold their place."[25]

You must keep in mind, as we continue with this analysis, that Publius' entire discussion of the judiciary takes place in the context of his view that federal judges ought to be granted tenure "during good behavior," a standard he describes as constituting "one of the most valuable . . . [m]odern improvements in the practice of government," and that during such service their salaries could not be reduced. Of equal importance, is that this "during good behavior" standard–for practical purposes amounting to lifetime tenure for federal judges–stands in stark contrast to the standard established for the legislative and executive branches of government: specific terms of office for members of the house, senate and the president. Indeed, the contrast between how Publius treats the tenure to be afforded judges and the other branches of government, is even greater if antifederalist sentiment is considered. The latter had criticized the constitution's tenure provisions for the executive and legislative branches as being too long. They instead favored, as had been the custom in many states, annual elections and rotation in office.[26]

Publius argues however that judicial tenure during good behavior will enable the people "to secure a steady, upright, and important administration of the laws."[27] Thus, tenure during good behavior was proposed by the framers not out of solicitude for those agreeing to be judges but rather because the framers believed such tenure was necessary to accomplish the end sought–judicial independence. That end was intended to better secure a *public interest*, not to elevate judges above legislators or to abandon the republican schema.

Let us now specifically turn to paper 78. Publius observes that when governments are created that seek to separate the legislative power (to make the laws), from the executive (to execute the laws) and judicial (to interpret the laws) powers, "the judiciary, from the nature of its functions, will always be the least dangerous to the political rights of the constitution; because it will be least in a capacity to annoy or injure them." He then explains that unlike the executive who "not only dispenses the honors but holds the sword of the community," and the legislature, which "not only commands the purse but prescribes the rules by which the duties and rights of every citizen are to be regulated," the judiciary has no specific concrete powers. Instead, "[i]t may truly be said to have neither force nor will but merely judgment; and must ultimately depend upon the aid of the executive arm even for the efficacy of its judgments." For these reasons Publius concludes that the judiciary is "beyond comparison the weakest of the three departments of power," specifically quoting Montesquieu's assessment that "'the judiciary is next to nothing.'"[28] Since judges possessed neither the power to make nor the power to enforce laws, and they rarely enjoyed independence, judges in the past had been frequently intimidated by legislators and executives. Thus, the Philadelphia delegates were concerned with the question of how "to enable [the judiciary] to defend itself against . . . [such] attacks" and were convinced that if judicial independence could be secured, "the general liberty of the people [would] never be endangered" from either of the two other branches. Shortly after saying that, however, Publius makes it perfectly clear that an independent judiciary *is in the American people's interest* because such independence is "peculiarly essential in a limited constitution."[29] He explains:

> [B]y a limited constitution, I understand one which contains specified exceptions to the legislative authority; such, for instance, as that it shall pass no bills of attainder, no *ex post facto* laws, and the like. Limitations of this kind can be preserved in practice no other way than through the medium of courts of justice, whose duty it must be to declare all acts contrary to the manifest tenor of the

> constitution void. Without this, all the reservations of particular rights or privileges would amount to nothing.[30]

Publius then explains that the power to declare "legislative acts void, because contrary to the constitution" had been misrepresented by antifederalist critics who wrongly contended that that power implied "a superiority of the judiciary to the legislative power." In rejecting that contention, he responds that the authority to declare acts of the legislature void rests on the "clear. . . [p]rinciple. . . that every act of a delegated authority, contrary to the tenor of the commission under which it is exercised is void." It follows therefore that "[n]o legislative act . . . contrary to the constitution, can be valid." It is, he declares, simply a matter of putting first things first. A constitution must be considered more important than an ordinary piece of legislation. "To deny this would be to affirm that the deputy is greater than his principal; that the servant is above his master; that the representatives of the people are superior to the people themselves; that men acting by virtue of powers may do not only what their powers do not authorize, but what they forbid."[31]

If an independent judiciary would be incapable of resolving the inevitable questions that would arise because of a unique constitution that for the first time delegated only certain sovereign powers to one government while the other retained all others, Publius asks, who could resolve such issues? Certainly the traditional caution that one should not be the judge of his own cause seemed particularly applicable. Neither the congress nor the executive therefore seemed a suitable repository for a power that would bind the other branches to its determination, although Publius does add–at least not where the legislative interpretation cannot "be collected from any particular provision in the constitution." Instead, he suggests that it is much more appropriate for the courts to serve as "an intermediate body between the people and the legislature in order . . . to keep the later within the limits assigned to their authority." After all, the "interpretation of the laws is the proper and peculiar province of the courts. A constitution is in fact, and must be regarded by judges as, *a fundamental law*."[32] Should conflicts arise between the constitution and legislative acts, "the constitution ought to be preferred to the statute, the intention of the people to the intention of their agents."[33]

Publius then repeats an earlier conclusion, that placing the power to declare acts of the other branches null and void neither suggests the superiority of the judicial power, nor does it imply that judges possess any special wisdom with respect to the making of ordinary public policy. He observes:

> it only supposes that the power of the people is superior to both, and that where the will of the legislature, declared in its statutes, stands in opposition of that of the people, declared in the constitution, the judges ought to be governed by the latter rather than the former. They ought to regulate their decisions by the fundamental laws rather than by those which are not fundamental.[34]

When these comments are taken together it is clear that Publius believed the constitution must be placed on a higher plane than ordinary legislation. When, for example, he speaks about "the intention of the people," he must be referring to the intentions of those who ratified the constitution.[35] He believes that the intentions of those who ratified the constitution must be preferred to "the intention of their agents," which he understood as the people's currently elected representatives. Why? Because when Publius' referred to "the intention of the people" I contend he could not possibly have been referring to the intentions of the *current population*. Under the Constitution, by simple majority vote, the current population (without any assistance from the judiciary), can exercise its will by legislating as it sees fit. Should the existing Constitution pose some barrier to the will of the current population, they could overcome that obstacle by using the amendment procedures. Publius however mentions neither alternative. Instead, he puts forth the proposition that in reviewing legislative acts judges must abide by the "power of the people . . . declared in the constitution."[36]

In subsequent paragraphs in paper 78 Publius contends that the judicial power to declare an act of the legislature void granted in the constitution is not terribly different than the typical statutory interpretative power where judges "fix [the] . . . meaning and operation [of laws]." That is, judges often resolve, for example, interpretive problems where two or more laws exist on the same subject but the legislature has not offered any specific guidelines as to which law should take precedence. Over the centuries, Publius explains, judges developed different rules to handle different types of interpretive situations. For example, in the instance noted above (when two laws conflict), the applicable principle would be that "the last . . [in] time shall be preferred to the first." Such guidelines are, he admits, "mere rules[s] of construction" and do not stem from any strict law, but he claims they are associated with "the nature and reason" of what judges do on a daily basis. These rules are followed because they provide a "reasonable" means for resolving "acts of *equal* authority."[37]

Logically then, when the act of a superior authority conflicts with an act created by a subordinate authority, "the prior act of a superior ought to be preferred." In such circumstances, he notes, it is anticipated that "it will be the duty of the judicial tribunals to adhere to the latter and disregard the former."[38] Could judges, he then asks, pretend some constitutional infirmity, and then illegitimately declare a piece of legislation void simply because they dislike it? Publius does not deny that possibility; he instead counters that such an assertion proves too much.[39] Since judges interpret statutes every day, what, he asks, prevents judges from doing that *all* the time?[40] Judges are ordinarily trusted with the power to interpret the law; why should they not be trusted with extraordinary applications of the same power. Presumably they will prefer the will of the people originally expressed in the Constitution over that of currently elected representatives, just as they are expected on a daily basis to prefer the will of the legislature above their own opinion. Any other line of reasoning, "if it proved anything, would prove that there ought to be no judges distinct from [the legislative] body," a position, he points out, that even critics of the proposed constitution reject because that had been one of the fundamental weaknesses of the Articles of Confederation.[41]

The proposed constitution, Publius maintains, addresses every aspect of an independent judiciary. It assures that judges remain independent by guaranteeing them tenure only during good behavior as well as assumes their salary cannot be reduced; it provides the means by which the judiciary can defend that independence, thereby serving the interests of all because the power to declare illegitimate legislative and executive acts is crucial if the natural tendency toward the consolidation of power is to be thwarted. But despite this comprehensive treatment of the problem, Publius notes, critics still raise objections, and they do so without offering some alternative and so he concludes their fear of judicial abuses lacks a reasonable basis.

But he is not quite finished yet. Publius observes that providing tenure during good behavior is perfectly consistent with the goal that "courts of justice are to [serve] . . . as bulwarks of a limited constitution against legislative encroachments." Without such a framework of independence he contends that judges probably could not protect "the rights of individuals," particularly when elected representatives, faced with one crises or another, might opt to oppress a "minor party in the community."[42] A majority, he notes, need not resort to some illegality to suppress a minority because that majority–being a majority–at any time could redefine the rights of the minority by "alter[ing (i.e., amending the constitution, which Publius describes as "that fundamental principle of republican government")] or abolish[ing] the established constitution." Despite its ultimate power to change even the fundamental law, however, Publius insists that until the majority actually did so by amendment, the majority or their elected representatives could not ignore what the Constitution had meant to those who had originally ratified it. Nor should courts, he warns, wink at possible infractions. Instead, he contends that "[u]ntil the people have, by some solemn and authoritative act, annulled or changed the established form, it is binding upon themselves collectively, as well as individually; and no presumption, or even knowledge of their sentiments, can warrant their representatives in a departure from it prior to such an act."[43] Thus, if the ratifiers' understanding of a constitutional phrase is clearly understood and discernible, I understand Publius' as maintaining that all Americans–legislators as well as citizens–remain morally and legally bound to that understanding.

Although Publius makes several additional points in paper 78, I end my analysis of it here as well as skip over paper 79, since the subjects discussed there do not immediately concern us.[44] In paper 80, however, Publius returns to more substantial issues although the focus of his remarks change, from demonstrating in paper 78 why little danger exists from the creation of an independent judiciary, to in paper 80, emphasizing how an independent judiciary might prove beneficial. For example, since the constitution contains explicit restrictions on the states (e.g., states are prohibited from issuing paper money or taxing imports), he asks if it is not foolhardy to assume that those restrictions always would be honored without some means of enforcement? Convention delegates believed they had only two choices: either the union had to have a "direct negative on state laws" or the "federal courts" had to be capable of overruling any state action "in manifest contravention of the articles of union."[45] The delegates wisely chose the latter.

In the pages that follow Publius provides additional examples where federal and state power might conflict, and for each, he carefully explains why the creation of an independent judiciary ought to prove beneficial. For example, he claims that no one state should be able to jeopardize the foreign relations of the united states. In another instance he argues that a dispute between two states needs some means of resolution. In yet again another instance, he suggests how the "privileges and immunities" and maritime trade clauses might be enforced, and why a particular word like "equity" was necessary.[46] After enumerating another list of types of cases the federal judiciary might hear, Publius concludes that should "some partial inconveniences appear to be connected with the incorporation of any of them into the plan it ought to be recollected that the national legislature will have ample authority to make such *exceptions* and to prescribe such regulations as will be calculated to obviate or remove these inconveniences."[47]

Publius begins paper 81 by quoting a critic of the proposed constitution, explaining here in more detail why he rejected as unfounded a criticism first reported in paper 78, namely, that if the proposed supreme court is "'separate and independent, [it] will be superior to that of the legislature.'"[48] He zeros-in on the specific antifederalist criticism that federal judges could construe "the laws according to the *spirit* of the constitution," and because under the proposed constitution judges would be answerable to no one (i.e., they are not elected), they might abuse their power. More specifically, these critics charged that the federal judiciary could "mould [a law] into whatever shape it may think proper; especially as its decisions will not be in any manner subject to the revision or correction of the legislative body." Thus, they concluded, the judicial power contained in the proposed constitution is "'as unprecedented as it is dangerous.'"[49]

In rejecting their assessment Publius replies that "[t]here is not a syllable in the plan under consideration which *directly* empowers the national courts to construe the laws according to the spirit of the constitution." Conceding that his position–that the constitution "ought to be the standard of construction for the laws" whenever any subordinate laws conflict–could not be deduced solely from the constitution, he asserts that his position is nevertheless consistent with "the general theory of a limited constitution."[50]

I skip over other arguments put forth by Publius at this juncture, which contend that the model for the judiciary contained in the constitution was not "as novel and unprecedented" as its critics suggested.[51] Instead, I want to concentrate on his conclusion–that the danger posed by the judiciary is manageable. Please examine his words carefully:

> that the supposed danger of judicial encroachments . . . is in reality a phantom. Particular misconstructions and contraventions of the will of the legislature may now

> and then happen; but they can never be so extensive as to amount to an inconvenience, *or in any sensible degree to affect the order of the political system.* This may be inferred with certainty from the general nature of the judicial power, from the objects to which it relates, from the manner in which it exercised, from its comparative weakness, and from its total incapacity to support its usurpations by force.[52]

In sum, Publius contends–after weighing benefits and possible costs–giving the judiciary the power to supervise the constitution's boundaries was both beneficial and perfectly compatible with its overall design. That conclusion, however, did not preclude the Philadelphia delegates from taking additional precautions. Publius points out that there is a very "important check" against any potential abuses from the judiciary: judges may be impeached. And significantly, the impeachment procedures contained in the constitution also should give judges pause–that is, the House of Representatives would indict an errant judge and the Senate would try them. Impeachment thus was a political not a judicial event. "This is alone a security. . . . [T]here never can be danger that the judges, by a series of deliberate usurpations on the authority of the legislature, would hazard the united resentment of the body intrusted with it, while this body was possessed of the means of punishing their presumption by degrading them from their stations."[53]

Apparently still dissatisfied that he has conveyed the full extent of the precautions taken at Philadelphia against the possibility of abusive judicial power, he again points out, as he did in paper 80, the power of congress to regulate or to place exceptions on the exercise of appellate federal jurisdiction.[54] This time he specifically quotes the applicable constitutional text, observing that "the supreme court would have nothing more than appellate jurisdiction 'with such *exceptions* and under such *regulations* as the congress shall make.'"[55] Then, several pages later he repeats the point, claiming that it is only proper that appellate jurisdiction first be couched in broad terms and then to provide "that this jurisdiction shall be subject to such *exceptions* and regulations as the national legislature may prescribe."[56] He also clearly describes why the delegates did so: "this will enable the government to modify [jurisdiction] in such a manner as will best answer the ends of public justice and security."[57] And two paragraphs later for the fourth and final time, Publius again refers to the right of Congress to regulate and make exceptions to federal appellate jurisdiction.[58]

His remarks in papers 80 and 81, leave little doubt that for Publius, given the impressive precautions taken against the possibility of judicial abuses, the nation had much more to gain than to fear from the constitution's creation of a truly independent judiciary–"that an ordinary degree of prudence and integrity in the national councils will insure us solid advantages from the establishment of the proposed judiciary without exposing us to any of the inconveniences which have been predicted from that source."[59]

Essay form does not permit any detailed consideration of paper 83, from which I conclude that Publius also anticipated that in practicing their interpretive craft judges would conform to a six hundred year tradition.[60] They would, therefore, follow interpretive guidelines that Publius variously called "rule[s] of interpretation,"[61] or "rules of legal interpretation,"[62] or just "rules."[63] At other times he used expressions such as "rules of construction"[64] or "*legal maxims.*"[65] The most complete description he offered is that "rules of legal interpretation are rules of *common sense*, adopted by the courts in the construction of the laws."[66] Clearly then the Philadelphia delegates believed that rules of interpretation were integral to the task of interpretation, and they also were quite aware that these rules could be manipulated and used inappropriately.[67]

Conclusion

At this juncture I want to review both the initial principles mentioned at the beginning of this article, and the content of papers 78, 80 and 81. Publius' entire discussion about judicial power takes place in the context of provisos for good behavior and a guarantee that judicial salaries could not be decreased.[68] These provisions are defended on two grounds. Firstly, there is nothing to fear. Judges lack any coercive power. They command no army; they have no money; they disperse no honors or patronage. Second, judges play a passive role: cases come to them through the ordinary processes of law. Judicial decisions are ultimately only as effective as are the quality of their judgments, and even then those judgments are dependent on the executive for enforcement.

Those two realities are at the heart of the framers view of the judiciary. And it is because judges lacked political and coercive power that Publius maintains that it is in *their* hands the power to interpret the law can safely be lodged. Judges depend on reason while the legislature and executive ultimately depend on the ability to coerce. If judges also possessed the physical power to coerce, how would their judgments differ from legislative or executive judgments? A physical power to coerce more likely than not evokes a physical power to resist. Civil war is its natural end. But reason in the hands of judges offers all parties (i.e., legislators, executives and citizens) another choice–to honor their oath "to support this Constitution."[69] All citizens owe allegiance to those who shed their blood to secure our right to self-government.

Publius maintains that an independent judiciary will reap substantial benefits. Not only will such independence enable judges to better perform their ordinary task of interpreting the law (i.e., to fix the meaning of ordinary statutes) without fear of legislative or executive retribution, but they now also can be entrusted with an extraordinary application of the interpretative task (i.e., the right to declare null and void those laws contrary to the intent of those who ratified the Constitution).[70] Publius points out that in a limited government surely that power must exist somewhere, and what better place than with the judiciary whose members already are familiar with the interpretive task, and who, under the proposed constitution, would be independent and secure–thus, more likely to protect the Constitution's meaning from momentary passion.

But let's make something very clear. Despite Publius' staunch support for an independent judiciary and for the power of judicial review, his support cannot reasonably be construed to assert that he or the framers sanctioned giving the judiciary legislative or executive powers. The latter powers are different in their nature, and in the Constitution they are specifically assigned to other departments. When any scholar comes to the opposite conclusion that scholar, I contend, has abandoned the framers' design and has substituted his own. Publius never abandoned the republican form of government and by some alleged subterfuge embraced an oligarchic one.[71] In fact, by characterizing the judiciary as next to nothing, and by his other observations, Publius leaves little doubt that although the judicial role would be an important one it also would be limited.[72] If any doubt persists Publius' explicit rejection of an institutional check on the legitimate exercise of legislative power, must put such doubts to rest.[73]

Finally, I contend that throughout his discussion of the judiciary, Publius applies the same principles he had applied to the legislative and executive branches. You may recall the most important of these principles, that the means provided should be commensurate with the ends sought.[74] Recall also that if that principle is applied, first one asks whether or not the power to be granted is necessary to accomplish the end sought, and then whether or not the granting of that power is consistent with the overall design. Once affirmatives are obtained on both scores any potential for abuse stemming from the granting of that power becomes a *secondary* issue, for unless some viable alternative is put forth to accomplish the end sought, it is far more realistic to grant the power than to forgo it. One then focuses on prudential efforts to protect against its abuse.[75]

These principles clearly are at play with respect to how the framers approached the judiciary, the role it was expected to play, and the powers granted it. Thus, when a constitution is written and purports to establish a limited government, Publius insists there must be some means to enforce its provisions. The power to review the actions of the other branches should be assigned to the judiciary because judges interpret the law all the time, and the power to declare acts unconstitutional is most akin to statutory interpretation.[76] Furthermore, he points out traditional rules of interpretive construction also would serve to reduce any arbitrariness. As might be anticipated, Publius then rejects all contentions that possible abuses of the power granted the judiciary (e.g., that judges would substitute their personal views for those of the legislature, that they would be guided by the spirit of the laws,[77] or that they would inappropriately use rules of construction) are determining. Such arguments fail to provide sufficient reasons to deny the power to declare void acts inconsistent with the Constitution to an independent judiciary. He reaches that conclusion, I suggest, not because those possibilities do not exist but because they do not warrant abandoning a power that is admittedly called for by a limited constitution, especially since no other viable alternative had been put forth that addressed the issues as comprehensively as did the proposed constitution.[78] After all, any power employed for the public good is a power that can be abused–that is the nature of power–and he drives that point home by reminding critics that logic leads to two conclusions they themselves reject, first, that "there ought to be no judges distinct from [the legislature]"[79] and second, that the same fears could be raised against all judges and the ordinary power exercised daily by judges–interpreting statutory law. As might have been anticipated, however, Publius instead discusses the practical checks against the possibility of judicial abuses. These include the controlling and regulating of the appellate jurisdiction of the federal courts, an observation he repeats no less than four times, and, of course, impeachment.

In sum, Publius applies the same principles to the exercise of judicial power that he had applied to the legislative and executive branches: what each branch must do, what powers are needed by each to do it, and how the potential for abuse of the powers granted each can be minimized. Judicial review then is defended by Publius as a partial republican cure for the universal tendency of all governments toward the consolidation of power. There is no evidence to support the belief that the framers' viewed judicial review as a means by which majority rule may be side-stepped and an oligarchic rule substituted. As long as majorities act within the powers granted their actions are constitutional ones. Judicial abuses, therefore, must be opposed on the level of principle, whether or not one believes what the judges are doing is good or bad. The majority's actions may not be moral ones; they may not be wise ones–but they certainly may be constitutional ones. With respect to immoral and unwise actions we must look to ourselves, for it is we–not elected representatives–who ultimately condone immorality and stupidity.

Final Comments

I am always looking for analogies to help explain my approach to constitutional law, and they sometimes come from unexpected sources. Attending church services one Sunday, a priest recounted that as a child he spent and learned to love summer days at Jones Beach, on Long Island, New York, and throughout his life he made it a habit to return there at least once every year. For those of you not familiar with Jones Beach it has an enormous parking lot, and on hot summer days unless you arrive very early in the morning, you face a considerable walk from the parking lot to the beach.

In any event this past summer he was returning from the beach to the parking lot, and just in front of him was a grandmother, loaded down with various beach paraphilia (chair, cooler, blanket and so on). Walking beside her was her five or six year old distraught granddaughter, carrying her own little beach chair. The child was very upset, bawling because she wanted her grandmother to also carry *her* to the car.

The grandmother refused. She told her granddaughter that she had to walk to the car and carry the chair she had used all day at the beach. The grandmother, added however, that as they walked, they could play a kind of game: her granddaughter could walk in her shadow, following all her movements.

Before long the bawling stopped and the child gleefully began walking in her grandmother's shadow. The priest deduced two lessons from the scene he witnessed. First, we all must carry our own burdens and should learn to do so without complaint; and second, that we all need someone's shadow to walk in. He then asked each member of his congregation, "whose shadow do *you* walk in? Who influences *your* life?"

In bringing this lecture to a close I raise the same question the priest did in his homily. In whose footsteps do we as a people walk? I contend that constitutional scholars must walk in the framers' footsteps, and it is our task to mark the boundaries of those shadows, to help explain to the American people when they are *obliged* to follow the footsteps of the founders, and just as important, to tell them when they are *not* so obliged. Insofar as judges walk in the founders' shadow their decisions are legitimate. They may in doubtful situations even stretch the boundaries of the shadows cast. They may not, however, deceive the American people, asking us for fidelity to shadows they themselves create.

Courts today often go far beyond their competency–they usurp the authority and responsibilities of legislators, which is to say that they undermine the rights of all citizens. Resistance to judicial abuses will grow only when the American people realize–as they did during the New Deal–that many of the public policies pronounced by the judiciary rest on no greater authority than what five justices think is good public policy, which in my view amounts to no authority at all. In the 1930s Franklin D. Roosevelt counseled, as I do counsel today, his fellow citizens to resist judicial abuses. He wished then, as I wish today, to put public policy-making back into the hands of accountable legislators. He understood then, as I do understand today, that questioning the legitimacy of Supreme Court decisions cannot be confined to the halls of academia. They are and must be the central issue of this nation's political life.

Notes

1. James Madison, Alexander Hamilton, John Jay, *The Federalist Papers* No. 23, 153 (Arlington House) [hereinafter cited as *Federalist*]. Publius elsewhere (though the authors of Papers 23 and 41 are different) adds:

> With what color of propriety could the force necessary for defense be limited by those who cannot limit the force of offense? If a federal constitution could chain the ambition or set bounds to the exertions of all other nationals, then indeed might it prudently chain the discretion of its own government and set bounds to the exertions for its own safety.
>
> How could a readiness for war in time of peace be safely prohibited, unless we could prohibit in like manner the preparations and establishments of every hostile nation? The means of security can only be regulated by the means and the danger of attack. They will, in fact, be ever determined by these rules and by no others.

Ibid., No. 41, 257. See also Leo Strauss, Natural Right and History (Chicago: University of Chicago Press, 1953), 160-161 (Publius' position is within the Aristotelian tradition).

2. *Federalist,* No. 22, 153. He continues, "the persons from whose agency the attainment of any *end* is expected ought to possess the *means* by which it is to be attained." Ibid.

3. Publius scolds critics, maintaining that those who oppose the powers granted the federal government "very little considered how far these powers were necessary means of attaining a necessary end." Instead, he charges, they chose "to dwell on the inconveniences which must be unavoidably blended with all political advantages; and on the possible abuses which must be incident to every power or trust of which a beneficial use can be made." He rejects opposition arguments as lacking in "good sense." Ibid., No. 41, 255.

Publius also observes the following:

> It may display the subtlety of the writer; it may open a boundless field for rhetoric and declamation; it may inflame the passions of the unthinking and may confirm the prejudices of the misthinking; but cool and candid people will at once reflect that the purest of human blessings must have a portion of alloy in them; that the choice must always be made, if not of the lesser evil, at least of the GREATER, not the PERFECT, good; and that in every political institution, a power to advance the public happiness involves a discretion which may be misapplied and abused.

Ibid., No. 41, 255-56.

4. Ibid., 256.

5. "Tyranny has perhaps oftener grown out of the assumptions of power called for, on pressing exigencies, by a defective constitution, than out of the full exercise of the largest constitutional authorities." Ibid., No. 20, 136-37.

6. *Federalist, supra* note 1, No. 47, 301. Professor Adair observes that in monarchies and aristocracies there is "an inveterate and incorrigible tendency to use the apparatus of government to serve the special selfish interests of the one or the few. However, the aristocratic form offered, so it was believed, the best possibility of *wisdom*, in planning public measures, while monarchy promised the necessary *energy, secrecy,* and *dispatch* for executing policy." Adair, "Experience Must Be Our Only Guide: History, Democratic Theory, and the United States Constitution," in R. A. Billington, *The Reinterpretation of Early American History* (San Marino, CA: Huntington Library, 1966), 143.

7. Ibid., 322.

8. Ibid.

9. George W. Carey, *In Defense of the Constitution* (Cumberland, VA: James River Press, 1989), 53: "that [it] was intentionally fused into our system to *thwart majority rule* in one way or another." (Emphasis added.) A revised and expanded edition of this work was published by the Liberty Fund in 1995. Publius labels the problem of governmental tyranny as the "*First*" problem. *Federalist, supra* note 1, No. 51, 323 (emphasis in original).

10. *Federalist, supra* note 1, No. 10, 80.

11. *Federalist, supra* note 1, No. 51, 323. Publius explicitly labels the problem of majority tyranny as, "*Second.*" He also mentions the following: "Different interests necessarily exist in different classes of citizens. If a majority be united by a common

interest, the rights of the minority will be insecure." Ibid.

12. Ibid., 323-24.

13. Ibid., 324. Publius describes that approach, in any event, "a precarious security," since the "will in the community independent of the majority" might in fact join with the majority or minority. Ibid., 323-24. See C. Wolfe, *Judicial Activism: Bulwark of Freedom or Precarious Security* (Pacific Grove, CA: Brooks/Cole Publishing Company, 1991) for an evaluation of the pros and cons of contemporary judicial activism. Cf. William Gangi, *Judicial Expansionism: An Evaluation of the Ongoing Debate*, 8 Ohio Northern University Law Review 1 (1981).

14. *Federalist, supra* note 1, 324. Publius adds: "Whilst all authority in [the United States] will be derived from and dependent on the society, the society itself will be broken into so many parts, interests and classes of citizens, that the rights of individuals, or of the minority, will be in little danger from interested combinations of the majority." Ibid.

15. Ibid., 324.

16. Ibid., No. 39, 240-41. Publius claims that "we may define a republic to be, or at least may bestow that name on, a government which derives all its powers directly or indirectly from the great body of the people, and is administered by persons holding their offices during pleasure for a limited period, or during good behavior." Ibid., 241. Elsewhere he makes this point:

> It is one thing to be subordinate to the laws, and another to be dependent on the legislative body. The first comports with, the last violates, the fundamental principles of good government; and, whatever may be the forms of the Constitution, unites all power in the same hands. The tendency of the legislative authority to absorb every other has been fully displayed and illustrated by examples in some preceding numbers. In governments *purely republican*, this tendency is almost irresistible. The representatives of the people, in a popular assembly, seem sometimes to fancy that they are the people themselves, and betray strong symptoms of impatience and disgust at the least sign of opposition from any other quarter; as if the exercise of its rights, by either the executive or judiciary, were a breach of their privilege and an outrage to their dignity.

Ibid., No. 71, 431. Emphasis added.

17. Publius makes the following comment:

> It is true that in controversies relating to the boundary between the two jurisdictions, the tribunal which is ultimately to decide is to be established under the general government. But this does not change the principle of the case. The decision is to be impartially made, according to the rules of the Constitution; and all the usual and most effectual precautions are taken to secure this impartiality. Such tribunal is clearly essential to prevent an appeal to the sword and a dissolution of the compact; and that it ought to be established under the general rather than under the local governments, or, to speak more properly, that it could be safely established under the first alone, is a position not likely to be combated.

Federalist, supra note 1, No. 39, 245-46.

18. U.S. Constitution, art. 3, sec. 1.

19. U.S. Constitution, art. 3, sec. 2.

20. U.S. Constitution, art. 3, sec. 3.

21. The reader might find equally surprising the fact that the Constitution does not specify the number of Supreme Court justices. For several thorough discussions of judicial review and related matters, see generally, W. F. Murphy and C. H. Pritchett, *Courts, Judges, and Politics* (NY: Random House, 1961), C. S. Hyneman, *The Supreme Court on Trial* (NY: Atherton Press, 1963), R. Berger, *Congress v. The Supreme Court* (Cambridge: Harvard University Press, 1969), H. J. Abraham, *The Judiciary: The Supreme Court in the Governmental Process*, 7th ed. (Boston: Allyn and Bacon, 1987) and L. W. Levy, *Original Intent and the Framers' Constitution* (NY: Macmillan, 1988).

22. See text accompanying endnote 30 ("to declare all acts contrary to the manifest tenor of the constitution void").

23. *Federalist, supra* note 1, No. 22, 150.

24. Ibid. The first issue is, "[t]he mode of appointing the judges," which Publius considers as having been already thoroughly discussed, since it "is the same with that of appointing the officers of the Union in general and has been so fully discussed in the two last numbers" (i.e., papers 76 and 77). The third, "[t]he partition of the judiciary authority between different courts and their relation to each other," he does not discuss until paper 81, and is not at the heart of our inquiry. Ibid.

25. Ibid.

26. "Antifederalists noted that under the proposed scheme of representation, the power of recall, frequent elections, and rotation of office were not built into the model." William B. Allen & Gordon Lloyd, *The Essential Antifederalist* (Lanham, MD: University Press of America, 1985), xiii [hereinafter cited as Antifederalist]. See also comment accompanying endnote 68 (no reduction of judicial salaries).

27. *Federalist, supra* note 1, 465. This proposal certainly seems to have been a bold one, given American distrust of monarchical devices, and even more striking is that it deviated from the normal inclination to put officials on a short-leash: regular elections. As we shall see, however, Publius makes powerful arguments that the deviation is warranted and in fact is in the common interest.

28. Ibid., 465-66, 466.

29. Ibid., 466. Elsewhere I argue more fully that contemporary abuses of judicial authority are not due to poor reasoning on Publius' part or to some defect in the framers' design, but to an unanticipated failure on the part of elected representatives to defend the people's right to govern themselves. For a complete exposition of my views, see William Gangi, *Saving the Constitution from the Courts* (Norman, OK: University of Oklahoma Press, 1995).

30. *Federalist, supra* note 1, 466.

31. Ibid., 467.

32. Ibid. Emphasis added.

33. Ibid.

34. Ibid., 467-468.

35. I refer the reader to Publius' explicit comments "that the representatives of the people are [not] superior to the people themselves" (see *supra* text accompanying note 31) and "the intention of the people [ought to be preferred] to the intention of their agents" (see *supra* text accompanying note 33).

36. Nearly a century later a unanimous 1872 Judiciary Committee Report put forth a similar understanding:

> In construing the Constitution we are compelled to give it such interpretation as will secure the result which was intended to be accomplished by those who framed it, and the people who adopted it. . . . A construction which should give . . . [a] phrase . . . a meaning different from the sense in which they adopted the Constitution, would be as unconstitutional as a departure from the plain and express language of the Constitution. . . . A change in the popular use of any word employed in the Constitution cannot retroact upon the Constitution, either to enlarge or limit its provisions. . . . Judge Thomas Cooley. . . wrote: "The meaning of the Constitution is fixed when it is adopted, and it is not different at any subsequent time. . . [T]he object of construction, as applied to a written constitution, is to give effect to the intent of the people in adopting it."

As quoted in Berger, '*Government by Judiciary*': *Judge Gibbons' Argument Ad Hominem*, 59 Boston University Law Review 783, 785n. 12 (1979) (Citations omitted).

37. *Federalist*, *supra* note 1, 468. "It is a rule not enjoined upon the courts by legislative provision but adopted by themselves, as consonant to truth and propriety, for the direction of their conduct as interpreters of the law." Ibid.

38. Ibid.

39. Ibid., 468-469. "It can be of no weight to say that the courts, on the pretense of a repugnancy, may substitute their own pleasure to the constitutional intentions of the legislature." Ibid.

40. Ibid., 469. ("The courts must declare the sense of the law; and if they should be disposed to exercise WILL instead of JUDGMENT, the consequence would equally be the substitution of their pleasure to that of the legislative body.")

41. Ibid., 469.

42. Ibid.

43. Ibid., 469-470. Publius is perfectly consistent here. If a limited constitution is to endure, it must be respected by all–even those authorized to change it. The capability of the present generation to change the Constitution does not warrant them or their elected representatives from abandoning–without using the appropriate procedures–the ratified limitations.

44. In No. 79, Publius discusses provisions for supporting the federal judiciary.

45. Ibid. At the Convention Madison supported a proposal for the federal government to have a veto over *state* laws. That veto was rejected, and its rejection apparently was linked to the creation of an independent judiciary. Professor Charles Hobson concludes:

> That the Supreme Court would be the ultimate line of defense was implicit in the jurisdiction of the federal judiciary as defined in Article III and was made explicit by the twenty-fifth section of the Judiciary Act of 1789, providing for appeals from state tribunals to the Supreme Court. As an additional precaution the framers wrote into the Constitution specific prohibitions and restraints on the states, including an absolute ban on coinage and paper money. Together, the supremacy clause, the judiciary article, and the restrictions on the states constituted the judicial substitute for the legislative negative on state laws.

Hobson, *The Negative on State Laws: James Madison, the Constitution, and the Crisis of Republican Government*, 36 William and Mary Quarterly 215, 228-29 (1979) [hereinafter Hobson]. Professor Hobson describes Madison as being "disappointed with the Convention's final draft." Hobson, 216. But in their introduction to *The Federalist Papers* Professors Kendall and Carey astutely observe that "[t]he Constitution was made possible . . . first and foremost because in the course of its proceedings the individual delegates became increasingly willing to 'write off' their own pet ideas, to subordinate their personal preferences, to the overriding necessity of arriving at a *consensus. Federalist, supra* note 1, xii. Their essay, "How to read *The Federalist*," also may be found in Willmore Kendall, *Contra Mundum* (New Rochelle, NY: Arlington House, 1971), 403, 410 .

46. *Federalist, supra* note 1, No. 80, 478-81.

47. Ibid., 480-81. Publius is specifically referring to the constitutional language in Art. III, sec. 2 (2), which provides for appellate jurisdiction "with such Exceptions, and under such Regulations as the Congress shall make." *Federalist, supra* note 1, No. 80, 481. See text accompanying endnote 20.

48. *Federalist, supra* note 1, No. 81, 482. For his initial rejection of the claim, see *supra* text accompanying endnote 30.

49. *Federalist, supra* note 1, No. 81, 482. Professors Allen and Lloyd recount the concern expressed by Agrippa:

> I appeal to the knowledge of everyone, if it does not frequently happen, that a law is interpreted in practice very differently from the intention of the legislature. Hence arises the necessity of acts to amend and explain former acts. This is not an inconvenience in the common and ordinary business of legislation, but is a great one in a constitution. A constitution is a legislative act of the whole people. It is an excellence that it should be permanent, otherwise we are exposed to perpetual insecurity from the fluctuation of government.

Antifederalist, supra note 26, p. 45.

50. *Federalist, supra* note 1, 482. Publius had made several points in No. 78, the most important being that the proposed constitution would be a written one, that a federal government with only limited powers had been created, and that the proposed constitution contained specific prohibitions directed at the federal government or the states, or both. Please also keep in mind that Publius' analysis here and in all the papers are made *in the absence of a Bill of Rights,* which of course eventually only added to the number of prohibitions entrusted to the judiciary for monitoring. See *supra* text accompanying endnote 29. But, as I defend elsewhere at greater length, the original or additional prohibitions did not increase the federal judiciary's power, only expanded its responsibilities. They, for example, were never authorized to expand the meaning such prohibitions had beyond the protections they afforded at the time of their adoption; and the judiciary certainly was never empowered to create new rights. See generally, Gangi, *supra* note 29.

51. Ibid., 483. He offers reasons for reaching the conclusion he does, but they cannot be detailed here. See ibid., 483-4.

52. Ibid., 484-85. Emphasis mine.

53. Ibid., 485.

54. See *supra* text and comment accompanying notes 47.

55. *Federalist*, *supra* note 1, No. 81, 488.

56. Ibid., 490.

57. Ibid., 490. His complete statement is as follows: "To avoid all inconveniences, it will be safest to declare generally that the Supreme Court shall possess appellate jurisdiction both as to law and fact, and that this jurisdiction shall be subject to such exceptions and regulations as the national legislature may prescribe." Ibid.

58. Ibid., 491. The pertinent phrasing is as follows: "that the Supreme Court will possess an appellate jurisdiction, both as to law and fact, in all the cases referred to them, but subject to any *exceptions* and *regulations* which may be thought advisable . . ." Ibid.

59. Ibid., No. 81, 491.

60. I also dismiss as uninformed contentions that the framers were unaware of the complexity surrounding the interpretative task:

> All new laws, though penned with the greatest technical skill and passed on the fullest and most mature deliberation, are considered as more or less obscure and equivocal, until their meaning be liquidated and ascertained by a series of particular discussions and adjudications. Besides the obscurity arising from the complexity of objects and the imperfections of the human faculties, the medium through which the conceptions of men are conveyed to each other adds a fresh embarrassment. The use of words is to express ideas. Perspicuity, therefore, requires not only that the ideas should be distinctly formed, but that they should be expressed by words distinctly and exclusively appropriate to them. But no language is so copious as to supply words and phrases for every complex idea, or so correct as not to include many equivocally denoting different ideas. Hence it must happen that however accurately objects may be discriminated in themselves, and however accurately the discrimination may be considered, the definition of them may be rendered inaccurate by the inaccuracy of the terms in which it is delivered. And this unavoidable inaccuracy must be greater or less, according to the complexity and novelty of the objects defined. . . .
>
> Here, then, are three sources of vague and incorrect definitions: indistinctness of the object, imperfection of the organ of conception, inadequateness of the vehicle of ideas. Any one of these must produce a certain degree of obscurity. The convention, in delineating the boundary between the federal and State jurisdictions, must have experience the full effect of them all.

Federalist, supra note 1, No. 37, 229.

61. *Federalist, supra* note 1, No. 32, 201. In No. 83 Publius recognizes that such rules can be abused, but that is no reason to deny their usefulness. He states that "certain *legal maxims* . . . [could be] perverted from their true meaning." Ibid., No. 83, 496. Furthermore, as will be discussed shortly, Publius is perfectly consistent with the approach he adopts throughout his discussions of the legislative and executive branches, that the potential for abuse is not in itself an adequate reason to deny a needed power. Professor Peter S. Onuf observes that the "Federalists . . . emphasized the document's similarity to the state constitutions, promising that traditional canons of construction would be applied to its provisions." Onuf, *Reflections on the Founding: Constitutional Historiography in Bicentennial Perspective,* 46 The William and Mary Quarterly 341, 369 (1989). Professor

Allen specifically discusses No. 83 and demonstrates that the framers' understanding of the "plain meaning rule" was more sophisticated than had been characterized by Professor Tushnet. Allen, *The Federalist's Plain Meaning: Reply to Tushnet*, 61 South Carolina Law Review 1701, 1712-13 (1988).

62. *Federalist, supra* note 1, No. 83, 496.

63. Ibid., No. 41, 263.

64. Ibid., No. 40, 248; No. 78, 468.

65. Ibid., No. 83, 496.

66. Ibid. Throughout the *Federalist* Publius provides examples of such rules:(1) "NEGATIVE PREGNANT," [ibid., No. 32, 200.]; (2) "Every expression ought, if possible, to be allowed some meaning," Ibid., No. 40, 248.]; (3) "Where the several parts cannot be made to coincide, the less important should give way to the more important part" [ibid. See also No. 41, 263; No. 83, 497.];(4) "The last in order of time shall be preferred to the first" [ibid., No. 78, 468.];and, No. 83]; (5)"'A specification of particulars is an exclusion of generals.'" [Ibid., No. 83, 496. See also No. 41, 263.]

67. Publius understood that such rules could be abused. See endnote 61. See generally, James G. Wilson, *The Most Sacred Text: The Supreme Court's Use of The Federalist Papers,* 1985 Brigham Young Law Review 65 (1985). Professor Lofgren quotes a long letter from James Madison to M. L. Hurlbert (May 1830), from which the following is excerpted:

> As there are legal rules for interpreting laws, there must be analogous rules for interpreting const[itutio]ns and among the obvious and just guides to the Const[itutio]n of the U.S. may be mentioned -
>
> 1. The evils & defects for curing which the Constitution was called for & introduced.
>
> 2. The comments prevailing at the time it was adopted.
>
> 3. The early, deliberate & and continued practice under the Constitution, as preferable to constructions adopted on the spur of occasions, and subject to the vicissitudes of party or personal ascendencies.

See also Charles A. Lofgren, *The Original Understanding of Original Intent,* 5 Constitutional Commentary 77, 110 (1988) (Publius contended that acquired expertise in the law should not be used to undermine common sense interpretation).

68. See *supra* text and comments accompanying endnotes 24-27. See also U.S. Constitution, art. 3, sec. 1 (providing that the compensation of judges shall not be diminished during their continuation in office).

69. U.S. Constitution, art. 6 , sec. 3.

70. The subject of interpretation is beyond the scope of this paper. The reader may turn to chapter five in Gangi, *Saving the Constitution From the Courts.*

71. See *supra* text and comments accompanying endnote 13.

72. While these matters are ultimately beyond the scope of this article several of the principles that govern my discussions elsewhere may be provided (see Gangi, *supra* note 29). The legitimate exercise of any power in the Constitution depends first on that power being conferred, and secondly that it be exercised within its intended scope. With respect to conferring a power, take the example of a congressional act purporting to establish a national church. All constitutionalists–whatever their personal views on the merits of such

proposal–would be obliged to speak out against its passage for several compelling reasons: the power to authorize a national church was never conferred, and it in fact was specifically prohibited. Without substantial contrary evidence (in this instance impossible to acquire) no other clause may be "interpreted" to cloud the framers' clear intent to prohibit a national religious establishment. Publius would argue, as we have seen, that even absent the first amendment the power to establish a church had never been granted. Indeed, *that is exactly what Publius would have argued since he opposed a bill of rights, arguing that its addition would merely muddy the waters.* We also have Publius' remark that "[t]his specification of particulars evidently excludes all pretensions to the general legislative authority, because an affirmative grant of special powers would be absurd as well as useless if a general authority was intended." *Federalist, supra* note 1, No. 83, 497.

The second aspect of constitutional legitimacy is more subtle but equally viable. Even conferred power may be abused if it is exercised beyond the scope of the framers' known intentions. For instance, the power to regulate the jurisdiction of federal courts undoubtedly was conferred upon Congress, but that power was abused when Congress sought to enlarge the Supreme Court's original jurisdiction. See e.g., Marbury v. Madison, 5 U.S. (1 Cranch) 137 (1803) and *Ex parte* McCardle, 74 U.S. (7 Wall.) 506 (1868). Or take another example: After adoption of the Constitution the states retained the power to tax but that power was abused when states attempted to use it to inhibit the operation of the federal government. See e.g., *McCulloch v. Maryland*, 17 U.S. (4 Wheat) 316 (1819).

The principles applicable to the granting of legislative power apply equally well to the judicial power. To concede that judicial review is legitimate does not and cannot foreclose on inquiry into whether or not in a specific instance that power had been abused by over extension. Over extension *constitutes an abuse equal to the exercise of a power never conferred.* For commentators to speculate (an assertion requires at least *some* evidence) that the framers intended to grant to the judiciary a general legislative power to address societal inequities appears totally unfounded, requiring us to conclude, that the power granted the judiciary, the judicial power, firstly, was a legislative power, and secondly that this judicial-legislating power was even more extensive than had been accorded Congress (enumerated in article 1, section 8). The granting of judicial-legislative power to unelected judges hardly would have left the American government a republican one, and we know from Publius that "no other form [but the republican one] would be reconcilable with the genius of the people of America; with the fundamental principles of the Revolution." *Federalist, supra* note 1, No. 39, 240. See *supra* text accompanying endnote 52.

73. See *supra*, text accompanying endnote 13.

74. *Federalist, supra* note 1, No. 23, 153 ("Not to confer in each case a degree of power commensurate to the end would be to violate the most obvious rules of prudence and propriety.")

75. See *supra* text accompanying endnote 5.

76. See *supra* text accompanying endnotes 59-64. Publius apparently viewed judicial review as a veto power akin to that granted to the executive. U. S. Constitution art. 1, sec. 7 (2). Cf. *Federalist, supra* note 1, No. 73 (executive veto). Several distinctions of course exist. Whereas the President is authorized to veto any legislation he considers either unconstitutional or *unwise* ["to increase the chances in favor of the community against the passing of bad laws, through haste, inadvertence, or design"] *(Federalist, supra* note 1, No. 73, 443), judges are not. Publius, you recall, states that the judiciary should declare an act of the legislature void only if the powers that had been granted it were exceeded and the

abuse had been "manifest." Application of those criteria, as we have stated before, does *not* entitle the Justices to "substitute their own pleasure to the constitutional intentions of the legislature." [Ibid., No. 78, 468-69]. On the contrary, as long as the legislature does not clearly overstep the powers granted, the judiciary has no cause to intervene. That is the only interpretation possible given the fact that the framers specifically denied the judiciary a general revisionary power, and the special power granted–the judicial power–is neither a general power to legislate nor does it extend to matters of wisdom or morals. Finally, the only authority to which the Justices legitimately may appeal to supersede that of the legislature, is the people; not as we already have stated the *current* population, who may themselves at any time employ the amendment process, but to the *people*, by which is meant the intentions of those who ratified the Constitution. See *supra* text and comments accompanying endnotes 34-41.

The judicial veto, like the executive one, also may be overturned by the legislature. But as one might expect from the fact that the two vetoes address different purposes, legislative revision must be consistent with both the different functions served by each branch and the need to maintain independent executive and judicial departments. Publius concedes that there is nothing "in the proposed constitution" that prohibits "revisal of a judicial sentence by a legislative act," but he concedes that the revision of cases already decided by the judiciary would be highly irregular. He concludes "the impropriety of the thing, on the general principles of law and reason, is the sole obstacle." *Federalist*, *supra* note 1, No. 81, 484. Besides Publius states explicitly that the Constitution provides a cure wherever particular judicial decisions are distasteful. Should they cause "some partial inconveniences," then "it ought to be recollected that the national legislature will have ample authority to make such *exceptions* and to prescribe such regulations as will be calculated to obviate or remove those inconveniences." Ibid., No. 80, 481. In fact, Publius' language in ibid., No. 80, 481, so much parallels a provision of the New York State Constitution [see ibid., No. 84, 512], that it is difficult not to conclude that the proposed congress, as the legislature of New York, had the absolute authority to change prior statutory or common law practice. He then explicitly affirms what had earlier been merely deduced: "The possibility of particular mischiefs can never be viewed, by a well-informed mind, as a solid objection to the general principle which is calculated to avoid general mischiefs and to obtain general advantages." Ibid., No. 80, 481.

77. See *supra* text and comments accompanying endnotes 47-48.

78. See comment *supra* endnote 43. It is only when Raoul Berger applied standards of interpretation to the Supreme Court did the conte*mporary de*bate over judicial power begin. See Raoul Berger, *Government By Judiciary* (Cambridge: Harvard University Press, 1977). See also Gangi, *supra* note 13.

79. See *supra* text accompanying note 40.

Chapter 6

Originalism and Criminal Procedure

Gerard V. Bradley

Unsympathetic critics of originalism–the method of constitutional adjudication which relies heavily upon the ratifiers' understanding of the provisions they ratified–have been hitting pretty hard with "the dead hand of the past." You know the line: originalism is unsustainable because it means rule of the present by dead guys who, to make matters worse, were all white and, in many cases, slaveholders. May God have mercy on their long departed souls. They will need it.

It is not clear what the operative portion of the criticism is. Is the validity of a law supposed to depend upon the longevity of its enactors? If so, say goodbye to New Deal legislation. Do laws expire if any *one* person essential to enactment dies? Presidential signature is essential to passage of a Congressional bill into law. What will be left of the U.S. Code when the Gipper finally goes to that great casting call in the sky?

It seems that dead folks *must* have a claim upon us, *if* they exercised public authority when they were alive. The real criticism might be that, because the Founders were unsound of morals, they did not exercise a morally legitimate authority. They were, one might say, like the Nazis. If one would have been morally justified–at least if there were a good chance of success–in revolting against and trying to overthrow the Nazi (or the slaveholder) regime, then it follows that *we* should not be ruled by them.

I grant the premise: one might well have been morally justified in revolting against the Nazis and the slaveholders. But the conclusion does not follow. No one really thinks that the Nazis had no law in the sense intended by the dead white slaveholder argument. Some of the directives Nazis enacted did facilitate cooperation for the common good. It was morally imperative for people to comply with them. Returning to the slaveholding regime, laws establishing and maintaining slavery should not have been embraced by conscientious persons. *Not* because the human sources of them were morally deficient (though they were) but because the laws themselves were unjust. It does not follow that all laws in the Old South, say those against rape or protecting freedom of worship, were unjust. Compliance with them was morally obligatory, too, because the laws served the common good.

Besides, any theory of legitimate public authority which ties the validity of laws to the state of the character of persons enacting them is troubling. Should we conclude that Watergate marked the demise not only of Nixon's political career, but of all the laws he signed?

Maybe the question is why should anyone rule us? It seems to me that the "dead hand" criticism, if it is more than colorful rhetoric, is kept aloft by either diffidence on, or a negative answer to, that question. I would rather ask what are the grounds for legitimate exercise of public authority. Either way, if the answer is negative or noncommittal, there is nothing wrong with originalism that is not wrong with any other theory of constitutional adjudication.

That must be what Laurence Tribe thinks. He says that concern for "methodology" (like originalism) is "irresponsible." With specific regard to accounts of how constitutional adjudication should proceed, Tribe says that "all legitimating theories [are] not simply amusing in their pretensions but, in the end, as dangerous as they are unconvincing."[1]

The salvageable element of the "dead hand of the past" riff is, I submit, its flip side expression: we need a "Living Constitution." Indeed, we do. Originalism, it is asserted, does not provide one. Therefore, we don't need–cannot have–originalism.

Living constitution notions worth entertaining do not suppose legitimacy is either impossible or dispensable. By and large, they are precisely attempts to legitimate constitutional law in the absence of (strictly speaking) the Constitution. The most reflective judicial effort of this kind is undoubtedly the *Casey*[2] joint opinion. Justices Kennedy, Souter, and O'Connor said that the "legitimacy" of the Court is "a product of substance and perception that shows itself in the people's acceptance of the Judiciary as fit to determine what the Nation's law means and to declare what it demands."[3] In the Justices' words, the *Casey* decision must stand or fall upon whether its principles are "sufficiently plausible to be accepted by the nation."[4]

There is here more than an echo of Justice Brennan's address to a Georgetown law class in 1985. Its title captures the animating feature of *Casey*: "Contemporary Ratification." Writes Brennan:

> When Justices interpret the Constitution they speak for their community, not for themselves alone . . . the Justices must render constitutional interpretations that are received as legitimate. The source of legitimacy is, of course, a wellspring of controversy in legal and political circles.[5]

Such statements as Brennan's and the *Casey* plurality's are purposely obscure, because the Justices are walking a gossamer line. They cannot sensibly proclaim themselves sole constitution makers. But they cannot yield very much to the people (and their representatives) without undermining their arguments for the judiciary's primacy in constitutional interpretation. One thing is clear. In some decisive way, these are confessions that the Framers are not enough, that constitutional law has so deviated from the Constitution that the glance back is insufficiently legitimizing. So the glance outward, at us. Our assent legitimatizes their proposal. But *how* do we register our opinions? The cases do not say.

One might suspect here a "process" of constitutional decision making, in which Justices are, apparently, conversation partners. With whom? Who has the final say? These theories are good at discerning contemporary ratification well after the fact. *Brown v. Board of Education*[6] is now confidently declared to be part of the Constitution. Is that an implicit concession that Orville Faubus and Lester Maddox were not acting illegally? That they, back when *Brown* was in its infancy (or in, shall we assume, a neonatal state) were instead agitated conversation partners?

People need to know what the law is not just in evaluating their grandparents' action but *when* the question of its guiding their conduct arises. That is, they need to know now. Is the doctrine of *Casey* a proposal–a judicially drafted bill–awaiting final approval? Are antiabortion demonstrators participating in the *lawmaking* process, exercising their constitutional veto, or are they engaged in illegal resistance to settle law?

The appeal of "living Constitution" theories is obvious, and they may well seem preferable to most–if not all–extant originalisms. But the notion at the heart of originalism–that *the* Constitution stands within or at least in back of all the judge-made constitutional law–has obvious appeal too. The appeal is not only to the naive, or to those edified by the quaint. Simply put, the appeal is so broad and so deep that, I submit, a candid confession by the Supreme Court that the Constitution has no bearing on its decisions, would bring on a constitutional crisis not seen since the Civil War.

In any event I should like to address here sympathetic critics of originalism; indeed I should like to meet just one–the main one, I think–of their reservations about originalism. Thus I come to Columbia Law School's Henry Monaghan.[7] The problem for Professor Monaghan is this: much of twentieth century constitutional law is completely beyond recall, yet much of that which is beyond recall cannot be squared with the original understanding. He offers many examples: structural features like the modern administrative state and Congressional penetration of state borders via the commerce power; many civil liberties decisions, most notably *Brown v. Board of Education*. The problem is to make sense out of a decidedly non-originalist universe. The melancholy ending to Monaghan's story is that he must defend, or at least accept, a constitutional law in which the sine qua non of legitimacy–the Constitution–is but one of many factors. Other factors include precedent, political equilibrium, and the need for change.

Monaghan's central assumption, hardly undefended but still not very carefully worked out, is that any originalism worth its name cannot be squared with enough of what is. Leave aside the problem of specifying how much is enough, and what originalism "worth its name" exactly means. Clearly, there is something to this criticism: any originalism worth its name may be sound (i.e. intellectually satisfying or correct) in an academic sense. But that's about it.

I deny Monaghan's criticism or, rather, I would slip through the horns of his dilemma. More–much more, I suspect –than he supposes can be squared with an originalism worth its name. I am prepared to argue that those cases (or lines of cases) which cannot be squared with originalism should be abandoned, and can be, without either ruining the Court's legitimacy or undermining the social fabric.

Given the limitations of this essay, I shall have to issue an IOU: the much wider case necessary to redeem that claim will be made in the book I am writing. Here, I hope to whet your appetite and lend an initial plausibility to my argument. I'm just trying to get past what the lawyers know as summary judgment. I aim to show that there is a live question about originalism's plausibility.

I shall offer a couple of basic distinctions, essential to a sound originalism, and then take a crack at one of the top three counts in the indictment of originalism: criminal procedure; specifically, the right to appointed counsel for indigent criminal defendants, the rules governing police interrogation, and the exclusionary rule for evidence obtained in violation of the Fourth Amendment. My agenda is to see if *Gideon v. Wainwright*[8], *Miranda v. Arizona*[9], and *Mapp v. Ohio*[10] can be sustained under an originalist constitutional theory.

The first basic distinction is between essential principles–provisions permanent and unalterable–and those which ought to be accommodated to times and events. This counsel was hardly lost on the Framers, and it helps us to develop a discriminating account of how constitutional law might evolve, how it might keep up with the times, without ceasing to be originalist. Most important here is the distinction between norms and their application. I do not cook it up to save originalism, nor have contemporary liberals done so to save the legitimacy of a constitutional law cut loose from its moorings. Justice George Sutherland was hardly a revisionist swashbuckler.[11] But he voted in *Euclid v. Ambler Realty* to uphold an ordinance that, he conceded, the Court would have rejected as arbitrary and offensive at an earlier date.

> Such regulations are sustained, under the complex conditions of our day, for reasons analogous to those which justify traffic regulations, which, before the advent of automobiles and rapid transit street railways, would have been condemned as fatally arbitrary and unreasonable. And in this there is no inconsistency, for while the meaning of constitutional guaranties never varies, the scope of their application must expand or contract to meet the new and different conditions which are constantly coming within the field of their operation. In a changing world, it is impossible that it should be otherwise.[12]

A simple illustration. Contrary to the prevailing judicial view, the original understanding of the Establishment Clause was that the government may not discriminate among religious sects.[13] But what was sect-neutral in the Christian America of 1790 is sect-preferential in today's more diverse society. Public school prayer may have been constitutional in 1791, but it is not now. Same norm, different results, due to changed facts.

The *Gideon* Court held that a criminal defendant must be afforded a lawyer regardless of his ability to pay. *Gideon* identified itself as a Sixth Amendment "right to counsel" case. But it cannot really be traced to that part of the Amendment. Historical recovery reveals that "In all criminal prosecutions, the accused shall . . . have the Assistance of Counsel" meant only that any defendant who retained counsel could actually bring that lawyer into court.[14] Tradition had it that defendants in treason trials, for example, had to appear alone. There is nothing about publicly appointed counsel in the Sixth Amendment, as understood by its ratifiers.

That does not necessarily mean that *Gideon* is wrongly decided. It means only that *Gideon* was wrongly reasoned. Can its rule–the right to publicly appointed counsel–find sure footing? Yes. The guarantee of a fair state trial has long been a component of the Due Process Clause. (Note that there are two Due Process Clauses–one in the Fifth and the other in the Fourteenth Amendment. One binds the states; the other binds the federal government. For convenience, I shall conflate them.) The Framers of the Due Process Clause, I grant, did not think an attorney was usually necessary to a fair trial. A lot has changed since they thought that in 1868. The law has grown much more complex, and now includes pretrial motions challenging evidence on constitutional grounds–confessions, identification procedures, tangible evidence–that may be dispositive of the trial. The prosecution is now–and long has been–conducted by professionally trained lawyers. Judges are now not so inclined to be proactive doers of justice, to help unrepresented defendants; judges now are neutral umpires. No longer are jurors acquainted with the parties and the witnesses. A prerequisite to their selection at present is their being strangers to the cause, or having only ineffectual knowledge of it. In sum and for a lot of reasons, a lawyer is now essential to a fair trial for the vast majority of criminal defendants. In 1868, it was not.

The more detailed originalist argument for publicly funded defense counsel for indigents goes something like this. As early as 1883 the Supreme Court in *Hurtado v. California* said that, while specifics might vary from jurisdiction to jurisdiction, "due process" is "a law which hears before it condemns, which proceeds upon inquiry, and renders judgment only after trial."[15] More compactly, per *Twining v. New Jersey* (1908), due process required "notice" and an "adequate opportunity to defend in the prosecution."[16] Notice and hearing were, per *Powell v. Alabama* (1932), essential to a court's jurisdiction to "passing an enforceable judgment." That is, "fair hearing"–a genuine as opposed to a sham trial or trial in form only–is a jurisdictional necessity and not, at least not only, a personal right of the accused.[17]

This principle–the seemingly simple guarantee of a fair trial–contains within itself the potential for a standard that requires an attorney in all criminal cases, depending upon the contingencies of matters very much within the competence of appellate courts, including the Supreme Court, to judge. By 1963, that the large majority of criminal defendants could not defend themselves in a way which secured the requisite adversarial testing of the prosecution's case was apparent to every member of the Supreme Court. So, too, was the incapacity of the Supreme Court to articulate standards short of a broad prophylactic rule that would assure a fair trial–and thus jurisdiction–in each criminal case.

By the time of *Gideon* all the premises were in place to sustain a prophylactic rule on Due Process grounds. The only interesting question is why the Court instead took a sharp "incorporationist" turn, that is, why it turned away from Due Process to a Sixth Amendment basis for its holding. I suspect this move had much to do with Justice Black's aversion to what he would have considered "substantive due process."

I think the same due process fair trial guarantee can sustain something like the *Miranda* rules. You know what they are, as everyone in America does, from Kojak and other police dramas. I say "something like" because the *Miranda* court made abundantly clear that the warnings' value was instrumental. They were not ends in themselves; they were designed to dispel the inherent coercion of custodial interrogation, to assure the "voluntariness" of any extrajudicial statement of a defendant received in evidence. The *Miranda* court said that other standards or techniques might work as well as or better than the warnings. But make no mistake about it: "voluntariness" is the underlying constitutional guarantee, much as a "fair trial" underlay *Gideon*.

An originalist defense of *Miranda* therefore means defending *some* standard or technique to assure the voluntariness of confessions. Whether the *Miranda* warnings are such a standard, I personally doubt. Whether they are, however, does not affect the vitality of originalism. That is, originalists can debate the *Miranda* warnings' cash value with nonoriginalists without putting originalism into play.

The *Miranda* court tied the familiar warnings to the Fifth Amendment Self-Incrimination Clause. The preponderance of historical evidence, though, shows that the privilege had to do only with forcing a criminal defendant to the stand in his own trial, and not with what happens in the station house under bright lights. Besides, the Fifth Amendment (like the rest of the Bill of Rights) was originally understood to bind the national government only, not the states. I should not care to defend the view that the privilege was "incorporated" by the Fourteenth Amendment, thus more applicable to the states. (Even if it was, there's still the first problem).

I propose here to mine further the guarantee of a "fair trial." The Supreme Court has always been concerned to carefully scrutinize confessions because of the grave consequences for the cause of justice if a confession received into evidence should prove to be untrue. Confessions were, and were recognized to be, very strong evidence of guilt. Once a confession was received in evidence, it was very likely to produce a conviction. Hence, courts concluded that great confidence in the truth of a confession was a prerequisite to its admission.

Here's the problem: courts have always also held that confessions are inherently unreliable. Why? I cannot improve upon the statement of the New York Court of Appeals, in a case from 1854–that expressed a view shared basically by the Supreme Court in its confessions cases.

> The mental disturbance produced by a direct accusation, or even a consciousness of being suspected of crime, is always great, and, in many cases, incalculable. The foundation of all reliance upon human testimony is that moral sentiment which almost universally leads men, when not under some strong counteracting influence, to tell the truth. This sentiment is sufficiently powerful to resist a trifling motive, but will not withstand the fear of conviction for crime. Hence, the moment that fear seizes that mind, the basis of all reliance upon its manifestations is gone. Speculation as to the effect of the declarations made, takes the place of a regard for truth; and this, too, in many cases, whether the party be innocent or guilty. If innocent, and yet conscious of the existence of circumstances tending to show guilt, there is the strongest temptation to make such statements, without regard to their truth, as will serve to conceal or break the force of these circumstances. Innocent persons have not infrequently been convicted upon false statements of precisely this character. The mind, confused and agitated by the apprehension of danger, cannot reason with coolness; and it resorts to falsehood when the truth would be safer, and is hurried into acknowledgments which the facts do not warrant. Neither false statements nor confessions, therefore, afford any certain evidence of guilt when made under the excitement of an impending prosecution for crime.[18]

Now we can join the two premises–the potency of confessions and their unreliability–into a grave threat to Due Process. Due Process requires some procedural protection which assures that the "disturbance" of which the New York Court spoke is ameliorated. That is what the *Miranda* court understood itself to be doing. I personally doubt whether the Court has succeeded. But the effort is justified, speaking as an originalist.

Lastly, the exclusionary rule. In *United States v. Leon*,[19] the first good-faith exception case, the majority described the exclusionary rule as "'a judicially created remedy designed to safeguard Fourth Amendment rights generally through its deterrent effect, rather than a personal constitutional right of the person aggrieved.'"[20] The majority did not respond to Justice Brennan's assertion, in his *Leon* dissent that deterrence was never a relevant concern "in the early cases from

Weeks to *Olmstead*." *Weeks*[21] is, by all accounts, the first sighting of the exclusionary rule. Yet the Court's *Leon* opinion contains not a single reference to *Weeks*, even by Justices ordinarily impressed with originalist reasoning, and who have never doubted the familiar claim that the exclusionary rule originated in *Weeks*. The majority brusquely disposed of any ties to pre-Burger Court precedent. It is a fair attribution to prefix their (previously quoted) version of the rule with, "Notwithstanding *Weeks* . . . ."

"Notwithstanding *Weeks*" is precisely what rankled Justices Brennan and Marshall who, perhaps unexpectedly for them, mounted an explicit "original understanding" defense of the exclusionary rule–original understanding of the rule in *Weeks*, that is. They quoted copiously from Justice Day's opinion and, to buttress their reading of the *Weeks* case, that reading favored a so-called principled basis for the rule–not a calculation of its deterrent effect.[22]

Weeks talk is incurably infected by the exclusionary rule synthesis in criminal procedure history. Because principles articulated by Justice Day in *Weeks*, after considerable refinement and external aid from the truly seminal *Boyd v. United States*[23] case, eventuated in the rule, *Weeks* itself is universally read as if it were talking about and justifying the exclusionary rule. It did neither. That it did not do so is at least suggested by the absence of any language in the opinion denoting its outcome as "exclusion" or "suppression."

Weeks itself did not employ that hallowed term. Further, even allowing for intergenerational definitional vagaries, *Weeks* contains no discussion of exclusion under any nomenclature. In Justice Day's words, the issue was "the right of the court in a criminal prosecution to retain for the purposes of evidence" unlawfully seized papers of the accused, when the defendant had filed a timely, pretrial petition for return.[24] "It is thus apparent that the question presented involves the . . . duty of the court with reference to the motion . . . for the return of certain letters, as well as other papers, taken from his room by the United States Marshal . . . ."[25] Removed from the analytical plan of the opinion was trial use of the evidence. That is, the "exclusionary rule" was but a parasite attached as a known consequence to the pretrial return motion that was the real subject of dispute. The result–there is *no* "original understanding" of the basis for the exclusionary rule.

Notes

1. Laurence Tribe, *Constitutional Choices* (Cambridge: Harvard University Press, 1985), 6.
2. *Casey v. Planned Parenthood*, 112 *S.Ct.* 2791 (1992).
3. *Casey v. Planned Parenthood*, 112 *S.Ct.* 2814.
4. *Casey v. Planned Parenthood*, 112 *S.Ct.* 2814.
5. William Brennan, *The Constitution of the United States: Contemporary Ratification*, 27 South Texas Law Review 433 (fall 1986).

6. *Brown v. Board of Education*, 347 U.S. 483 (1954).

7. See H. Monaghan, *Stare Decisis and Constitutional Adjudication*, 88 Columbia Law Review 723 (1988).

8. *Gideon v. Wainwright*, 372 U.S. 335 (1963).

9. *Miranda v. Arizona*, 384 U.S. 436 (1966).

10. *Mapp v. Ohio*, 367 U.S. 643 (1961).

11. See generally H. Arkes, *The Return of George Sutherland* (New Jersey: Princeton University Press, 1994).

12. *Euclid v. Ambler Co.*, 272 U.S. 365, 387 (1926).

13. *See* Gerard V. Bradley, *Church-State Relationship in America* (New York: Greenwood Press, 1987).

14. *See* William M. Beaney, *The Right to Counsel in American Courts* (Ann Arbor, MI: University of Michigan Press, 1955).

15. *Hurtado v. California*, 110 U.S. 518, 535-6 (1883).

16. *Twining v. New Jersey*, 211 U.S. 78, 112 (1908).

17. *Powell v. Alabama*, 287 U.S. 45, 69 (1932).

18. *Hendrickson v. People*: 10 NY (6 Selden) at 33 (NY CT. APP. 1854).

19. *U.S. v. Leon*, 468 U.S. 897 (1984).

20. *U.S. v. Leon*, 468 U.S. 906.

21. *Weeks v. United States*, 232 U.S. 383 (1914).

22. See generally *U.S. v. Leon*, 468 U.S. 928-960.

23. *Boyd v. United States*, 116 U.S. 616 (1885).

24. *Weeks v. United States*, 232 U.S. 393.

25. *Weeks v. United States*, 232 U.S. 389.

Chapter 7

When Constitution and Precedent Collide

Christopher Wolfe

The last three decades or so have been a distinct "era" in the perennial debate about the fundamental nature of constitutional interpretation and judicial review in American government. Since Alexander Bickel's *The Least Dangerous Branch* most constitutional scholars have argued or assumed that judicial review does not consist essentially in a careful reading and application of the Constitution–what I would call the textualism or "interpretivism" of *Marbury v. Madison.*[1] Thomas Grey's distinction between "interpretivism" and "noninterpretivism," and the later usage by many scholars of "originalism" and "nonoriginalism," assume that judges do not act as "mere" mouthpieces of the law, but rather as creators of it, as legislators.[2]

The combination of the extensive judicial activism of the Warren Court and increasingly candid recognition among legal scholars that judicial review was a legislative power led to a significant backlash against "modern" judicial review and the articulation of a theory of judicial review that claimed to be a return to earlier American political principles. This theory was generally referred to as a theory of "original intention," though that term was understood somewhat differently by various representatives of the position.[3] But in general the original intent approach aimed at eliminating the strong element of judicial *will* (as opposed to judgment) in the interpretive process. Judges ought to aspire, it was said, to give effect to the will of the lawmaker, without permitting their own wills–their political preferences or beliefs–to shape their decisions.

In my earlier work, I have tried to provide the outline of an interpretive history of judicial review in America. *The Rise of Modern Judicial Review* described a "traditional" judicial review, dominant in the founding and during most of the nineteenth century, that was closely tied to a fair reading of the text and quite limited in scope, and a "modern" judicial review that was essentially a broad delegation of power to the judiciary to engage in the essentially legislative task of giving specific content to allegedly indeterminate generalities of the Constitution.[4] In my subsequent *Judicial Activism: Bulwark of Liberty or Precarious Security*, I tried to provide a dialectical argument regarding the strengths and weaknesses of modern judicial review ("judicial activism") and traditional judicial review (one distinctive form of "judicial restraint"), concluding that, in the final analysis, traditional judicial review is not only closer to the intentions of the authors (and ratifiers) of the Constitution, but also the more prudent principle.[5]

Even with the completion of this history of judicial review and a defense of a particular normative position on the question, however, there remains one final task to complete this project. Even assuming that it were possible, over time, to secure the appointment of originalist justices to the Supreme Court–an admittedly unlikely development–what would these justices do, confronted with a large body of constitutional law that is tenuously, if at all, rooted in the Constitution itself? If the justices merely applied precedents, their originalist convictions, as mere historical curiosities, would have little impact on constitutional law. If they maintained precedents, but avoided extending or even applying them (grasping at grounds to distinguish precedents, however unpersuasively), they would help to create an incoherent and unprincipled constitutional law. If they insisted on the Constitution as the standard (over precedent), and were willing to uproot precedent, then they would be the authors of a radical revolution in American law. If they at times did the former and at other times the latter, on what principled basis could they choose to draw the line between appropriate maintenance and appropriate overruling of precedents?

The Burger court–in ways that I have discussed elsewhere[6]–fairly typically chose the route of incoherence. It was notably reluctant to overturn precedents explicitly, though it occasionally did so, as in *Garcia v. San Antonio Metropolitan Transportation Authority* (overturning its own earlier decision in *National League of Cities v. Usery*). But it was also notably reluctant to extend many liberal Warren court precedents, as it refused in *San Antonio v. Rodriguez* (which turned down an equal protection challenge to local school financing, despite wide disparities in the wealth of school districts, holding that education was not a "fundamental right") to apply the reasoning of cases like *Shapiro v. Thompson* (which held that one-year residency requirements for welfare unconstitutionally burdened the "fundamental right" to travel). The result was a body of law in which many cases whose underlying principles seemed incompatible with each other were all "good" constitutional law, on the basis of unpersuasive "distinctions" between them.[7]

The Rehnquist Court seems, on the whole, to be similarly inclined. The Court is divided into "conservatives" generally oriented toward originalism (Scalia, Thomas, Rehnquist), "liberals" oriented toward some form of modern judicial review (Stevens, Ginsberg, Breyer, and increasingly Souter), and "moderates" (O'Connor, Kennedy, sometimes Souter). This last group typically provides the key votes on divided issues and, while they are moderately conservative on many issues, they are not consistently committed to originalism in principle. The "center of gravity" of the Court, then, lies in a moderate form of modern (essentially legislative) judicial review–a Court that is reluctant to extend past activist decisions or produce new ones, but is also opposed to uprooting activist precedents and is occasionally willing to engage in some judicial legislation. A particularly disconcerting result of this balance of forces is the lack of a truly principled jurisprudence–notwithstanding the many arguments elaborated by classic defenders of modern judicial activism such as Alexander Bickel and Ronald Dworkin that support an expanded modern judicial power because of a special judicial capacity to articulate principles.[8]

In this paper I would like to examine the question of how an originalist Court would approach the task of judicial review today, when (arguably) most of the controlling precedents typically at issue are at best tenuously rooted in the Constitution and often lack constitutional foundations at all.

I will start by examining two contrasting recommendations from originalist scholars, and then move on to examine some materials from earlier American constitutional statesmen (James Madison and Abraham Lincoln), and finally try to provide some conclusions of my own.

One Extreme Alternative

Gary Lawson of Northwestern University Law School provides us with a striking and powerfully stated position in "The Constitutional Case Against Precedent."[9] He lays out the reasoning of *Marbury v. Madison*: judges are called upon to decide cases according to law, the Constitution is the supreme law, and therefore in cases where the Constitution and a statute (or an executive act) are incompatible the Court should apply the Constitution, refusing to give effect to the law (or executive act). This reasoning, he says, provides a parallel argument to deny precedent *any* weight in constitutional adjudication.[10] If the precedent is correct (its reasoning is persuasive), then there is no need to rely on precedent. The weight of precedent is therefore an issue precisely in cases where the precedent was wrongly decided. If the previous judicial decision was wrongly decided, judges in a new case are in essence faced with the choice of giving effect either to the Constitution or to the incorrect prior judicial opinion. Just as the judges must place the Constitution above an unconstitutional law or executive act, so must they place it above a decision of a previous court that is contrary to the Constitution:

> If a statute, enacted with all of the majestic formalities for lawmaking prescribed by the Constitution, and stamped with the imprimatur of representative democracy, cannot legitimately be given effect in an adjudication when it conflicts with the Constitution, how can a mere judicial decision possibly have greater legal status?[11]

Reliance on incorrect precedent is not only *not* obligatory–it is affirmatively *unconstitutional.*

Several questions might be raised regarding this argument. First, Lawson's argument seems to be just as effective against the legitimacy of "vertical precedent," in which a lower court is compelled to follow the incorrect precedents from higher courts. An argument that effectively "saves" the practice of vertical precedent–and it is hard to imagine our legal system without such a practice–may very well provide grounds for a doctrine of horizontal precedent as well.[12]

Second, Lawson's argument appears to draw a simple either/or picture of constitutional decisions. They are either clearly right or clearly wrong. Does he give sufficient weight to the fact that some decisions are less clear?

He does take up the issue, to some extent, when he acknowledges that his "argument rests on the premise that the Constitution has, at least in principle, an objectively ascertainable meaning."[13] (This is a premise, in which I strongly concur.) He rightly dismisses critics who assert the total indeterminacy of constitutional meaning, and points out that "the absence of right answers in some cases affects the practical scope of my argument but not its formal soundness. The use of precedent will still be unconstitutional in any case in which a right answer is ascertainable."[14]

Lawson goes on to argue that "the constitutional case against precedent is precisely coterminous with the constitutional case for judicial review. To the extent that indeterminacy undermines the argument against precedent, it also undermines the case for judicial review in the first instance."[15] Again, I think that he is correct in assuming that the indeterminacy of the Constitution in a given matter removes an essential condition for the exercise of judicial review, which is premised on the existence of a clear conflict between the law or act and the Constitution. The question is whether there is anything in between an interpretation being clearly right or wrong and its being "indeterminate."

Another Extreme

Virtually no one says that precedent is completely sacrosanct. *Cooper v. Aaron* does seem to argue that Supreme Court precedent is authoritative *vis-à-vis* all other political actors; that is, the decision identifies the oath to uphold the Constitution with an oath to uphold the Supreme Court's interpretation of the Constitution.[16] For reasons cited below (in Lincoln's discussion of the authority of court decisions), I think this is clearly wrong, but for the moment I want to point out that even this extreme claim does not make precedent absolute, for the court did not bind *itself* to follow its own precedents in every case.

Professor Henry Monaghan, in his "Stare Decisis and Constitutional Adjudication,"[17] goes quite far in attributing weight to constitutional precedent, even from an originalist perspective, and his thoughtful article is worth considering. Monaghan contends that there have been "significant and irreversible departures from original understanding" of the Constitution (e.g., *Brown v. Board of Education*, the scope of the national commerce power, the growth of the administrative state, and the transformation of presidential power).[18] Stare decisis certainly helps to explain why some of these decisions are and should be maintained. Monaghan argues that there are sound grounds for this power of stare decisis. "At its most general level, stare decisis operates to promote systemwide stability and continuity by ensuring the survival of governmental norms that have achieved unsurpassed importance in American society."[19] In addition, stare decisis helps to legitimate judicial review (especially among elites) by contributing to the rule of law argument, "the important notion that the law is impersonal in character."[20]

The *source* of stare decisis is either the "judicial power" of Article III or "constitutional common law," that is, in "the natural result of judicial powers and duties established in the text and ultimately subject to the control of Congress."[21] The *content* of stare decisis is more complex. Briefly, it can be said that "[i]n the American common law, stare decisis states a conditional obligation: precedent binds absent a showing of substantial countervailing considerations."[22] But Monaghan uneasily concedes that "it may not be possible to go further and formulate relatively determinate implementing criteria, however general, that would guide, if not constrain, judgment."[23] The *meaning* of precedent includes the court's rule or standard and also (because judicial opinion ought to be a reasoned elaboration of principle) the underlying reasoning.

What are the implications of this weighty but conditional authority of precedent for originalism? Monaghan argues that "we cannot know the framers' original understanding on the subject under discussion: deeply ingrained transformative change." Even conceding that they expected an adherence to original understanding, "our task is to make sense out of a nonoriginalist universe," in which the constitutional text plays "only a role, and an increasingly subordinate one at that."[24] He concludes that

> neither originalism nor the constitutional text has mystical qualities that compel a return to the fold in the face of transforming departures from the original understanding. At this point in our history, when adherence to stare decisis promotes the underlying values of stability and continuity better than does adherence to the original understanding, the latter cannot prevail.[25]

Monaghan carries the logic of his case to a consistent conclusion: it not only justifies maintaining transformative change, but also licenses (prospectively) "disregard of original understanding when the court is satisfied that change is necessary to maintain systemic equilibrium," and disregard of precedents themselves for similar reasons.

Despite a final assertion that we cannot dismiss the Constitution of 1789, then, Monaghan's article ends by apparently abandoning originalism. If precedents have such great weight, constituting in at least some cases *de facto* constitutional amendments, the fixed standard of the Constitution, the "anchor" for interpretation, seems lost. Originalist justices are reduced to defending not the Constitution but previous, illegitimate constitutional decisions. Precedent seems like a one-way ratchet moving away from the Constitution.

Some Historical Materials

I would like to turn now from modern scholarship to earlier thinkers, in particular James Madison and Abraham Lincoln. Both of these constitutional statesmen can contribute in important ways to our understanding of the question.

On various occasions, Madison dealt explicitly with the question of the force of precedent in constitutional cases. Probably the most important of these was the attack on him for inconsistency at a time, later in his life, when he rejected the doctrine of nullification, though his critics alleged that he had embraced such a doctrine in the Virginia Resolutions of 1798. Critics said that Madison had manifested such inconsistency throughout his career, and they cited especially his prominent opposition to the national bank, on constitutional grounds, in the early 1790s and his later signing of a bill establishing a national bank when he was president.

In response, Madison strongly denied the charges of inconsistency. On the bank question, he said that he signed the bank bill

> in conformity to an early & unchanged opinion, that in the case of a Constitution as of a law, a course of authoritative, deliberate, and continued decisions, such as the Bank could plead was an evidence of the Public Judgment, necessarily superseding individual opinions. There has been a fallacy in this case as indeed in others in confounding a question whether precedents could expound a Constitution, with a question whether they could alter a Const. This distinction is too obvious to need elucidation. None will deny that precedents of a certain description fix the interpretation of a law. Yet who will pretend that they can repeal or alter a law?[26]

And to another correspondent he wrote:

> the inconsistency is apparent only, not real; inasmuch as my abstract opinion of the text of the Constitution is not changed, and the assent was given in pursuance of my early and unchanged opinion, that, in the case of a Constitution as of a law, a course of authoritative expositions sufficiently deliberate, uniform, and settled, was an evidence of the public will necessarily overruling individual opinions. It cannot be less necessary that the meaning of the Constitution should be freed from uncertainty, than that the law should be so. That cases may occur which transcend all authority of precedents must be admitted, but they form exceptions which will speak for themselves and must justify themselves.[27]

Madison, then, clearly understood precedent to have force, even in cases where his "abstract opinion" remained that the meaning of the Constitution had been misstated by the precedent.

Lincoln's contribution to our topic is more indirect. It occurs in the context of a discussion of the authority of Supreme Court precedents, which was part of his response to the *Dred Scott* decision. Lincoln's position was quite nuanced. He distinguished between the *decision of the case* and the *interpretation of the Constitution* on which that decision was based. Republicans had no intent to disturb the decision in the particular case, he said. He went even further, conceding that normally the decisions of the Court should control not only the particular cases decided, but the general policy of the country, subject to be disturbed only by amendments. Nonetheless, as Lincoln argued in his First Inaugural:

> the candid citizen must confess that if the policy of the government, upon vital questions, affecting the whole people, is to be irrevocably fixed by decisions of the Supreme Court, the instant they are made, in ordinary litigation between parties, in personal actions, the people will have ceased, to be their own rulers, having, to that extent, practically resigned their government, into the hands of that eminent tribunal.[28]

Lincoln took a middle position on the question of the authority of Supreme Court precedents: "judicial decisions are of greater or less authority as precedents according to circumstances." Lincoln listed a variety of circumstances that undermined the authority of the *Dred Scott* decision, though there is no indication that he intended the list to be exhaustive. They include: the lack of unanimity of the decision; its apparent partisan bias; its discordance with educated public (especially legal) opinion and with the steady practice of the different branches of government throughout our history; its foundation upon false historical opinions (e.g., that the Declaration's "all men are created equal" meant "all white men are created equal"), and (given the presence of these factors) the lack of authority that comes from being affirmed and reaffirmed over time.

Although Lincoln was addressing the question of the authority of Supreme Court precedents for other actors in the political system (e.g., legislators), the factors that affect that authority of Supreme Court precedents for them would presumably also be at least some of the factors in the Court's own judgment about its precedents.

Some Basic Principles

With these materials to help us examine the question of the legitimate force of precedent for an originalist, I would like to try to sift through the various arguments and provide what I think are some reasonable guidelines.

The first factor to note in evaluating the weight of precedent is that *settled* precedents, especially, carry weight in constitutional adjudication. Lincoln's list of factors that undermine the authority of Supreme Court precedents provides us with a good starting point. The more divided the court, the less weight its opinion carries;[29] the greater the appearance of partisanship, the less weight; the more the opinion "surprises" or goes against the grain of educated (especially legal) expectations and the less it is supported by the practice of other branches of the government, the less weight; the more dubious the historical arguments on which it is based, the less weight; the more recent the contested decision, the less weight. Settled decisions, then, will be especially those that are agreed to by large or unanimous Court majorities, that conform to the expectations of the educated public, that are supported by the practice of government generally, and that have been reaffirmed over time.

These considerations seem to overlap with Madison's reasons for the force of precedent. His reasoning gives weight to the need for "deliberate, uniform and settled" constitutional meaning. But he connects these factors to a deeper *political* argument derived from the nature of our republican form of government: "a course of authoritative expositions sufficiently deliberate, uniform, and settled" is "evidence of the public will necessarily overruling individual opinions," "evidence of the Public Judgment, necessarily superseding individual opinions." The ultimate rulers in republican government are the people, and it is their opinion that is finally authoritative. When by various signs it becomes clear that a decision has become "settled," that is a kind of tacit consent argument that the people have determined the matter. (At the same time, recall–as I will discuss further below–that Madison indicates that there may be cases that "transcend all authority of precedents.")

It is important to note here that settled precedent reflects not only the reaffirmation by the Court of its earlier decisions, but also the acceptance of those decisions by the other branches of government. Justice Scalia made a form of this argument in *Pennsylvania v. Union Gas Co.*:

> Moreover, unlike the vast majority of judicial decisions, *Hans* has had a pervasive effect upon statutory law, automatically ensuring that private damages actions created by federal law do not extend against the States. Forty-nine Congresses since *Hans* have legislated under that assurance. It is impossible to say how many extant statutes would have included an explicit preclusion of suits against States if it had not been thought that such suits were automatically barred. Indeed, it is not even possible to say that, without *Hans*, all constitutional amendments would have taken the form they did [citing the Seventeenth Amendment].[30]

Precedents may have become part of the fiber of the law, the assumptions on which other branches of government have based the performance of their duties.

A second factor in considering the weight of precedent must be its "distance" from the Constitution. The further the precedent is from the Constitution, the less its weight. A decision that is *clearly* wrong will have less weight than one that is at least a plausible interpretation or application of the document.

Lawson argues that indeterminacy of the Constitution adds nothing to the weight of precedent, since the case for judicial review is precisely coterminous with the case for precedent. If the meaning or application of the Constitution is indeterminate, then an essential ground for judicial review is absent, and the resultant precedent carries no weight.

While I strongly agree that indeterminacy makes judicial review inappropriate in the first instance, that indeterminacy may cut the other way when it is a question of overruling precedent. It seems to me that precedent should carry greater weight, especially when judges are confronted with a precedent that is not so much "affirmatively unconstitutional" (i.e., clearly wrong in its substantive interpretation of the Constitution) as it is "unjustifiable," that is, not clear enough to justify judicial review although its substantive interpretation of the Constitution may be quite plausible (but not compelling).

For example, I would argue that the constitutional question in *Champion v. Ames* could have gone either way. The minority opinion, which would have struck down the prohibition of the interstate shipment of lottery tickets, could rightly appeal to Marshall's admonition in *McCulloch v. Maryland* that the Court would be compelled to strike down laws when enumerated powers were used as a "pretext" for regulating matters intended to be left to the states. (What about a Congressional law that prohibited the interstate transportation of people not married or divorced in accord with Congressional specifications?) On the other hand, the majority rightly pointed to Marshall's statement in *Gibbons v. Ogden* that the abuse of an enumerated power–given that those powers were "plenary"–could only be rectified by electing new representatives. Both positions are reasonable.

Because the law was not *clearly* unconstitutional, the Court was correct in upholding it. Why should the court's preference between two concededly reasonable constitutional interpretations take precedence over the legislature's? Suppose, however, that the Court had wrongly struck down the law, and that this decision had become a settled precedent. What should a later Court then do in a case where the precedent was invoked? It seems to me that there are reasonable grounds to say that precedent, if settled, should have stronger weight in such a case, even though the original act of judicial review would have been unjustified.

Lawson might possibly agree with this, since the "unjustifiable" decision (as opposed to the *substantively* mistaken one) can be viewed as not positively violating the Constitution, and hence as not unconstitutional. Perhaps this is simply another limit on the scope of his argument.

However, it seems more likely that he would disagree, arguing that what I am calling an "unjustifiable" decision is substantively wrong in a broader sense in that it constitutes a judicial usurpation of the legislative power granted by the Constitution. From that perspective, he might argue that today's Court cannot, on the basis of the previous unjustifiable decision, continue to restrict legitimate legislative power.

But Madison notes that it is "necessary that the meaning of a Constitution should be freed from uncertainty" just as it is true that ordinary statutes ought not to be left uncertain in meaning. This necessity inheres in the nature of law, for an unsettled and changing law is harder to know and to apply consistently and impartially.

Combined with the argument that constitutional law properly regarded as "settled" can be viewed as having received public acquiescence, this provides a reasonable ground for recognizing the force of precedent in constitutional decisions.

But what is the source of this recognition of the "nature of the law" that justifies giving precedent weight? The most plausible contender would appear to be "the judicial power" of Article III. Lawson contends that invoking this provision begs the question. Since the judicial power turns on what the sources of law are in deciding cases, and since the Constitution is hierarchically superior to any other source of law, Article III contains no basis for a judicial power to prefer incorrect precedent to the Constitution. Lawson does concede, however, that Article III grounds a case-deciding power that is final, so that the executive must enforce a judicial decision even when he believes it to be unconstitutional. But if the executive can be required to enforce a wrong judicial decision, on grounds relating to an Article III case-deciding power, why cannot courts be required to give weight to precedents (even when incorrect) as part of an Article III judicial power understood to include the respect for precedent indisputably at the core of Anglo-American judging?

Another level of this problem of indeterminacy emerges when we ask "exactly how 'indeterminate' is the Constitution on the point at issue?" This is a variation of the question "*how* plausible or reasonable are competing interpretations of a constitutional provision?"

The very important qualification that Madison adds to his position–that some cases will transcend all authority of precedent–seems to suggest that it is too simple to distinguish only between "clearly wrong decisions" and "decisions where the Constitution is indeterminate." Madison's abstract opinion on the constitutionality of a national bank never changed–in that sense, his decision to uphold the constitutionality of the bank was "clearly wrong." And yet, the fact that Madison found that wrong decision about the bank in some sense tolerable–it did not fit in the category of cases that transcended all authority of precedent–suggests, perhaps, that the opinion was "reasonable" in at least some weak sense of that term.

Perhaps we can say that Madison believed in a certain kind of constitutional humility. He was willing to defer to what he saw as long-term popular agreement to a constitutional position, even one he considered wrong in the abstract. He acknowledged that his opinion was subject to a form of popular overruling. This suggests that those popularly supported opinions are "reasonable" in some sense, especially since they can be contrasted with some decisions that–even with the support of precedent–are not authoritative, that are in some sense so "unreasonable" as to lack authority.

What are these limits that apply to even the popular authority manifested to settled precedent? The most plausible interpretation of this Madisonian position is that some constitutional principles are *so* "fundamental" that even precedent cannot displace them; precedent would not authorize maintaining decisions based on principles incompatible with the essential nature of our form of government.

We do know that this category does *not* include the important question of a national bank–though Madison's language on the bank issue was very strong. He argued in House debate that accepting the bank meant permitting Congress to choose *any* means to achieve its constitutionally specified ends, and thus "the essential characteristic of the Government, as composed of limited and enumerated powers, would be destroyed."[31] Would cases that transcended all authority of precedent have to go beyond *that* somehow?

I take Madison's deference to settled precedent on the bank as a tacit admission that his earlier case is overstated. The power of Congress to have plenary power to choose means to the ends entrusted to it by the Constitution–rather than have those means limited in some implied way–was, after all, compatible with a government of limited, enumerated powers. Of course, the power to choose means *might* be pushed so far as to change the nature of the Constitution. As Marshall said in *McCulloch v. Maryland*, Congress might improperly use the power to choose means as a pretext for pursuing *ends* that were not granted it by the Constitution, and if it did so, judges ought to strike down such laws.[32] But the constitutional interpretation on which the bank was based did not make that inevitable.

Madison's acceptance of the bank precedent reflects in part, I think, the fact that the constitutional differences among the founders, however great, were generally contained within boundaries set by their common agreement on rules for interpreting the Constitution.

The more difficult question–given that the founders did not have to confront the question of what Monaghan calls "deeply ingrained transformative change"–is what Madison would say about precedent in our "nonoriginalist universe," that is, a later America in which most constitutional law has been systematically detached from the anchor of the written document. Would these cases (or some of them) be cases that transcend all authority of precedent?

Precedents and the Originalist Today

It was established early in American history that "the judicial power" of Article III referred to the decision of "cases" and "controversies." Judges, for example, were not to issue "advisory opinions."[33] The "judicial power" to which the framers referred was not a newly devised power, but one that had been exercised for centuries in the country from which America took root. In particular, the judicial power reflected the influence of the common-law system, in which judges acknowledged the great weight of precedent.[34] Alexander Hamilton gives testimony to this in *Federalist* No. 78:

> There is yet a further and weighty reason for the permanency of the judicial offices; which is deducible from the nature of the qualifications they require. It has been frequently remarked with great propriety, that a voluminous code of laws is one of the inconveniences necessarily connected with the advantages of free government. To

> avoid an arbitrary discretion in the courts, it is indispensable that they should be bound down by strict rules and precedents, which serve to define and point out their duty in every particular case that comes before them; and it will readily be conceived from the variety of controversies which grow out of the folly and wickedness of mankind, that the records of those precedents must unavoidably swell to a very considerable bulk, and must demand long and laborious study to acquire a competent knowledge of them.[35]

The necessity of the authority of precedents, to limit the discretion of judges, is assumed by Hamilton to be an ordinary and essential part of the judicial power.[36]

Should constitutional cases be somehow exempted from the ordinary attributes of the judicial power? A more plausible case for this might be made if the power of judicial review were a distinct and independent power of American judges. But the fact is that judicial review is nowhere mentioned in the Constitution, and is actually a *derivative* power, something that flows from the ordinary power of judges to decide cases. This suggests that it ought to be exercised according to the usual forms of judicial power. That is, the nature of judicial review differs from ordinary common-law adjudication; but since judicial review is exercised in the context of such adjudication, it ought to be exercised in the common-law mode–always remembering that the ground for judicial review is judicial judgment, not will, and the principle of legislative deference thereby entailed.

Precedent, however, was not an *absolute* principle in the common-law system. Also, in addition to the countervailing considerations in common law, special considerations exist related to the nature of constitutional adjudication. Justice Louis Brandeis' qualification of precedent is one of the best known:

> Stare decisis is usually the wise policy, because in most matters it is more important that the applicable rule of law be settled than that it be settled right . . . This is commonly true even where the error is a matter of serious concern, provided correction can be had by legislation. But in cases involving the Federal Constitution, where correction through legislative action is practically impossible, this Court has often overruled its earlier decisions. The Court bows to the lessons of experience and the force of better reasoning, recognizing that the process of trial and error, so fruitful in the physical sciences, is appropriate also in the judicial function.[37]

An originalist can be concerned about part of the argument–the reference to experience suggests the kind of adaptability that is characteristic of modern, nonoriginalist judicial review[38]–but the references to the difficulty of correcting errors in constitutional cases and to the force of better reasoning seem to be sensible admonitions that qualify the force of precedent somewhat.

The conclusion that I would draw from these observations is that there ought to be, as Monaghan says, a presumption in favor of precedent. The burden of proof is on the one who seeks to overturn precedent.

How heavy that burden will be, however, very much depends on how settled a precedent is. Once a precedent is very settled in the terms we noted above–large

Court majorities have affirmed and reaffirmed the decision over a long period of time, in accord with educated public opinion and with the apparent acquiescence of the other branches–the burden of proof will be a heavy one. But if a precedent is young, controversial, and subject to substantial and ongoing debate, it does not seem to qualify for the kind of respect and deference that Madison ascribed to settled precedent.

Likewise, the greater the distance between the precedent and the "true law" of the Constitution, the less deference it deserves. A "clearly wrong" precedent needn't automatically be overturned, but other things being equal, it ought to be more vulnerable to overturning than a constitutional precedent that is a close call.

What cases seem most fairly to fall into Madison's category of cases that transcend all authority of precedent? *Roe v. Wade* would clearly be a major instance, since, besides the federalism issue, it implicates the question of the right to life, one of the most fundamental principles of our form of government. *Roe*, moreover, is already extremely vulnerable because it has clearly never been "settled" (and that can still be said after *Planned Parenthood v. Casey*, I believe) and because its basic principle is a substantial distance from the command of the Constitution (being a dubious interpretation of a privacy right that is already on its own terms a dubious interpretation).

Another example might be the extreme form of the incorporation of the Bill of Rights into the Fourteenth Amendment that applies virtually all of its rights (now dramatically expanded) to the state *and* does so "jot-for-jot and tittle-for-tittle." Such a dramatic transformation of federalism, it might be reasonably argued, cannot be closed off to reconsideration.

Hypothetically, were the Supreme Court to adopt the extravagant claims of recent Presidents about the war making power of the President (e.g., that a United Nations resolution is a sufficient basis for the president to commit troops to war, apart from any Congressional authorization), those claims would involve such a transformation of separation of powers that they would have to be considered open to revision.

Perhaps most fundamentally, judicial decisions that commit the Court itself to the ongoing exercise of nonjudicial power would seem open to question. On this ground it was sensible for the Court to reconsider its free exercise doctrine, which under *Sherbert v. Verner* and *Wisconsin v. Yoder* had required constant judicial balancing or policy-making, and to return to the more traditional doctrine reinstituted in *Employment Division v. Smith*, which relieved it of the task of constant legislating in this area.

The Pragmatic Case for Precedent

There is another, more minimalist form of the case for precedent today. There seem to be no sound reasons for committing originalist judges to what might be called "Don Quixotism." It *is* a form of tilting at windmills to try to fight battles that are decisively and irreversibly lost. Of course, it may not always be easy to say when defeat is indeed final. But sometimes it will be clear, and there are at least strong practical grounds for the originalist judge not to contend against well-settled precedents. For example, *Brown v. Board of Education*, at least as to the fundamental principle of prohibiting genuine legal segregation (that is, understanding *Brown* on its own terms rather than the way subsequent Courts have interpreted it since 1969) does seem to be a literally irreversible decision. There is virtually no support for its overruling and no sound reason, as a matter of broad public policy principles, to want it overruled. Even originalists who regard it as a judicial modification and extension of the Fourteenth Amendment, therefore, are right not to press for its overruling.

Likewise, one could mount a powerful case against the existence of substantially independent federal agencies exercising quasi-legislative, quasi-executive, and quasi-judicial power. (Are the "quasi-"s just a way of trying to downplay the reality that separation of powers is being violated?) Yet the administrative state, as Monaghan points out, is clearly with us to stay–it is so deeply embedded that it cannot be uprooted–and so it would be a foolish exercise to try to declare these agencies unconstitutional. Nor, to give a third example, is there any likelihood that the incorporation of the Bill of Rights into the Fourteenth Amendment due process clause, despite its dubious textual and historical basis, can be completely uprooted. And, finally, even if there is strong evidence that the original First Amendment freedom of speech was a prohibition of prior restraint, the extension of that protection of speech to most forms of subsequent punishment seems irreversible.

This position does, however, leave some room for judges to *limit* (as opposed to simply rejecting outright and fully) such settled precedents. In fact, that is one of the strongest arguments for permitting judges to accept the weight of precedent to some degree: if they are not bound in principle to dissent from all decisions based on incorrect precedents ("wasting" their votes on positions that have no practical chance of being adopted), judges generally committed to originalism will be free to provide (perhaps necessary) votes for positions that are at least *closer* to the proper interpretation of the Constitution.

It is possible, for example, to accept that a given precedent is settled in part, but in other respects not fully settled. *Brown* may be settled, but later school desegregation cases are not. It may be simply settled that the First Amendment (as to both its speech and religion positions) applies to the states. Is it clear that there must be a completely uniform standard applied to both? I do not think so. It is not at all unthinkable that, for example, given the traditional state police power regarding regulation of morals (and the absence of a general federal police power), different obscenity standards apply to the states (and localities) and to the federal government.[39] It seems settled that the most basic search-and-seizure requirements apply to both federal and state governments, but the rather indeterminate language of the clause (no "unreasonable" searches and seizures) and the different demands of criminal law enforcement and the constitutional principle of federalism make different minimum standards for them plausible.

Some hard questions remain here as to what exactly has been "settled" by precedent and what remains subject to revision. And since this ground for giving weight to precedent is a practical one (the futility of opposing what seems to be beyond dispute), it is subject to change if the empirical judgment on which it is based ("x is a lost cause") turns out to be wrong. Causes that seemed hopelessly lost have on occasion, surprisingly, been resuscitated.

Conclusion

This kind of discussion is necessarily a very dissatisfying one for an originalist. Originalism is a theory whose roots generally reside in the recognition that republican principles are incompatible with unchecked (or insufficiently checked[40]) judicial power.[41] While traditional constitutional jurisprudence was never a "mechanical jurisprudence" that claimed to eliminate completely the need for a certain measure of political prudence in judges, it certainly tried to confine judges to the interpretation (rather than the making) of law. The general guidelines for originalist judges discussed above recognize that there is no absolute rule on precedent: it is neither always illegitimate to uphold incorrect constitutional precedents nor always illegitimate to overturn them. They tell originalist judges to give considerable weight to precedent that is settled and less sharply opposed to (or less dramatically an extension of) the Constitution. They also say that practical necessity will require conceding great precedential weight to cases that seem so deeply rooted that opposition to them would accomplish nothing. On the other hand, they also recognize that many decisions are not fully settled and that some principles are so fundamental that contrary decisions can never be exempted from reconsideration. In the final analysis, then, originalist judges will have to make prudent determinations about what precedents to consider beyond debate and which to regard as open to challenge. If this is an uncomfortable position for originalist judges–and it is–that may simply be an inevitable feature of living in what Monaghan calls a "nonoriginalist universe."

Notes

1. This is not to say that it is universally or even generally accepted that *Marbury* describes a form of judicial review closely tied to text and framers' intention. Many constitutional commentators, as well as judges, seem to assume that the judicial review described in *Marbury* is the same as the judicial review with which we are familiar today, i.e. they assume that *Marbury* authorizes judges (ultimately, the justices of the Supreme Court) to give determinate content to the uncertain generalities and ambiguities of the Constitution. My point is that since Bickel there has been an implicit assumption that the authoritative meaning of the Constitution is not necessarily tied to its original meaning. Bickel rightly understood that this required a new basis for judicial review.

2. Thomas Grey, *Do We Have an Unwritten Constitution?* 27 Stanford Law Review 703 (1975).

3. Raoul Berger, for example, placed primary emphasis on the historical intention in the minds of the original framers of the Constitution and of subsequent amendments. Others (myself, for instance) tended to give greater weight to the text of the document itself, though allowing a more limited and subordinate place for historical evidence of intention or meaning. I explore some of the differences between the two forms of "original intention" in "Between Scylla and Charybdis: Powell and Berger on the Framers' Intentions," a paper delivered at the American Political Science Association annual meeting, September, 1992.

4. Christopher Wolfe, *The Rise of Modern Judicial Review: From Constitutional Interpretation to Judge-Made Law* (New York: Basic Books, 1986); second, revised edition (Lanham, MD: Rowman and Littlefield, 1994).

5. Christopher Wolfe, *Judicial Activism: Bulwark of Liberty or Precarious Security?* (Pacific Grove, Ca.: Brooks/Cole Publishing Co., 1991).

6. See Wolfe, *The Rise of Modern Judicial Review*, chapter 13, and "Burger Court Disappointments," *This World,* Fall 1986, 59.

7. One of the most salient instances of this process occurred in the area of church-state law. After years of tug-of-war on the court between "stricter separationists" and "accommodationists," attempts to make sense out of the court's precedents regarding what was "a primary effect that advanced or inhibited religion" seemed impossible. Perhaps the ultimate expression of this occurred in *Lynch v. Donnelly*, 465 U.S. 668 (1984), in which the court upheld the constitutionality of a nativity scene contained in a larger municipal Christmas display. Chief Justice Burger, writing for the court, said that the benefits for religion of a municipal creche scene were not greater than the benefits of many other programs that had been upheld (e.g., textbooks and transportation for parochial schools, grants for buildings at religiously affiliated colleges, tax exemptions for church property, Sunday closing laws, released time programs for religious education). "We are unable," said Burger, "to discern a greater aid to religion deriving from inclusion of the creche than from these benefits and endorsements previously held not violative of the establishment clause."

His assertion was quite right, but beside the point. It would also have been easy enough to say that the effect of the creche advanced religion no *less* than a string of *other* cases the court had decided (e.g., overturning state provision of maps and field-trip transportation and other "secular" services to private, nonprofit–including parochial–schools and tax credits for parents of students in those schools, public school "nondenominational" prayer–none of which could be said to single out and support *particular* religious views, as the creche scene clearly did).

8. See Bickel, *The Least Dangerous Branch* (Indianapolis: Bobb-Merrill, 1962), chapter one, and Ronald Dworkin, *Taking Rights Seriously* (Cambridge: Harvard University Press, 1977), chapters four and five.

9. Gary Lawson, *The Constitutional Case Against Precedent*, 17 Harvard Journal of Law and Public Policy 23 (1994).

10. Lawson explicitly confines his analysis to *federal* cases involving *horizontal precedent* (i.e., precedent made by an equal or inferior, not a superior, court) and dealing with *constitutional* issues (not common-law adjudication).

11. Lawson, *The Constitutional Case Against Precedent*, 27.

12. Akhil Reed Amar makes this point in his response, *On Lawson on Precedent*, 17 Harvard Journal of Law and Public Policy 41 (1994). He makes a similar point respecting Lawson's acceptance of *res adjudicata*–that the final judicial decision in a case is binding as to the parties to that case. But if the decision is binding on the parties even if it is based on an incorrect reading of the Constitution, then it is not *always* inadmissible to give effect to a decision contrary to the Constitution, as Lawson's argument suggests it is.

13. Lawson, *The Constitutional Case Against Precedent*, 31.

14. Ibid.

15. Lawson, *The Constitutional Case Against Precedent*, 31-32 (emphasis omitted).

16. *Cooper v. Aaron*, 358 U.S. 1, 18 (1958).

17. Henry Monaghan, *Stare Decisis and Constitutional Adjudication*, 88 Columbia Law Review, 723 (1988).

18. Monaghan, *Stare Decisis and Constitutional Adjudication*, 727, 724.

19. Monaghan, *Stare Decisis and Constitutional Adjudication*, 749.

20. Monaghan, *Stare Decisis and Constitutional Adjudication*, 752 .

21. Monaghan, *Stare Decisis and Constitutional Adjudication*, 754 . The notion of constitutional common law was developed more fully by Monaghan in an earlier article, *The Supreme Court 1974 Term–Foreword: Constitutional Common Law*, 89 Harvard Law Review 1 (1975).

22. Monaghan, *Stare Decisis and Constitutional Adjudication*, 757.

23. Monaghan, *Stare Decisis and Constitutional Adjudication*, 761.

24. Monaghan, *Stare Decisis and Constitutional Adjudication*, 770, 771.

25. Monaghan, *Stare Decisis and Constitutional Adjudication*, 772.

26. Madison to N. P. Trist, December 1831, *The Writings of James Madison*, ed. Galliard Hunt (New York: G.P. Putnam's Sons, 1900-1910), 9:476-77.

27. Madison to C. E. Haynes, 25 February 1831, *The Writings of James Madison*, 9:442-43.

28. *The Political Thought of Abraham Lincoln* (Indianapolis: Bobbs-Merrill, 1967), 175-76. This is a restatement of a position taken earlier in his speech on the Dred Scott decision in Springfield, Illinois, 26 June 1857.

29. Madison agreed with this point. See his letter to Spencer Roane, 2 September 1819, *The Writings of James Madison*, 447-48, wishing that the court had given seriatim opinions in *McCulloch v. Maryland*, since "[t]his might either by the harmony of their reasoning have produced a greater conviction in the Public mind; or by its discordance have impaired the force of the precedent now ostensibly supported by a unanimous & perfect concurrence in every argument & dictum in the judgment pronounced."

30. *Pennsylvania v. Union Gas Co.*, 105 L.Ed.2d 1, 37 (1989).

31. *History of Debates in Congress* (Washington, D.C.: Gales and Seaton, 1834-56) (debate of 2 February 1791), 1947.

32. *McCulloch v. Maryland,* 4 Wheaton 423 (1819).

33. See Wolfe, *The Rise of Modern Judicial Review*, 102-03.

34. It might be argued that the Constitution does not explicitly adopt common-law judicial procedure, and that my reliance on the importance of precedent in the common law is therefore inadmissible. I believe that this reads the Constitution too narrowly. At some points, the Constitution's text itself seems to *presume* a common-law background, e.g., the Seventh Amendment: "In Suits at common law. . ."; Article III, section 2: "The judicial

Power shall extend to all Cases, in Law and Equity. . ." (the reference to "Law and Equity" being more plausibly a reference in the context of the Anglo-American legal system than to more generic uses of the term, e.g., in Aristotle's *Politics*). This, and similar language, only confirms a noncontroversial historical fact that our legal system "flowed out of" the English legal system, and initially bore its general features, except where the colonists and founders took steps to change it. (One of those areas was, of course, judicial review itself. But even here, it is important to recognize that the power of judicial review is not a distinct and independent prerogative of the judiciary, but a power derivative from, and limited to the context of, their more fundamental task of deciding cases.)

35. Hamilton, Madison, Jay, *The Federalist Papers*, ed. Gary Wills (New York: Bantam, 1982), 398-99.

36. While there is no specific mention of precedent in it, I believe that another passage makes similar assumptions. Hamilton says in *Federalist* No. 81, 411 that the danger of judicial usurpation on legislative authority "can never be so extensive as to amount to an inconvenience, or in any sensible degree to affect the order of the political system. This may be inferred with certainty *from the general nature of the judicial power*; from the objects to which it relates; *from the manner in which it is exercised*; from its comparative weakness, and from its total incapacity to support its usurpations by force" (emphasis added). The italicized passages, especially the second one, seem very likely to include an implicit reference to a system of case law in which great weight is given to precedent.

37. *Burnet v. Coronado Oil & Gas Company*, 285 U.S. 393, 406-08 (1931) (internal citations omitted).

38. See Wolfe, *The Rise of Modern Judicial Review*, chapters nine and ten.

39. See, for example, Justice Harlan's dissent and concurrence in *Roth v. U.S.* and *Alberts v. California* 354 U.S. 476, 496 (1957).

40. One does not have to consider judicial power completely unchecked to regard it as excessive and dangerous. It is sufficient that it not be *adequately* checked.

41. Originalism, that is, while initially a theory of interpretation of the Constitution, naturally extends into a theory of adjudication as well. A large part of the reason for this is that an originalist examination of the constitutional foundations of judicial review in the Constitution will recognize the very limited form judicial review should take in order to make it compatible with the overall republican design. I discuss this in chapters 3 and 4 of *The Rise of Modern Judicial Review*.

Chapter 8

The Operational Irrelevance of Originalism

Sanford Levinson

My essay in many ways is complementary to that offered by Christopher Wolfe, who writes about the delicate problems that occur "when Constitution and precedent collide." One can understand this title only by recognizing that Wolfe is one of those constitutional theorists labeled as "originalists." Fidelity to constitutional meaning is best achieved by attempting to discern, and then to enforce, the likely understandings held about the constitutional passages in question by the original ratifiers of those passages. The most famous, or at least notorious, of such originalists is almost certainly Robert Bork, who has proclaimed "original understanding" as the "only" approach meeting "the criteria that any theory of constitutional adjudication must meet in order to possess democratic legitimacy. Only that approach is consonant with the design of the American Republic."[1] Any other approaches presumably produce only pretend versions of the Constitution, as it were, and not the real thing.

Yet Wolfe himself notes that this limitation of constitutional legitimacy to originalist decisions scarcely accords with the respect almost all of us pay, at least some of the time, to one or another past decision of the Supreme Court that cannot plausibly be defended as particularly faithful to original understanding, and the brunt of his eloquent and elegant paper is to try to accommodate the claims of originalism and precedent alike. I do not intend to retrace all of Wolfe's tracks. But I do want to use his paper as grist for my own argument that the opportunity actually to be a thoroughgoing originalist–even assuming that originalism is a coherent theory of constitutional interpretation, an assumption that I will leave blessedly unexamined in my remarks[2]–is in fact quite limited in regard to most analysts. This is true both for non-lawyers, like Wolfe, and, I shall argue, even more so for lawyers, whether they are engaged in ordinarily legal practice in the bar, serve on the bench, or even teach the young as members of the legal academy.

I don't want to go quite so far as to say that the argument between Bork and Wolfe, on the one side, and their anti-originalist critics (including myself), on the other, is "full of sound and fury, signifying nothing," for that would be surely hyperbolic. But I do argue that there is far less to the dispute than may first appear, that what political scientists, in their more positivist moments, call the operational importance of originalism, is really quite limited. Thus one of my central theses is that there is a surprisingly general consensus–most definitely including Bork and Wolfe–that originalism simply won't do as an exhaustive, or even a necessarily privileged, theory of constitutional interpretation. What this means, simply, is that they agree that originalism, whatever its claims, at least sometimes legitimately loses out to some other theory about how we ascertain that complex web of understandings we call the United States Constitution.

I don't want to be heard as simply dismissing originalism, for at some suitably abstract level almost everyone is an originalist in at least some limited sense. Few can be heard to proclaim that they just don't care, under any circumstances, what those who drafted, or those who voted for, a text probably thought the text meant. Even though I am probably more indifferent than are many to original understandings, I scarcely disdain appeals to history, especially if one wants to figure out why a particular clause was placed in the Constitution in the first place. My own best known piece of legal writing, for example, is almost certainly an essay on the Second Amendment and its controversial right to "keep and bear arms."[3] Much of my argument there depends on a reconstruction of 18th-century civic-republican thought, knowledge of which is, I believe, a *sine qua non* for understanding why it is in the Bill of Rights in the first place and even for interpreting the Amendment as we approach the 21st Century. Indeed, when Garry Wills recently offered an originalist account of the Amendment that had the consequence of basically removing from it any real point, I had no hesitation in writing a response based on what I thought was a sounder historical account. Moreover, I also concede, as a practical matter, that interpretations that demonstrably stray too far from pragmatically plausible original understandings sometimes pay a real price in support from those members of the public who, naively or not, identify constitutional meaning with original understanding. It is no small matter, rhetorically speaking, to profess indifference to what the authors of a given writing probably meant.

However, even if I want to argue that "we (or at least most of us) are all originalists," I also want to go on to argue that "we (or at least most of us) are also Ackermanians," and it is this tension–or what some might call outright incoherence–that makes contemporary constitutional theory such a challenge. In describing someone as "Ackermanian," I am referring to the extremely interesting and important work of Yale Professor of Law Bruce Ackerman, whose work I have publicly described as "[t]he most important project now underway in the entire field of constitutional theory" and, indeed, "the most significant work in constitutional theory to be published . . . in the past half-century."[4] I believe that anyone analyzing our constitutional system as it has actually operated over the past 200 years must recognize that constitutional change–including, most definitely, "amendment–is a far more complicated process than might be suggested by reference simply to constitutional text or original understanding. Ackerman has been devoting himself for more than a decade to teasing out the implications of our operational system of constitutional change, and by "Ackermanian" I refer to anyone who accepts, even if only with reluctance, the legitimacy of significant constitutional change quite contrary to the wishes of the framers and perhaps indefensible by any ordinary means of interpretation that has occurred outside the boundaries presumably set by Article Five.

How do I justify this proposition that almost all of us have an Ackermanian streak? I begin my defense by reference to James Madison, surely one of the central figures in our constitutional Pantheon. Perhaps the most important feature of the casebook on constitutional law that I co-edit with Paul Brest is that it begins, practically speaking, not with *Marbury v. Madison*, but, rather, with Madison's speech to the 1791 House of Representatives explaining why the bill before Congress that would charter the Bank of the United States was, for better or worse, unconstitutional. The record of the congressional debate, written in indirect form, states that "[Madison] had entertained this opinion from the date of the Constitution. His impression might, perhaps, be the stronger, because he well recollected that a power to grant charters of incorporation had been proposed in the general convention and rejected."[5] Thus the man often called "the father of the Constitution" is telling his colleagues, in effect, "I was there. I know what we meant. We can't do this," even though, ironically enough, he had been one of the strongest, albeit unsuccessful, supporters of a strong national government–and concomitantly weakened states–in the Philadelphia convention. As every student knows, though, the Senate and the House disagreed with Madison, in part because of the defense of the Bank authored by Madison's co-author of *The Federalist*, Alexander Hamilton,[6] and the Bank was chartered. That is interesting in itself, especially for those who proclaim their commitment to originalism, but it is not my main point.

What is my main point is that it was President James Madison himself who some twenty-five years later signed the bill authorizing the establishment of the Second Bank of the United States, the charter for the first Bank having expired, unrenewed, in 1811. Why did Madison sign the legislation, especially since we know that he was thoroughly capable of vetoing bills that he supported, as a policy matter, but thought, alas, unconstitutional? This occurred, for example, in 1817, when he vetoed an "internal improvements" bill, even though it might provide "signal advantage to the general prosperity" of the United States, because the bill was beyond the powers assigned to Congress by Article I of the Constitution.[7] Had Madison, then, changed his mind about the merits of his 1791 speech and concluded that he had been wrong and that Hamilton had in fact been correct in defending the constitutional propriety of the Bank? You will find no such admission. Instead, Madison stated that the issue of congressional power had been settled "by repeated recognitions, under varied circumstances, of the validity of such an institution."[8]

Madison's argument is a version of precedent-oriented doctrinalism. What this means is that decisions that violate the tenets of originalism at time T become accepted as part of our constitutional fabric at T1. I think that this version of doctrinal argument, which is at the very heart of ordinary legal reasoning, is basically similar to the most general (and thus compelling) version of Bruce Ackerman's argument. I understand Ackerman's most fundamental point to be that it is literally impossible to understand American constitutionalism as it has actually been practiced for the past 200 years if you say (something like), "Look. There is a set of decisions that are legitimate only because they can be traced back to original understandings. Then there are changes that come through and only through Article Five. Otherwise, there is nothing else that a well-trained legal analyst should be willing to recognize as American constitutional law."

That certainly does not seem to describe James Madison's view of what made the bank legitimate by 1816 in a way that it was not in 1791. Instead, I think that Madison is in effect arguing that the course of practice had affected a de facto constitutional amendment. To be sure, Madison didn't express Ackerman's kind of delight in this fact, but, ultimately, that is beside the point. The question before us is more strictly positivist: What is the best way of understanding the actualities of American constitutionalism, whether or not one is delighted by what one finds? Consider in this context James Boyd White's frank description of Marshall's opinion in *McCulloch v. Maryland*,[9] which of course upheld the constitutionality of the bill that Madison signed. White has termed the opinion "less an interpretation of the Constitution than an amendment to it, the overruling of which is unimaginable."[10]

As the literary theorist Jonathan Culler has written, "The history of readings is a history of misreadings, though under certain circumstances these misreadings can be and may have been accepted as readings."[11] Jack Balkin, formerly of Texas, now, alas, at Yale, has persuasively argued that Culler's comment aptly describes what we ordinarily think of as The Rule of Law, especially insofar as that concept includes paying due regard to decided cases. Indeed, Balkin compares "constitutional decision making" to "the party game where each guest whispers a message into the next person's ear, and finally the first and last incarnations of the message are compared." To the extent that "the Constitution obeys the Rule of Law, it must contain its own possibilities of cumulative misunderstanding . . . ."[12]

Whether or not we agree with White's specific description of *McCulloch* or Balkin's evocation of "cumulative misunderstandings" as the best description of our constitutional history, I suspect that each of us has a nomination for a case, well integrated into the corpus of American constitutionalism, that is "less an interpretation of the Constitution than an amendment to it." To stick only to 20th century examples, some might pick one of the central cases that, taken together, comprise the so-called "constitutional revolution" of 1937;[13] others might choose *Bolling v. Sharpe*,[14] the companion case to *Brown v. Board of Education*[15] that in effect read the Equal Protection Clause of the Fourteenth Amendment into the Fifth Amendment as a limitation on the federal government. Many, of course, would name *Roe v. Wade*,[16] though there might be considerably more debate on whether it is in fact well integrated into the constitutional fabric. We could, presumably, go on and on giving examples of cases that under one or another plausible originalist argument were wrongly decided, but nonetheless have become encrusted and are followed by the conscientious judge.

This theme certainly pervades the (in)famous joint opinion of Justices O'Connor, Souter, and Kennedy in *Planned Parenthood v. Casey* arguing in behalf of stare decisis regarding a woman's right to choose to have an abortion.[17] Their plurality opinion managed to argue for page after page that *Roe* ought not be overturned (even while overturning many of its specifics) without ever once saying that it had been rightly decided. Professor Gerard Bradley of Notre Dame, in another essay in this collection, eloquently denounced this opinion and the role it appears to assign the Supreme Court as the drafter of a "new constitutional covenant" to replace the old one when it is found wanting.[18] But none of these three justices has ever proclaimed an originalist faith, so they perhaps do not serve as the best example of my point above about the pervasiveness of "Ackermanianism."

Consider, then, Robert Bork himself. It was he, after all, who both denounced *Bolling* as essentially lawless and, yet, promised the Judiciary Committee that he would not vote to overrule it were he confirmed as a member of the Supreme Court.[19] Similarly, Bork has indicated his belief that "it is too late to overrule . . . those decisions validating certain New Deal and Great Society programs," for that "would be to overturn most of modern government and plunge us into chaos."[20] This prudential argument would obviously be beside the point if he believed that those decisions were legitimate from the beginning; it would also be obviously beside the point if he believed that the conscientious judge owed strict fidelity only to original intent.

I therefore believe that Bork is literally incoherent when he first concedes his agreement with Ackerman that "the Constitution's interpretation has undergone radical shifts in the past that cannot be accounted for by classical or lawyerly reasoning," including "the constitutional revolution worked by the New Deal Court," but then attempts to distance himself from his former Yale colleague by saying that he, unlike Ackerman, refuses to "concede its legitimacy."[21] Perhaps this means that Bork, like other conservatives, laments the revolution and regards it as a bad thing, politically speaking. But the far more important point is that Bork seems to believe that conscientious judges are now bound by many of these "radical shifts" and that voting to overrule them would constitute almost as egregious a display of judicial activism as the original decisions themselves. Surely this is all that a positivist analyst like Bork could mean by "legitimacy," and he has sworn under oath that, however begrudgingly, he finds *Bolling* and the Supreme Court decisions of 1937 legitimate at present even if they were illegitimate at birth. Q.E.D. that Robert Bork is Bruce Ackerman in disguise.[22]

So the central point is that the present Yalie Ackerman and the former Yalie Bork in fact have more in common than either would like to concede. Indeed, I might add one more former Yalie to this list: Clarence Thomas. Although Justice Thomas wrote, in his *Lopez* concurrence[23] and *U.S. Term Limits* dissent,[24] perhaps the most uncompromising originalist opinions in decades, he nonetheless joined in the majority opinion in *Adarand Constructors, Inc. v. Pena*,[25] which requires "strict scrutiny" of congressional statutes that use race as a classification. That opinion literally makes no sense unless one gives full credit to *Bolling* as a reading of the Constitution (and, incidentally, rejects Andrew Kull's telling of the original history of the Fourteenth Amendment).[26] One notes that Thomas took nary a sentence in his uncharacteristically short concurrence in *Adarand*[27] to indicate if he disagrees with Robert Bork as to the historical provenance of *Bolling* or to explain why, if he in fact agrees with Bork, it is nonetheless binding on him now in a way that other precedents of the Court seem not to be. Dare one suggest that Thomas's own political (or moral) preferences are more important to him, at least on this occasion, than fidelity to original understanding?

I offer one more example of what I am calling the Ackermanian consensus, this time from a young and as yet generally unknown, scholar, Peter McCutchen, who recently published an interesting article, *Mistakes, Precedent and the Rise of the Administrative State: Toward a Constitutional Theory of the Second Best*.[28] It begins with a very dramatic statement: "In exercising executive, legislative and judicial power, administrative agencies combine powers that the Constitution separates . . . . In short, the administrative state is unconstitutional."[29] McCutchen immediately goes on to note that the Supreme Court has been unwilling to invalidate the post-New Deal administrative state, largely on "pragmatic" grounds, including the possibility that the Court "might not have the political capital necessary to realize its objective."[30] The naive reader, especially if he is aware that McCutchen is a member of the Federalist Society, which numbers originalists like Bork and former Attorney General Edwin Meese among their heroes, might believe that this analysis will shortly translate into the proposition that we must immediately begin, perhaps with all deliberate speed, to dismantle the constitutionally illegitimate administrative state. After all, I assume that most Federalists can easily write a paragraph castigating the ill-disguised political calculations known as "pragmatism" as a proffered reason for refusing to enforce the Constitution as originally understood.[31]

But look how McCutchen proceeds: "[T]he Court should tolerate structures or practices that are conceded to be unconstitutional when such structures or practices have become institutionalized."[32] I quickly note that this is a very sensible notion. After all, as yet another would-be originalist, Professor Henry Paul Monaghan of Columbia, has written, "insistence upon original intent as the only legitimate standard for judicial decision making entails a massive repudiation of the present constitutional order,"[33] and such a repudiation would simply cost too much in terms of the stability of our now-existing institutional structures of government. So, says Monaghan, the task of the contemporary constitutional analyst, whatever his or her abstract preference for originalism, is "to make sense out of a nonoriginalist universe,"[34] a task accepted, however ambivalently, by McCutcheon and, as a practical matter, by almost everyone else.

But, once again, I think that all of this is a version of the Ackermanian argument. To be sure, many of us might quibble whether Ackerman has gotten it exactly right with his particular theory of non-Article Five amendment, the complexities of which are not the topic of my remarks today. But such quibbles are beside the point. Far more important, I think, is that all of these distinguished people–James Madison, Robert Bork, Henry Paul Monaghan, and Peter McCutchen–join with Ackerman in saying that one simply cannot understand American constitutionalism as actually practiced unless one complements originalism and Article V with some theory of non-Article V amendment. Maybe you would respond that Madison, Bork, and McCutchen are talking about "constitutional change" rather than "constitutional amendment." But I insist that that purported distinction must itself be subjected to close analysis rather than blithely asserted. As I have written elsewhere, it is quite naive–indeed, I have described it as almost literally thoughtless–to describe the United States Constitution as having exactly 27 amendments, unless one limits one's notion of "amendment" only to the relatively uninteresting category of "numbered textual addition" to an original text. If, on the other hand, "amendment" refers to any change in the operative legal culture that cannot plausibly be ascribed simply to relatively conventional "interpretation" or elaboration of pre-existing legal materials, then I believe, and I will be so bold as to suggest that most of you in fact believe, that our constitutional history manifests more "amendments" than those found in the numbered listing following the 1787 text of the Constitution.

I have now come to the conclusion of my first argument as to why originalism is less important than it's sometimes cracked up to be. To be sure, emphasis on the importance of precedent does not genuinely stop the discussion, for part of our constitutional practice is that on occasion precedents can in fact be overruled. It would be nice to have some theory as to what justifies overruling precedents. I must say, though, that I am not familiar with any very good theory of how we decide which precedents are respect-worthy and which should be consigned to the dustbin of history. And it is certainly no one's theory–or, perhaps more accurately, the theory of no one viewed as within the "mainstream" of contemporary constitutional debate–that precedents ought to be overruled merely because they violate original understandings.[35]

Now for my second major point: We have this whole time made what I consider to be one of the cardinal mistakes of the way American academics–and most other people–approach the study of constitutional law. That mistake is to reduce the subject matter of constitutional interpretation to the interpretive practices of judges–in reality to only one group of judges, those on the United States Supreme Court. Many of us are much too often just like Ronald Dworkin, who writes about a mythic judge named Hercules rather than about the actual practices of the American (or British) judiciary in all of their complexity. It is far easier to ignore that complexity and to obsess about the interpretive practices of a single justice on the Supreme Court (and therefore ignore even the legitimate requirements of "teamwork" and "compromise" that are often necessary in order to gain five votes to make a majority opinion). This, of course, was one of the reasons the Bork hearings were so riveting, because everyone assumed that he would indeed have a great deal of interpretive freedom were he confirmed. And it is often tempting to cast arguments in the form, "How would you decide the case were you on the Supreme Court?"

I don't want to deny that that is an interesting question, no less interesting, for example, that asking one of our friends or colleagues what he or she would do as President of the United States. But, for better or worse, such questions are almost always literally fantastic. The reality, of course, is that there are very few seats available on the Supreme Court (and even fewer in the Oval Office). Far more seats are available on so-called "inferior courts," which I quickly point out is a constitutional term.[36] What does it mean to be a member of an inferior court? Well, one of the things that means is that one is viewed as part of a command structure in which superior courts–and especially the Supreme Court–gives the orders that the lower courts are required, whether with pleasure or sullenly, to enforce. Last year I heard Judge Frank Easterbrook, a conservative member of the Seventh Circuit Court of Appeals, tell a Federalist Society audience that he was a loyal and faithful servant of non-overruled opinions written by William J. Brennan that are based on interpretive theories that Easterbrook most definitely does not adopt. What is one's reaction to this confession?

The Supreme Court itself could not be clearer in emphasizing that it does not want inferior court members to think for themselves in regard to what the Constitution requires. The Court rejects Andrew Jackson's altogether sensible notion that opinions of the Court "have only such influence as the force of their reasoning may deserve."[37] Indeed, if you want to see hierarchical thought played out, just read an opinion of the U.S. Supreme Court when an inferior court does develop a mind of its own. Thus, after the Fourth Circuit more or less ignored an existing Supreme Court decision and found cruel and unusual a 40-year sentence that had been imposed for possessing with intent to distribute and distributing nine ounces of marijuana,[38] the Supreme Court granted certiorari and didn't even bother to write a signed opinion in reversing the Circuit Court for its having "failed to heed our decision in *Rummel*."[39] It used a per curiam opinion, the most contemptuous sort of opinion it can use to indicate to an inferior court exactly how inferior it is, to say that "the Court of Appeals could be viewed as having ignored consciously or unconsciously the hierarchy of the federal court system created by the Constitution and Congress." As you might quickly infer, this is not a good thing. "[U]nless we wish anarchy to prevail within the federal judicial system, a precedent of this Court must be followed by the lower federal courts no matter how misguided the judges of those courts may think it to be."[40]

So now we come to a key question: What would it mean to be an originalist–or, indeed, any other kind of "ist," save a doctrinalist, on an inferior court–if your superiors insist on giving you what you consider to be dumb, wrongly decided, non-originalist opinions? So long as one adopts Easterbrook's bounded view of his own authority, I think the answer to the question is, not much or, at the very least, far less than might be the case, arguendo, for a member of the U.S. Supreme Court.

I should confess, incidentally, that I am one of those relatively few people who in fact are not so appalled by the notion of members of inferior courts thinking for themselves and feeling themselves free to overrule misguided decisions–or at least to challenge misguided decisions of the U.S. Supreme Court by refusing to follow them.[41] But I have discovered in making this argument that most people do find persuasive the language of the U.S. Supreme Court and consider my position little short of the anarchy against which the Court warns. To the extent that is true, then all such critics must be rejecting originalism in the name of the quite different value of institutional stability.

We must ask, therefore, whether anybody other than that numerically insignificant group of individuals who in fact make it to the United States Supreme Court really engage in these great passionate debates about what approach to constitutional interpretation is the one true one. On the contrary, I think it is fair to describe almost all "inferior judges," whatever their eminence–Easterbrook was a member of the University of Chicago law faculty, and former Dean Guido Calebresi of the Yale Law School has now joined the Second Circuit Court of Appeals–as disabled from paying any serious attention to originalist arguments should their masters on the Supreme Court have decided in a direction contrary to that desired by James Madison and other framers. To be sure, if a "case of first impression" ever arises, then even inferior court judges can have the fun of trying to decode original intentions. But the point is that very few such cases are thought to arise in a legal system as rich and complicated as our own.

I now turn to my final point as to why originalism is, most often, not so much "wrong" as irrelevant for those who actually practice law in the United States. The explanation for this irrelevance is very simple: A lawyer's duty is to make the best arguments one can for his or her client, where "best" is defined, for better or worse, in the crassest, most instrumental terms possible. The best argument is the one that is in fact likely to be accepted by the lawyer's audience, not the one that he or she might select as a member of the United States Supreme Court. To be sure, some members of the Supreme Court are interested in originalist arguments, and every lawyer practicing at that level must therefore be prepared to present an originalist argument. But the point is that every lawyer must be prepared to make non-originalist arguments as well. (I am reminded of the old story of the three persons being interviewed for a job teaching math. The appointments committee asked every applicant the same question: What is 2+2. The philosopher answered, "It depends on the base system you're using." The engineer answered, "4." And the lawyer answered, "What do you want it to be?") If you accept my description of the lawyer's role, then the obvious question is whether it makes sense to imagine someone practicing as a systematically "originalist attorney"? Can you imagine, for example, a lawyer telling her clients that she will make only originalist arguments, even if there are respectable non-originalist arguments that would serve the client better? More to the point, can you imagine any client that would in fact retain such a lawyer? Even if you agree entirely with Christopher Wolfe and Robert Bork as to what judicial integrity requires, would you want a principled "Wolfian" or "Borkian" to represent you in your own case if in fact originalist argument cut against you and some other kind of argument would support the outcome you desired?

It is the case, then, that every practicing lawyer has to be able to speak in all of the possible forms of the language of constitutional law, what my friend Jack Balkin and I refer to as "constitutional grammar."[42] We adopt the notion from the book written by my colleague Philip Bobbitt, *Constitutional Interpretation*.[43] There he focuses on the various forms of law talk–he calls them "modalities"–that are admissible in lots of courts in the land, especially over time and before some judges at any time. One of these modalities, to be sure, is "historical" argument, which is functionally similar to originalism. But it is only one of six identified by Bobbitt. Perhaps the most relevant of the two other modalities that are most relevant to this discussion are "doctrine"–the reliance on previously decided cases–and "ethos"–reference to the fundamental notions underlying our constitutional norms. (And some analysts would suggest the legitimacy of recourse even to natural law–the appeal to transcendental standards of justice.)

Unless one is hired by clients who will allow their lawyers simply to ignore a plethora of admissible legal arguments, one would be manifestly incompetent in refusing to use every one of these modalities when it would help one's client. Every lawyer must know how to make a fundamental values argument, even if his stomach turns at the idea and even if, were he named to the Supreme Court, he would rule out any such arguments. But one can't do that as a lawyer. The point is that lawyers often beg judges to follow decisions of hierarchical superiors that may make them retch, as legal theorists. Once again it turns out that one really cannot afford to be a very strong "ist" of any kind, lest one truly incapacitate herself to be a lawyer.

There may be a few decision makers who can be "ists." As already noted, Supreme Court justices may have that prerogative, whether or not they demonstrate any genuine consistency across time in regard to the particular "ism" of their choice. Perhaps the same is true for members of the United States Senate or House, not to mention the most important officials of all in a constitutional republic, free-standing citizens who stand in judgment over the constitutional fidelity of their governmental agents. (Law professors, in their sometime mode of judges manque, can also write articles encouraging the adoption of originalist outcomes.) Otherwise, however, as practicing lawyers, law professors preparing students to be lawyers, or judges, we almost always are playing specific roles in which originalism is only one of several necessary methods of decision making and of argument.

It is far past time to integrate the role of role into our jurisprudential understandings, to recognize, that is, the extent to which the ability to adopt any given form of argument is contingent on the position one holds. Once one does this, the limited relevance of originalism is, for better or worse, all too clear. The debate will no doubt go on, but it should be recognized that it relates to a surprisingly small part of the legal firmament.

Notes

1. Robert Bork, *The Tempting of America: The Political Seduction of the Law* (New York: Free Press, 1989), 143 (emphasis added).

2. For well expressed and, I think, convincing critiques, see Paul Brest, *The Misconceived Quest for the Original Understanding*, 60 Boston University Law Review 204 (1980); Mark Tushnet, *Following the Rules Laid Down: A Critique of Interpretivism and Neutral Principles*, 96 Harvard Law Review 781 (1983). I should also note, though, the extremely interesting and influential argument by Steven Knapp and Walter Benn Michaels, "Against Theory," *Critical Inquiry* 8 (1982): 723, arguing that all coherent interpretation rests on some notion of an agent's intent. See also Knapp and Michaels, "Intention, Identity, and the Constitution: A Response to David Hoy," in *Legal Hermeneutics: History, Theory, and Practice*, ed. Gregory Leyh (Berkeley: University of California Press, 1991), 187. See also the eloquent comments of Steven D. Smith, "Law Without Mind," in *Against the Law*, ed. Michael C. Eberhardt (New York: NAL-Dutton, 1995).

3. Sanford Levinson, *The Embarrassing Second Amendment*, 99 Yale Law Journal 637 (1989).

4. See the back cover of Bruce Ackerman, *We The People: Foundations* (Cambridge: Harvard University Press, 1991), for my enthusiastic blurb.

5. Paul Brest and Sanford Levinson, *Processes of Constitutional Decision Making*, 3rd ed. (Boston: Little, Brown and Co., 1992), 10-11.

6. See Alexander Hamilton, Opinion on the Constitutionality of an Act to Establish a Bank (1791), in *8 Papers of Alexander Hamilton* 97 (New York: Columbia University Press, 1965).

7. The veto message is reprinted in Richard B. Morris and Jeffrey B. Morris, eds., *Great Presidential Decisions* 81 (New York: Richardson, Steinman & Black, 1988).

8. Quoted in Brest and Levinson, *Processes of Constitutional Decision Making*, 18.

9. *McCulloch v. Maryland,* 7 U.S. (4 Wheat.) 316 (1819).

10. James Boyd White, *When Words Lose Their Meaning: Constitutions & Reconstitutions of Language, Character and Community* (Chicago: University of Chicago Press, 1985), 263. I discuss this quotation and its implications in Sanford Levinson, "How Many Times Has the United States Constitution Been Amended? (A) <26; (B) 26; © 27; (>27): Accounting for Constitutional Change," in Levinson, ed., *Responding to Imperfection: The Theory and Practice of Constitutional Amendment* 22 (Princeton, NJ: Princeton University Press, 1995).

11. Jonathan Culler, *On Deconstruction: Theory and Criticism After Structuralism* (Ithaca: Cornell University Press, 1982), 176, quoted in J. M. Balkin, *Constitutional Interpretation and the Problem of History*, 63 New York University Law Review 911, 933 (1988)(review of Raoul Berger, *Federalism: The Founders' Design* (Norman, OK: University of Oklahoma Press, 1987)).

12. Ibid., 934.

13. See, e.g., William Leuchtenburg, *The Supreme Court Reborn: The Constitutional Revolution in the Age of Roosevelt* (New York: Oxford University Press, 1995).

14. *Bolling v. Sharpe*, 347 U.S. 497 (1954).

15. *Brown v. Board of Education*, 347 U.S. 483 (1954).

16. *Roe v. Wade*, 410 U.S. 113 (1973).

17. *Planned Parenthood v. Casey*, 112 S.Ct. 2791 (1992).

18. See Gerard V. Bradley, "The New Constitutional Covenant," *The World & I*, March 1994, 359-375. I respond to Bradley in "The Constitution and the Supreme Court," *The World & I*, March 1994, 380-384.

19. For the denunciation, see Senate Committee on the Judiciary, *Nomination of Robert H. Bork to be Associate Justice of the Supreme Court of the United States Hearings*, 100th Cong., 1st sess., 1987, 286-287; for the reassurance, see ibid., 288.

20. Bork, *The Tempting of America*, 158

21. Ibid., 215.

22. It may be only fair at this point to note Suzanna Sherry's argument that Ackerman is more than a little bit Borkian himself insofar as his theory of constitutional moments includes the duty of judges to enforce the new norms that an aroused people have, through one means or another, placed into the Constitution. These norms must be followed by judges, whether or not they agree with them as a political matter, simply because the people adopted them at some earlier time and, presumably, intended them to be implemented by judges and other officials who have taken oaths to obey "the Constitution." This is why I am willing to assert that almost all of us pay homage to some kind of originalism.

23. *Lopez*, 115 S.Ct. 1624, 1642 (1995).

24. *U.S. Term Limits*, 115 S.Ct. 1842, 1875 (1995).

25. *Adarand Constructors, Inc. v. Pena*, 115 S.Ct. 2097 (1995).

26. Andrew Kull, *The Color-Blind Constitution* (Cambridge: Harvard University Press, 1992).

27. Ibid., 2119.

28. Peter McCutchen, *Mistakes, Precedent and the Rise of the Administrative State: Toward a Constitutional Theory of the Second Best*, 80 Cornell Law Review 1 (1994).

29. Ibid., 2.

30. Ibid.

31. See Edwin Meese III, "Address before the D.C. Chapter of the Federalist Society Lawyers Division," in Sanford Levinson and Steven Mailloux, *Interpreting Law and Literature: A Hermeneutic Reader* (Evanston, IL: Northwestern University Press, 1988), 25.

32. McCutchen, *Mistakes, Precedent and the Rise of the Administrative State*, 2-3.

33. Henry P. Monaghan, *Stare Decisis and Constitutional Law*, 88 Columbia Law Review 723, 727 (1988).

34. Ibid., 743. See also Boris Bittker, *Interpreting the Constitution: Is the Intent of the Framers Controlling? If not, what Is?*, 19 Harvard Journal of Law & Public Policy 9 (1995).

35. The closest exception would be Raoul Berger, whose commitment to original intent does indeed go this far. See Berger, *The Judicial Manipulation of the Commerce Clause*, 74 Texas Law Review 695 (1996) in which he breaks from Bork (and Clarence Thomas) and indeed seems to endorse invalidating the New Deal insofar as it violates original intent.

36. See U.S. Constitution, article 3, section 1.

37. See Andrew Jackson, Veto Message of July 10, 1832, reprinted in Brest & Levinson, *Processes of Constitutional Decision Making* , 50.

38. See *Davis v. Davis*, 646 R.2d 123 (1981), affirming by an equally divided vote *Davis v. Zahradnick*, 432 F. Supp. 444 (1977). The procedural history is more complex than might be suggested by this citation. Zahradnick had first been overruled by a panel of the Court of Appeals, but then affirmed en banc in *Davis v. Davis*, 601 F.2d 153 (en banc, 1979). The Supreme Court then granted certiorari and remanded for reconsideration in light of its decision in *Rummell v. Estelle*, 445 U.S. 263 (1980). See *Hutto v. Davis*, 445 U.S. 947 (1980). As noted, the Fourth Circuit adhered to its original (en banc) decision, though only by an equally divided vote. The history is set out in *Hutto v. Davis*, 354 U.S. 370, 372 (1982).

39. *Hutto v. Davis*, 354 U.S. 370, 372.

40. Ibid., 375 (1982).

41. See Sanford Levinson, *On Positivism and Potted Plants: "Inferior" Judges and the Task of Constitutional Interpretation*, 25 Connecticut Law Review 843 (1993).

42. J.M. Balkin & Sanford Levinson, *Constitutional Grammar*, 72 Texas Law Review 1771 (1994).

43. Philip Bobbitt, *Constitutional Interpretation* (Cambridge, MA: Blackwell, 1991).

Part III

Contemporary Issues in American Constitutionalism

Chapter 9

The New Understanding of the President's War Power

Robert Scigliano

The Understanding

A new understanding of the president's war power has emerged since the Second World War. The president, in this new understanding, may engage the country in war without the consent of Congress. This understanding appeared most recently, as of this writing, in the events that preceded the attack by an American-led coalition of nations against Iraq in January, 1991, for the purpose of compelling that nation's withdrawal from Kuwait, which it had occupied the previous August. Iraq's action had been condemned by the United Nations Security Council in several resolutions, the most important of which, adopted in November, 1990, called on member nations to use "all necessary means" to compel its withdrawal if it did not do so by January 15, 1991.

Repeatedly during this period, President George Bush and other administration officials claimed authority for the president to take action against Iraq. In October, the president, in a meeting with congressional leaders, acknowledged Congress' power to declare war but observed that the Constitution designated him as commander in chief of the armed forces, implying that the document provided alternative ways of going to war.[1] In early December, the secretary of defense told a congressional committee that he did not think the president needed "additional authorization" from Congress–that is, any authorization, as he had received none as of that time–before committing American forces assembled in the Gulf region to action.[2] When the president finally invited Congress to act on the matter of war with Iraq, on January 8, 1991, a week before the expiration of the Security Council deadline, he did not seek that body's consent but rather invited its "support"–he used the term several times–for whatever action he might take. Although Congress rejected the President's invitation and instead authorized hostilities, on January 12, the President, in approving the legislation, referred to it as support, not authority, and reasserted his own position.[3]

George Bush was not the first president to claim for himself, or to have claimed for him, a power to engage the country in war, as I will show. I will try to show the basis of this understanding of the war power by recourse to the Constitution and, especially, the practice of government. Certain actions of Franklin Roosevelt taken shortly before this nation's entry into the Second World War will have an important place in my account. The question is an important one, for it relates to the constitutional balance between the presidency and Congress in the conduct of foreign policy. For example, the committee that reported the War Powers Resolution of 1973 to the Senate claimed that "the residual authority over the entire domain of foreign policy–not just the war power–was placed in Congress by the Constitution."[4] The question's importance can be seen in the debate that preceded Congress's decision to give President Bush authority to act against Iraq. A prominent senator warned the president that he would precipitate a "constitutional crisis" if he went to war against Iraq without it, and there was some murmuring of possible impeachment.[5]

The Constitution

I need not spend much time in considering whether the Constitution allows the president to engage in war. The document is clear on this point. It states that "the Congress shall have power . . . To declare war, grant letters of marque and reprisal, and make rules concerning captures on land and water" and that "the president shall be commander-in-chief of the army and navy of the United States, and of the militia of the several states, when called into the actual service of the United States." Why does it give Congress authority to declare war, subject to the president's veto as in the case of other legislative acts, if the president may engage in war on his own authority? As Alexander Hamilton explained the matter, "it is the peculiar and exclusive province of Congress, *when the nation is at peace*, to change that state into a state of war."[6] The president's authority, to borrow again from Hamilton, "would amount to no more than the supreme command and direction of the military and naval forces, as first General and Admiral of the Confederacy; while that of the British king extends to the *declaring* of war."[7]

To my knowledge, no early American ever suggested that the Constitution invested the President with the power to initiate war. Nor have modern advocates of presidential war-making power, such as those persons I have quoted, ever supported their claim with arguments drawn from the document. So far as the Constitution is concerned, the claim rests on assertion.

The Practice of Government

Instead of relying on arguments drawn from the Constitution, supporters of recent presidential initiatives in war making have cited precedents. For example, in the debate over President Bush's authority to go to war against Iraq, the president's supporters, relying on a report prepared by the Congressional Research Service in 1989, referred to over 200 instances in which presidents had used the armed forces abroad "in situations of conflict or potential conflict."[8]

This list of precedents descended more or less lineally from others used in earlier contests over the president's war powers. In 1973, for instance, Senator Barry Goldwater produced an enumeration of "153 Military Actions Taken by the United States Abroad Without a Declaration of War" (some of which, he conceded, were "arguably" based on legislation or treaty), to bolster his opposition to enactment of the War Powers Resolution.[9] In 1966, the State Department supported the claim made by President Lyndon B. Johnson two years earlier of authority to go to the aid of South Vietnam with a list of "at least 125 instances" in which other presidents had "ordered the armed forces to take action or maintain positions abroad without prior congressional authorization."[10] Still earlier, in 1950, the State Department defended President Harry S Truman's action in going to the defense of South Korea against invasion from its northern neighbor with a list of "eighty-five instances of the use of American armed forces without a declaration of war."[11] On several of these occasions, supporters of the president have punctuated their argument with the statement that in all of American history Congress has declared war only five times.

Past practice may properly be invoked to justify current actions, no matter what one may think the Constitution intended, especially if that practice has been of long duration and generally accepted. Precedents do go a long way towards conferring legitimacy. As an opinion of the Supreme Court put the matter, "a systematic, unbroken, executive practice, long pursued to the knowledge of the Congress and never before questioned . . . making as it were such exercise of power part of the structure of our government, may be treated as a gloss on 'executive power' vested in the president" by the Constitution.[12] So, too, in the specific case of the president's war making power. The argument that presidents have used the armed forces so often "in situations of conflict or potential conflict" or in "military hostilities" or "without a declaration of war" over the course of American history, with Congress having declared war so seldom appears to make an impressive case for the legitimacy of that power.

In saying that Congress has declared war in only five instances, supporters of a presidential war power imply that if the Constitution and not precedents had been followed, war would have been declared in all or most of them. Rarely do they discuss these instances and never do they do so in any detail. It is my purpose here to examine the actions behind the numbers to see whether in fact a long history of precedents support the position that the president has an independent power to make war.

To begin, it is beside the point and misleading to speak only of the number of times Congress has declared war, for Congress may authorize war by means other than a declaration. The difference between a war that is declared and one that is authorized by ordinary acts of legislation corresponds to the difference, well understood by early Americans, between general war and limited war, between war that "destroys the national peace and tranquillity" and war that "interrupts it only in some particulars."[13] As the Congressional Research Service's 1989 list reports, Congress declared war against Great Britain in 1812, against Mexico in 1846, against Spain in 1898, against Germany in 1917, and against Germany, Italy, and Japan in 1941.[14] But the list fails to mention that Congress authorized war by ordinary statutes on more than a dozen occasions, most of which occurred in the first few decades of the nation's history and in those following the Second World War. In the 1790s, when the Indians along the frontiers were formidable enough to command respect, in part because they had ties with European powers, Congress authorized expeditions against the Miami and related tribes in the Ohio territory (and declined to authorize any against tribes to the south of the Ohio River). The so-called "Undeclared War with France," which was fought between 1798 and 1800 and which has frequently been singled out in recent decades by advocates of presidential power, was authorized by several congressional acts. Other early limited wars authorized by Congress include those with Algiers in 1794 (not fought), with Tripoli in 1802, with any Barbary power that committed hostilities against the United States in 1806 (also not fought), with any country that attempted to possess Spanish Florida, by a secret law in 1811 (Andrew Jackson drove the British out in 1814), and again with Algiers in 1815. The only one of these wars that the 1989 list acknowledges as having been authorized is the second war with Algiers.

Since the Second World War, Congress has authorized hostilities on several occasions. It empowered President Eisenhower to protect Formosa and countries in the Middle East from external aggression, in 1955 and 1957, respectively. It empowered John F. Kennedy to use armed force against Cuba in 1962, and Lyndon B. Johnson to use it, in 1964, to assist nations in Southeast Asia in defense of their freedom, although neither president thought he needed legislative permission. More will be said about these congressional authorizations a little later. In 1983, to give a more recent example, Congress authorized Ronald Reagan to maintain for an additional year and a half the marines he had sent to Lebanon as a peace keeping force a year earlier, having decided they were now exposed to hostilities. Like Kennedy and Johnson, Reagan denied that he needed approval. And in January, 1991, Congress authorized George Bush to go to war against Iraq.

In both its wars with Germany and in that with Japan, Congress proclaimed it was formally declaring war as a result of war having been "thrust upon" the United States. In the case of Mexico, it did not declare anything but rather, at the request of President James K. Polk, merely "recognize[d]" the existence of war, because, or so Polk claimed, Mexico had started the war by attacking an American army detachment on American soil, in Texas.

Congress' action in the Mexican War reflects the view that Congress' power to declare or otherwise authorize war is that of deciding whether the United States should go from peace to war, as I quoted Hamilton earlier. But, to continue with Hamilton, "when a foreign nation declares or openly and avowedly makes war upon the United States, they [the United States] are then by the very fact already at war, and any declaration on the part of Congress is nugatory; it is at least unnecessary."[15] Abraham Lincoln acted on this understanding when he "call[ed] out the war power of the government" after South Carolina attacked Fort Sumter, a federal fortress in Charleston harbor, in April, 1861. The Supreme Court agreed with him and upheld the legality of the blockade that he imposed on Southern ports immediately thereafter.[16] Congress may, as Hamilton indicated, still act–it may declare that war exists or recognize its existence, or, as it did in July, 1861, it may approve and make legal (in case there was any question) all things done by the president prior to its own action.

It is pertinent to ask here, what did early Americans understand to constitute war? I take my bearing from an early Supreme Court opinion, which defines foreign war as "a contention by force between two nations, in external matters, under the authority of their respective governments."[17]

By this definition of war, most of the incidents on the lists cannot be considered precedents for what presidents in recent decades have done or claimed the power to do. Indeed, some of them did not involve the use of force against anyone. Take the small party of soldiers, under Lieutenant Zebulon M. Pike, that was sent west in 1806 to explore the domain that the United States had recently acquired from France. Even if the party intentionally entered into land that was in dispute between the United States and Spain–Jefferson said it had strayed there–its entry hardly constituted an act of war. And yet the 1989 list says that Pike and his men "invaded Spanish territory." Or take the employment of American troops in 1922 to supervise Panamanian elections, at the request of local political parties. How could this incident be counted as a precedent for later presidential war-making?

Nor do all uses of force constitute acts of war. Most often prior to the Second World War, in the period we are considering, the United States used force abroad, or was prepared to use it, in limited ways in order "to secure adequate safety and protection for its citizens and their property." This is how a State Department memorandum issued in 1912 and updated in 1934 described it in enumerating eighty-five such incidents between 1812 and 1933.[18] This appears to have been the first of the lists of presidential actions taken abroad. It cannot be said that the United States was engaged in war when its navy chased pirates and other adventurers on the high seas or punished inhabitants of Pacific islands for threats or attacks against American citizens and their property. Generally such incidents involved action by single naval vessels. Nor was it war when marines or other forces were sent onto the soil of other countries for the purpose of protecting Americans during disturbances at the request or with the acquiescence of the authorities there. Such incidents were rather common at one time, especially in Latin American and Far Eastern port cities, as the lists testify, and they still happen, as when American helicopters flew into Cyprus in 1974 to evacuate Americans and other foreigners during fighting between Turkish and Greek Cypriot forces.

Constitutionally speaking, does it matter whether American forces enter another nation's territory with or against the permission of its government, or whether their efforts are directed against unruly mobs or the government itself, if the latter cannot effectively oppose the American interventions? Does a "contest by force" take place in any meaningful sense in such situations? A congressional committee gave this answer in 1824 in considering the question of the pursuit of pirates by American naval parties onto Spanish territory: "Powerful nations never permit feeble neighbors to enter their territory for this purpose but enter without scruple in pursuit of their enemies the territory of such neighbors . . . . Practically, the question is one not of right but of relative power."[19]

It is not always easy to draw a line between those uses of military force that fall short of war and come within the president's authority, and those that cross the line and require the consent of Congress. This is true also of line-drawing in other areas. Consider, for example, the related area of treaty-making. Which international arrangements made by the president must be submitted to the Senate and which, falling short of treaties, may be made by the president alone as executive agreements? By the early twentieth century an accumulation of precedents had made the distinctions tolerably clear in both areas. William Howard Taft offered his successors in the presidency a rule of thumb for deciding on which side of the line a contemplated military action fell. It depends on whether you can make do with using (shipboard) marines or whether you must send in the army.[20] And Hamilton, always prudent in matters of statecraft, offers this cautionary advice: In a "delicate" case, "one which involves so important a consequence as that of war–my opinion is that no doubtful authority ought to be exercised by the President."[21]

I do not suggest that no president prior to the Second World War engaged in acts of war when there was time to go to Congress or, where emergency action was necessary, declined to go there after taking it. Lincoln thought President Polk had engaged in war unconstitutionally against Mexico by sending American troops onto soil that belonged to Mexico or, at least, to which it had a strong claim. (If Mexico had committed hostilities, it would have been a different matter.) Taft thought that his successor in the presidency, Woodrow Wilson, had committed an act of war against Mexico in 1914 in ordering the American navy to attack and the army to occupy the Mexican city of Vera Cruz because Mexican authorities would not make what Wilson considered to be a proper apology for the brief arrest of some crew members from an American naval vessel. Perhaps we could add President William McKinley's despatch of about 3,000 American troops to northern China in 1900 to assist forces sent by other nations in protecting foreign nationals from attacks during the Boxer Rebellion, and President Theodore Roosevelt's naval threat off Panama in 1903 that assured its independence from Columbia and American rights to construct a canal across the isthmus.

Whatever their precise number, the instances in which presidents prior to the Second World War made war independently of Congress were few. Moreover, except in the case of the Mexican War, they were not of the magnitude of the instances that have occurred since that time. They certainly do not provide the precedential support for war making by the executive that recent presidents and their partisans have claimed for them. In particular, they do not make of the Constitution's "commander-in-chief" clause an alternate means of going to war.[22]

I will leave it to the reader to apply the distinction between war and non-war to such recent presidential actions as Ronald Reagan's military intervention in Grenada in 1983 and the air attack he ordered on Libya in 1986, George Bush's intervention in Panama in 1989 and in Somalia in 1992, and Bill Clinton's air strikes against Iraq in 1993 and 1996.

The Roosevelt Precedent

In the debate in Congress over going to war with Iraq, one House member said that the United States was in the fortieth year of a constitutional crisis, begun when Harry Truman sent troops to Korea without the authority of Congress. He might have looked a little farther back, to actions that Franklin Roosevelt sanctioned during the months of 1941 preceding formal American entry into war against the Axis powers. In the spring of that year Roosevelt ordered the occupation of Greenland after Denmark, which exercised sovereignty over the territory, was overrun by Nazi Germany. Roosevelt wished to prevent the Germans from establishing a military garrison there. In July a military force was sent to Iceland and Roosevelt announced that the navy would escort convoys of merchant ships between Iceland and the United States. Encounters between American destroyers and German submarines followed and American merchant ships came under attack. According to what Prime Minister Winston Churchill revealed to the British cabinet at the time, Roosevelt told him when the two met off Newfoundland in August, 1941 that he would "wage war" but he would "not declare it."[23] The next month Roosevelt announced that American vessels and aircraft would henceforth "shoot on sight" German and Italian submarines and other war vessels anywhere in American defensive waters, which were defined to extend most of the way across the Atlantic. In October he announced that the "shooting" had begun.

An important debate took place in the Senate following Roosevelt's decision to send forces to Iceland and to provide convoy escorts. In it, Tom Connally, the administration's main spokesman in Congress on matters of foreign policy, defended the president's actions in the face of charges that they would lead inevitably to war and that the president had, consequently, usurped Congress's authority to declare war. Connally produced a list of eighty-five incidents occurring between 1812 and 1933 to justify what the president had done, interpreting them to mean that the executive could send the armed forces wherever he believed "the interests of the nation" required. [24]

Connally's list of incidents was taken in its entirety from the State Department memorandum of 1912, updated to 1933. That memorandum, as I have shown, was concerned with measures taken by presidents to protect Americans and their property abroad–that is, nearly always with minor uses of force against pirates or island natives or lawless mobs or weak governments. What Connally did was to make these incidents into more than they were in order to claim sustained government practice for what was, in fact, a break with the past. The list that the State Department issued in 1950 to justify President Truman's going to war in Korea was identical to Connally's list. But whereas Connally avowed in Senate debate that only Congress could make war, Dean Acheson, who was Truman's secretary of state, cited the 1950 list to support his belief that Truman had "constitutional authority to do what he did."[25] And yet war, at first limited and then full scale, resulted from Roosevelt's actions, inevitably as some had predicted at the time. The broad terms in which Connally had defended the president's right to act in foreign affairs–wherever the national interests were concerned –were used by Roosevelt's successors and their supporters to stake out greater claims of presidential power. President Bush, for example, referred to "the president's constitutional authority to defend vital U.S. interests" in discounting the authority that Congress had given him to use force against Iraq.[26]

The modern understanding of the president's war power has its origin in the presidency of Franklin Roosevelt. In this as in other important ways, Roosevelt cast his influence upon the future. The president's right to use the armed forces as he deemed necessary–including their employment in war–became an article of belief among New Dealers. And then, gradually, as with other innovations wrought by the New Deal, its influence spread into the ranks of conservative Democrats and liberal Republicans, and then further. Indeed, eventually the Republicans became the bearers of Roosevelt's legacy regarding the president's use of military power, at a time when Democrats were reconsidering their position and rejecting their legacy.

Harry Truman was the first of Roosevelt's successors to view his powers through the prism provided by his great predecessor. After he had taken his initial emergency measures, Truman did not go to Congress for authority to engage American forces in support of South Korea against invasion from the north in June, 1950. Truman would have had the approval of many Republicans in Congress as well as his own party. Senator Robert A. Taft, the most influential Republican in the Senate at the time, stated on the floor of that body about a week after Truman acted that, had Truman so requested, he would have voted for legislation approving of what the president had done and providing supplies for the war.[27] According to

Acheson, Truman did not go to Congress because he wished to avoid "the possibility of endless criticism" (ironic, in view of the criticism that dogged the rest of his presidency for his failure to go there) and because he was determined "to pass [his office] on unimpaired by the slightest loss of power or prestige."[28]

Dwight Eisenhower had no such constitutional qualms. In asking for authority to act in defense of Formosa against invasion from China in 1955, he stated that he might be able to do some things if that happened–he referred to "emergency action [that] might be forced upon us"–but that suitable legislation "would clearly and publicly" establish his authority to employ the armed forces if it became necessary.[29] In explaining why he wanted authority to act in defense of nations of the Middle East, the President was not as clear, perhaps because he was sensitive to the need for Democratic support, and the Democrats, as he noted later, were criticizing him for seeking Congress' approval.[30] He referred both to the greater effect that would result from "a consensus of executive and legislative opinions" and to his "regard for constitutional procedures."[31]

In the Eisenhower years, support for a presidential war-making power came mainly from liberals, that is, from Democrats, and Congress was under their control in 1955 and 1957. In the House of Representatives, John W. McCormack, the floor leader for the Democrats, stated in the Formosa debate that "the general feeling is that the President has the power inherent in the authority of the commander in chief to issue the necessary orders to take such action as might follow the passage of the pending joint resolution." In the Senate, Mike Mansfield, the assistant Democratic floor leader and a leading spokesman for his party on matters of foreign affairs, made a similar declamation on the president's power to act without Congress. In committee consideration of the Middle East resolution, for example, he asked Eisenhower's secretary of state, "Mr. Secretary, why does the President want to limit his power, thereby abrogate the Constitution to an extent, and create a precedent which may become recognized as a part of the Constitution through custom, especially in this hydrogen age?"[32] This view was even more strongly held by constitutional scholars at the time. It was observed in Senate discussion of the Middle East resolution that "practically all" such persons thought that Eisenhower already possessed the powers he had asked for.[33]

A Republican senator expressed the predominant view held by conservative members of Congress, especially by those of his own party, on the matter of presidential war-making when he stated during debate on the Formosa resolution that passage of the resolution would "restore a long line of precedents which, over the past ten years, have been disregarded, unconstitutionally in my judgment . . . . What I cannot understand is why some members of the Congress are so eager to deny that we have any right to participate in this momentous decision."[34]

President Eisenhower got his way in regard to Formosa and the Middle East. Congress approved of the actions he might undertake through joint resolutions–acts submitted to his approval having the force of law. They did not issue concurrent resolutions, which are approved only by the two houses and are typically employed as expressions of congressional opinion. If Congress wished merely to register its support for actions the president might undertake on his own authority, the latter method was the way to do it. Those in Congress who believed the president needed authority to engage in acts of war, mostly Republicans, won out, although they were in a minority, because the majority of Democrats were unwilling to go against a popular president. Their victory was more clearly marked in the Formosa resolution, for it "authorized" the president to employ the armed forces in combat, whereas the Middle East resolution was intentionally evasive–a compromise of contending views providing that, "if the President determines the necessity thereof, the United States is prepared" to employ the forces in this way.[35] Those who believed in a presidential war power might have been reconciled to voting for the joint resolutions by the argument that foreigners would be more impressed by an action that showed the unity of the two branches of government. Besides, some of them probably asked themselves, what difference does it make by what form Congress acts if we are not giving the president any power that he did not already have?[36]

Roosevelt's precedent was reestablished in the White House in the presidencies of John F. Kennedy and Lyndon B. Johnson. Kennedy and Johnson had as members of Congress sustained Truman's action in Korea and questioned Eisenhower's turn to the legislative branch in the Formosa and Middle East situations, and they acted on their earlier views when they became president. In September, 1962, as the Cuban Missile Crisis began to develop but before there was incontrovertible evidence that the Soviet Union was arming Cuba with missiles, Kennedy did not ask Congress to consent to take military action against Cuba and possibly its ally, the Soviet Union. When members of Congress began to press for a joint resolution to authorize him to take such action, he sought to divert their efforts. "As commander in chief," he said, "I have full authority now to take such action" as might be necessary against Cuba, although it would be "useful" for members of Congress, "if they desire," to "express their view" on the situation.[37] Nor did Johnson ask for consent to use the armed forces in defense of South Vietnam prior to sending them there in May, 1965. Indeed, when Johnson's undersecretary of state testified before a congressional committee in August, 1967, that the Southeast Asia resolution, adopted three years earlier, was "a functional equivalent" of a declaration of war, the president repudiated the statement, insisting that in conducting hostilities in Vietnam "we did not think the resolution was necessary to do what we did and what we are doing. We think we are well within the grounds of our constitutional authority."[38]

However, Congress acted in both cases by joint resolution. Kennedy accepted one that cloaked the question of authority in compromise language similar to that used in the Middle East resolution. It said, "The United States is determined, by whatever means may be necessary, including the use of arms," to prevent Cuba from carrying out revolutionary activities elsewhere in the hemisphere or from permitting on its territory a foreign (that is, Soviet) military capability dangerous to the United States. Johnson actually proposed a joint resolution to Congress: "It could well be based upon similar resolutions enacted by Congress in the past," though he thought of it as a means for "expressing the support of the Congress for all necessary action " that he might take to protect American forces in Vietnam and to help nations in the region to defend themselves. As enacted, the resolution declared that "the United States is prepared, as the President determines, to take all necessary steps, including the use of armed force" to help those nations.[39]

In discussing the Southeast Asia resolution, many members of Congress tended to regard it as President Johnson did, as a way of registering their support for the president. This view helps explain why some members of Congress complained later that they did not realize what they were doing at this time or, more often, that they had not authorized Johnson to do what he was doing in Vietnam and hence that the war there was unconstitutional. But it would be more correct to say that these members were confused as to the constitutional issue. J. William Fulbright, who guided the measure through the Senate, explained it to his colleagues in this way: "[The resolution] would authorize whatever the commander in chief feels is necessary," including the landing of large American armies in Vietnam or China. Yet it "would [not] in any way be a deterrent, a prohibition, a limitation or an expansion of the President's power to use the armed forces in a different way or more extensively than he is now using them." And, "we are not giving the President any powers he does not have under the Constitution as commander in chief." Finally, when Fulbright was asked by another senator if Congress was giving the president advance authority to do whatever he thought was necessary in the defense of South Vietnam, his answer was, "I think that is correct."[40]

Many who were influenced by the precedent that Franklin Roosevelt created by his actions in the North Atlantic believed there were limits to how far a president might go on his own, but they were not very specific about them. Perhaps typical of their views was the remark made by a Democratic senator in the Formosa debate: "Of course, if he [the President] undertook to engage in a major war, he would be expected to ask Congress for a declaration of war."[41] And yet belief in the value of Congress' power to declare war had undergone erosion. This erosion can be seen in the remark that Senator Fulbright–an early adherent to the Roosevelt precedent–made on the Senate floor back in 1945. He did not see why the war power should be retained in Congress, he said, when it had never been "important."[42]

Democrats in and out of Congress were induced to rethink their view of the president's war power when they moved from support of the Vietnam War to opposition. The process was undoubtedly helped by the accession of a Republican, Richard Nixon, to the presidency in 1969. They now became "the party of the Constitution," some of them with the fervor of converts as they discovered the document's grant of war-making power to Congress to be clear and relevant, where once they had found it ambiguous and obsolescent. The Republicans became defenders of presidential war-making, speaking of the precedents that sustained it and of the need for flexibility in interpreting the Constitution. In short, the Republicans, most of them, became heirs of the Roosevelt legacy and praised him and also Truman and Kennedy, and sometimes Johnson, for their leadership in foreign affairs.

The new political division regarding the president's power to engage in hostilities can be seen in the vote that took place on that subject in the House of Representatives on January 12, 1991. Congress had shortly before rejected legislation that would have continued sanctions imposed earlier on Iraq by the United States and other nations and it would shortly afterwards approve legislation authorizing hostilities against that country. The House vote in question was on a concurrent–non-binding–resolution that contained two propositions: that the Constitution vests the power to declare war in Congress and that the president must obtain Congress' approval before undertaking military action against Iraq. (The resolution did not come to a vote in the Senate.) The resolution was adopted by a vote of 302 to 131, with 260 Democrats and 1 Independent (associated with them) voting in favor and 5 Democrats voting in opposition and with Republicans opposing by a margin of 126 to 41 members.

The New Understanding of Defensive War

It has generally been accepted that the Constitution allows the president to meet war with war when "a foreign nation declares or openly and avowedly makes war upon the United States," as I quoted Hamilton in my earlier discussion of the subject. Even those who would not go this far have acknowledged a right in the president to engage in measures strictly of defense until Congress could decide what to do. During the Second World War the idea of self-defense began to assume a broader meaning, to include the defense of other nations. This meaning was incorporated into the Charter of the United Nations, whose Article 51 recognizes the right of nations to engage in collective as well as individual self-defense in case of armed attack. The defense treaties into which the United States entered following the war, which in the main were directed at the Soviet Union and communism generally, all embraced the idea of collective defense. Typical of the others, the North Atlantic Treaty, ratified by the Senate in 1949, stated as follows: "The parties agree that an armed attack against one or more of them in Europe or North America shall be considered an attack against them all."[43]

Just as several of the joint resolutions we have considered avoided specifying just who would decide on going to war, so too did the mutual defense treaties now under review. In the Southeast Asia Collective Defense Treaty, for example, it was agreed that in the event of an attack upon a state covered by the treaty, each party would "act to meet the common danger in accordance with its constitutional processes."[44] It was easy for some people to think the President was the one to make this decision inasmuch as he was the one looked to when the nation itself was attacked. In the new thinking, an attack upon an ally or, by extension, upon any country whose security was important to that of the United States (the United States had no treaty with South Korea in 1950) was considered to be tantamount to an attack upon the

United States. The circumstances of the Cold War played a large part in this thinking. For example, it was explained in the Senate in 1950, when Truman decided to go to the assistance of South Korea, that "the basic reason" for his decision was that if the communists had been successful there they would have carried out similar invasions elsewhere and "our own ultimate safety would then have been threatened."[45] In a similar vein, the committee that reported the Formosa resolution to the House saw in Communist China's threat to the island not only the fate of Formosa but that of "the non-communist peoples of Asia, and of our own defensive line."[46] So long as the war the United States fought in defense of an ally or friend was defensive, it was thought, there was no need to have recourse to Congress. In explaining why the president had not requested a declaration of war to fight in Vietnam, the State Department gave as one reason the circumstance that the struggle had to be won primarily in South Vietnam, and it "is in that context a defensive military effort."[47] Similarly, President Bush's supporters in Congress argued in early 1991 that the United States would not be engaging in "offensive action"–would not be *going* to war–against Iraq, inasmuch as Iraq started the war when it occupied Kuwait.[48]

This is not to suggest that presidential war-making in defense of others has a basis in the Constitution; it does not. Nor that it has acquired constitutional status through the accretion of uncontested precedents; as we have seen, it has not. But it does help explain how intelligent and responsible persons, starting with Senator Connally and other supporters of Franklin Roosevelt's anti-Axis policies, could come to the position they did.

The connection between the security of the United States and that of other nations lost much of its compelling force when the long confrontation between the United States and the Soviet Union dissolved in the latter's collapse at the beginning of the 1990s. The right continues to be asserted by American politicians but in a different way. In support of their position regarding Iraq, President Bush and other administration officials cited the United Nations Charter and Security Council resolutions that called for Iraq to withdraw from Kuwait and then called for other nations to compel its withdrawal. When President Truman went to war in Korea, his action was justified by the citation of Article 51 of the United Nations Charter and Security Council resolutions calling on North Korea to withdraw from South Korea and asking other nations to help bring about that result. But the connection between Iraq's action and American security was not very apparent. Indeed, the president emphasized an emerging new world order in which aggression would be shown not to pay in defending his right to force Iraq out of Kuwait. Congress challenged the president's right to act for the nation in the Iraq case, whereas it had not at the time of Korea; it, too, cited the United Nations Charter and Security Council resolutions, as if seeking to wrest from the president any legitimacy they might confer.

Thus the new idea of defensive war seems to have a broader dimension than I have yet stated: the action of all peace-loving nations against aggressors. This aspiration, too, exists in the United Nations Charter. When the Charter was before the Senate for ratification in 1945, one of that body's leading advocates, Warren R. Austin, expressed it in this way: "We recognize [in the Charter] that a breach of the peace anywhere on earth which threatens the security and peace of the earth is an attack upon us."[49] This conformed to Franklin Roosevelt's vision of the United Nations: it was to be an organization in which the United States would play a major part in policing a new world order, helping the cause of human rights everywhere.[50] Long submerged in the more pressing concern for security and survival during the period of the Cold War, this idea was never absent even then. It is not without significance that Senator Austin's remarks, quoted above, were reproduced by the State Department in the memorandum that justified President Truman's going to the aid of South Korea. The idea seems to be gaining strength in the world at present. As to who will decide on the disposition of American forces in this new world, I cannot predict. Senator Austin, however, was sure back in 1945 that he knew. "I am bound to say that I feel that the president is the officer under our Constitution in whom there is exclusively vested the responsibility for maintenance of peace."[51]

Notes

1. Reported in "Uncertain Congress Confronts President's Gulf Strategy," in *Congressional Quarterly Weekly Report*, 17 November 1990, 3879.

2. Senate Committee on Armed Services, *Crisis in the Persian Gulf Region: U.S. Policy Options and Implications, Hearings*, 101st Cong., 1st sess., September 11, 13; November 27, 28, 29, 30; December 3, 1990, testimony of Secretary of Defense Dick Cheney, 3 December 1990, 701-702.

3. George Bush, Statement on Signing the Resolution Authorizing the Use of Military Force against Iraq," *Weekly Compilation of Presidential Documents, January-March, 1991*, 27, no. 3 (21 January 1991): 48-49.

4. Senate Committee on Foreign Relations, *War Powers*, 93d Cong., 1st sess., 1973, S. Rept. 220, 13.

5. Senate, Senator Kennedy of Massachusetts, 102d Cong., 1st sess., 1991, *Congressional Record* (3 January 1991), 137, no. 1, S13.

6. Alexander Hamilton, "The Examination, No. I," Dec. 17, 1801, in Hamilton, *The Papers of Alexander Hamilton*, ed. Henry C. Syrett et al. (New York: Columbia University Press, 1977), 25:455.

7. The Federalist No. 69 in Alexander Hamilton, James Madison, and John Jay, *The Federalist: A Commentary on the Constitution of the United States*, Introd. Edward M. Earle (New York: Modern Library, 1937), 448. Emphasis in the original.

8. "Instances of Use of United States Armed Forces Abroad, 1798-1989," CRS Report for Congress, Dec. 4, 1989, *Congressional Record*, 102d Cong., 1st sess., 1991, 137, pt. 8:S130-35. See, e.g., House of Representatives, Rep. Bruce A. Morrison, H404, 102d Cong., 1st sess., 1991, *Congressional Record* (12 January 1991), 137; Senate, Senator John W. Warner, Committee on Armed Services, Hearings, *Crisis in the Persian Gulf Re-*

gion, 27 November 1990, 112-13; Secretary of Defense Dick Cheney, Committee on Armed Services, Hearings, *Crisis in the Persian Gulf Region*, 3 December 1990, 702, also 730-31.

9. Senate Committee on Foreign Relations, *War Powers Legislation, Hearings*, 92d Cong., 1st sess., 1971, March 8, 9, 24, and 25; Apr. 23 and 26; May 19; July 26 and 27; and Oct. 6, 1971, 379. This and earlier enumerations are taken up in Francis D. Wormuth and Edward B. Firmage, "Lists of Wars," ch. 9 in *To Chain the Dog of War: The War Power of Congress in History and Law* (Champaign: University of Illinois Press, 1986), 133-49.

10. Department of State, Office of the Legal Adviser, T*he Legality of United States Participation in the Defense of Viet Nam,* (March 4, 1966), 36.

11. "Authority of the President to Repel the Attack in Korea." Department of State Memorandum of July 3, 1950," *Department of State Bulletin*, July 31, 1950, 174.

12. *Youngstown Sheet and Tube Company v. Sawyer*, 343 U.S. 579 (1952), Justice Felix Frankfurter concurring, at 610-11. My attention was drawn to this statement by Harold H. Koh, in *The National Security Constitution: Sharing Power after the Iran-Contra Affair* (New Haven, CT.: Yale University Press, 1990), 71.

13. *Case of the Resolution*, 2 Dall. 12, 20 (1781).

14. The 1989 list did not concern itself with declarations of war against Germany's lesser allies in the two World Wars, nor will I notice them.

15. Alexander Hamilton, "The Examination, No. I," in Hamilton, *Papers*, 456.

16. Abraham Lincoln, "Special Session Message," July 14, 1861, *Compilation of the Messages and Papers of the Presidents, 1789-1897*, ed. J.D. Richardson (Washington, D.C.: Government Printing Office, 1897), 6:23; *The Prize* Cases, 2 Bl. 635 (1863).

17. Alexander Hamilton, "The Examination, No. I," in Hamilton, *Papers*, 456.

18. Department of State, Memorandum of the Solicitor (Reuben J. Clark, Jr.), *Right to Protect Citizens in Foreign Countries by Landing Forces*, Oct. 5, 1912, 3rd rev. ed., with supplementary appendix up to 1933 (Washington: Government Printing Office, 1934), 33.

19. House of Representatives Committee on Foreign Relations, *Piracy and Outrage on Commerce of the United States by Spanish Privateers*," 18th Cong., 2d sess., Rept. 398, in *American State Papers, 1, Foreign Relations*, 5:586.

20. William Howard Taft, *Our Chief Magistrate and His Powers* (New York: Columbia University Press, 1916), 95.

21. Alexander Hamilton to James McHenry, 17 May 1798, in Hamilton, *Papers*, 21:462.

22. Using the incidents reported in the State Department's 1967 list as their basis, Wormuth and Firmage conclude in *To Chain the Dog of War* that American presidents have unconstitutionally engaged American forces in war or acts of war (they distinguish between the two) probably between a dozen and two dozen times, which they think disproves the claims made for such lists in recent decades. But their understanding of the president's constitutional power to use force is much narrower than the one I and those statesmen I have cited in this essay (e.g., Hamilton, Lincoln, William Howard Taft, and Robert A. Taft) have used. These two authors do not believe the Constitution allows the president ever to intrude the public force onto foreign territory. See 147-49.

23. British war cabinet minutes, cited in Thomas A. Bailey and Paul B. Ryan, *Hitler vs. Roosevelt: The Undeclared Naval War* (New York: Free Press, 1979), 166.

24. *Congressional Record,* 77th Cong., 1st sess., 1941, 87, pt. 6:5927-30. Connally said he was unable to put his hand on a longer list that would have brought the total to more than one hundred incidents, apparently by including actions prior to 1812.

25. Ibid., 5927; Dean Acheson, *Present at the Creation: My Years at the State Department* (New York: W.W. Norton, 1969), 414.

26. Bush, *Statement on Signing the Resolution,* 48.

27. *Congressional Record,* 81st Cong., 2d sess., 1950, 96, pt. 7:9320.

28. Acheson, *Present at the Creation,* p. 415. President Reagan's secretary of state gave a similar reason for his president's refusal to acknowledge Congress' grant of authority to him in 1983 to keep marines in Lebanon. The President had no intention of turning over to Congress his constitutional responsibilities as commander in chief. Secretary of State George Schultz, cited in "A Reluctant Congress Adopts Lebanon Policy," *Congressional Quarterly Almanac 1983* (Washington, D.C.: Congressional Quarterly, Inc., 1984), 117.

29. *Congressional Record,* 84th Cong., 1st sess., 1955, 101, pt. 1: 601.

30. Eisenhower, *The White House Years: Waging Peace, 1957-1961* (Garden City, N.Y.: Doubleday, 1965), 182.

31. Ibid., 179, 273.

32. *Congressional Record,* House of Representatives, 84th Cong., 1st sess., 1955, 101, pt. 1:659; *Congressional Record,* Senate, 84th Cong., 1st sess., 1955, 101, pt. 1:622; U.S. Congress, Committees on Foreign Relations and Armed Services, *The President's Proposal on the Middle East, Hearings, pt. 1,* 85th Cong., 1st sess., 1957, 118.

33. Senate, Senator Kennedy of Massachusetts, 85th Cong., 1st sess.,*Congressional Record* (4 March 1957), 103, pt. 3:2878.

34. Senate, Senator Bricker, 84th Cong., 1st sess., 1955, *Congressional Record* (28 January 1955), 101, pt. 1:953, 954.

35. Senate Committee on Foreign Affairs, Subcommittee on National Security Policy and Scientific Development, *Background Information on the Use of United States Armed Forces in Foreign Countries,* 91st Cong., 2d sess., 1970, Committee Print, 59-60. The Middle East, Cuba, and Southeast Asia (Tonkin Gulf) resolutions are also reproduced here, 58-62.

36. See, e.g., Senate Committee on Foreign Relations, S. Rept. 13, to accompany S.J. Res. 28, January 26, 1955, 84th Cong., 1st sess., 9; Prepared Statement and Testimony of Secretary of State John Foster Dulles, Senate Committee on Foreign Relations and Committee on Armed Services, *President's Proposal,* pt. 1:9-10, 21.

37. John F. Kennedy, Presidential Press Conference, September 13, 1962, *Congressional Record,* 87th Cong., 2d sess., 1962, 108, pt. 14:19537, 19539.

38. Lyndon B. Johnson, Presidential Press Conference, August 21, 1967, *Congressional Record,* 90th Cong., 1st sess., 1967, 113, pt. 17:29393. Perhaps reflecting some confusion or uncertainty on his part, President Johnson stated later in his remarks both that the resolution authorized the president and expressed the Congress' willingness to go along with the president in doing whatever was necessary to deter aggression.

39. Lyndon B. Johnson, Message to Congress, August 5, 1964, *Congressional Record,* 88th Cong., 2d sess., 1964, 110, pt. 14:18132.

40. *Congressional Record,* 88th Cong., 2d sess., 1964, 110, pt. 14: 18403, 18407, 18409.

41. Senate, Senator Sparkman, 84th Cong., 1st sess., 1955, Congressional Record, (28 January 1955), 1101, pt. 1:933.

42. *Congressional Record*, 79th Cong., 1st sess., 1945, 91, pt. 8:11396.

43. "North Atlantic Defense Treaty Between the United States of America and Other Governments," 4 April 1949, in U.S. Congress, House of Representatives, *Collective Defense Treaties*, 91st Cong., 1st sess. (Washington, D.C.: Government Printing Office, 1969), 77.

44. Senate Committee on Foreign Relations, *Background Information Relating to Southeast Asia and Vietnam*, 4th rev. ed., 90th Cong., 2d sess., Committee Print, 100-102.

45. Senate, Senator Douglas, 81st Cong., 2d sess., 1950, *Congressional Record*, 96, pt. 7:9649.

46. House Committee on Foreign Affairs, *Authorizing the President to Employ the Armed Forces of the United States for Protecting the Security of Formosa, the Pescadores, and Related Positions and Territories of that Area*, 24 January 1955, 84th Cong., 1st sess., 1954, Rept. 4, 4.

47. Senate Committee on Foreign Relations, *The Question of a Formal Declaration of War in Vietnam*, State Department Position Paper, 19 November 1965, *Background Information*, 168.

48. See, e.g., House of Representatives, Representative Hyde, 102d Cong., 1st sess., 1991, *Congressional Record* (12 January 1991), 137, pt. 8:H391.

49. Senate, Senator Austin, 79th Cong., 1st sess., 1945, *Congressional Record*, (July 26, 1945), 91, pt. 6:8065.

50. Cf. Willard Range, *Franklin D. Roosevelt's World Order* (Athens, GA: University of Georgia Press, 1959), esp. ch. 11.

51. Senate, Austin, 8065.

This is a revision of an essay published under the title of "Politics, the Constitution, and the War Power," in *The Politics of American Foreign Policy*, ed. David A. Deese (New York: St. Martin's Press, 1993).

Chapter 10

From Presidential Shield to 'Go Ahead, Make My Day': The Presidential Veto and the Constitutional Balance of Power

Robert J. Spitzer

On February 26, 1992, the president pro tempore of the U.S. Senate took the floor and spoke for over six hours to address a matter he considered of the utmost importance. West Virginia Senator Robert Byrd's speech was not a filibuster, nor an attempt to influence the fulsome flow of federal patronage to his home state. Instead, Byrd's speech, reminiscent of grand Senate orations of an earlier age, was an extended discourse on the genesis and evolution of the modern British state (beginning before the Norman conquests), the development of the British Parliament, the relationship between these and the American Constitution, a comparison between Parliament and Congress, and a detailed discussion of contemporary American budget dilemmas. Byrd's theme tying this all together was "the centrality of power over the purse to the overall scheme of Constitutional American liberty."[1]

Yet the more precise focus of Byrd's peroration was far more specific and political. He was seeking to persuade the Senate to defeat a rather ingenious effort, sponsored by the Bush administration, to grant the president item veto powers by statute. Labeled "veto rescission" or "enhanced rescission," this power if enacted would have allowed the president to line out budgetary items from appropriations bills up to 20 days after the bills had been passed by Congress. Any items so excised would be permanently deleted from the legislation, unless Congress restored the deleted items by majority vote within 20 days. The president could then veto the restored deletions, and Congress in turn could override that veto by a two-thirds vote.

That the Senate fell 16 votes short of approving this measure[2] is probably attributable less to Byrd's eloquence and more to the concern in the Senate that they were tampering with a fundamental governmental relationship, the effects of which would 1) do little or nothing to solve the country's drastic fiscal dilemma, and 2) could only further strengthen the executive branch's political advantages over Congress. That Congress resisted the temptation to approve a proposal that would have yielded to Congress some short-term symbolic political advantage–by seeming to respond to the enormous pressure to take some action that would at least seem decisive in stopping the federal budgetary hemorrhage–speaks well, in my estimation, for Congress' refusal to relinquish its vital role in the constitutional separation of powers, and more specifically in its constitutionally mandated role as keeper of the national purse.

I preface this essay with this anecdote as a basis for supporting my argument that the presidential veto power, far from being an unimportant or marginal weapon in the president's arsenal, has been in fact a central power of the presidency of 1992 no less than that of 1792. To be sure, much has changed in the presidential-congressional relationship in 200 years,[3] as is true of the veto power itself. But analysts of the Constitution and the institutions it spawned often focus so much attention on modern political arrangements that they overlook or underestimate the potency of key powers like the veto. The Executive and Legislative branches are no less constitutional departments today than in centuries gone by.

Background

Most of the Constitution's founders agreed that the president should possess a veto power, and it was a feature of the presidency as described in the Virginia Plan at the start of the convention.[4] On the other hand, the founders struggled to define the presidency with greater precision. Like a student who avoids the difficult work until the very end of the semester, the founders put off completing the wording for Article II until the final weeks and even days of the convention.

The debate over the nature of the veto power reflects nicely the intellectual and political struggles of the founders. Some argued with great force that the president's veto should be absolute–that is, not subject to congressional override. Championed by such articulate and brilliant thinkers as Alexander Hamilton and James Wilson, the absolute veto idea was nevertheless doomed by its close identity with the odious British monarchical veto, and because of the more general concern about the presidency, expressed by George Mason, that "We are not indeed constituting a British Government, but a more dangerous monarchy, an elective one."[5] An executive chosen independently of Congress was acceptable to the convention; an independent executive with an absolute veto was not.

Many at the convention supported a proposal that the veto should be exercised jointly with the Supreme Court in a body called a "council of revision." This proposal was not as novel as it might sound to the twentieth century, as it had been the system used by New York's governor the previous decade (and continued to be so until 1821). Its proponents thought that this unity between the executive and judicial branches would be necessary to help fend off possible legislative encroachments. Despite repeated efforts by James Madison and others, the proposal failed, mostly on the grounds that it violated separation of powers, and would give the judiciary two chances to rule on legislation (the second being through judicial review).[6]

Even more intriguing was Madison's advocacy of the proposal incorporated in the Virginia Plan to give Congress an absolute veto over state laws. By one account, this idea "occupied a central place in his [Madison's] plan for extending the sphere of republican government."[7] Madison was eventually forced to abandon this cherished idea; but little imagination is required to construct how different the evolution of the republic might have been had Congress been able to block any state law.

In any case, these deliberations reflect the founders' efforts to strike an appropriate balance between the branches. And the veto itself was understood first and foremost as a necessary device for executive self-protection. The concern with executive defense is even more clear in the case of the pocket veto, a power that undeniably has an absolute veto effect. The apparent contradiction between the repeated rejection of an absolute veto by the Constitution's founders and the existence of the pocket veto is understood again by the principle of executive defense: the founders feared that Congress might try to duck a veto by passing a bill for which a veto was expected and then quickly adjourning before the president had a chance to return the bill. Remember, there can be no veto unless the president can return the bill to Congress, absent the pocket veto.

The Evolution of the Veto

As the law recognizes, intentions and expectations are one thing, laws and actions are another. Even though the founders thought the veto would be used rarely and to ward off overly aggressive legislative enterprises, the text of the Constitution in Article I, Section 7, sets no conditions on the veto as to manner, frequency, or style of use–although it does pose particular restrictions on the pocket veto, which may only be used when "Congress, by their Adjournment prevent its [a bill's] Return, in which Case it shall not be a Law." Early veto use was marked by little frequency but great controversy. The nation's tenth president, John Tyler, was actually threatened with impeachment for nothing more than using his veto five times in an admittedly politically inept, but not illegal, manner. Through the end of

Abraham Lincoln's term (1865), presidents had applied a total of only 59 vetoes. From then to the present, presidents have vetoed over 2400 bills.

If the veto proved to be a key defensive tool for presidents in the early years of the republic (basing this judgment on the political import of bills vetoed rather than the sheer number), its importance seemed to recede with the dawn of the twentieth century. No contemporary analysis of executive-legislative relations fails to dutifully mention the veto, yet its significance seems to have faded when analysts consider the ample array of political resources available to modern presidents seeking to shape and sway the national agenda. Agenda-setting, central clearance, liaison, lobbying, party leadership, patronage, and the ability to rally public support all summarize a presidential arsenal that dwarfs expectations of executive leadership of the early nineteenth century.

Do I agree that the veto is now but a marginal tool? No. I would make two points about the importance of the veto. First, it was a core power that opened the door to greater presidential involvement in the legislative realm. In the early nineteenth century, presidents were not only expected to refrain from active involvement in the legislative process, but were sharply criticized for merely expressing an opinion on legislation before Congress. President James Monroe, for example, was sharply criticized for suggesting that he would veto an internal improvements bill should it cross his desk, and for recommending that Congress remedy the situation through constitutional amendment. In 1817, a congressional committee responded with a report which asserted that the president's views should have no influence on congressional deliberations, and that if they did, "the Presidential veto would acquire a force unknown to the Constitution, and the legislative body would be shorn of its powers from a want of confidence in its strength."[8]

Yet the very existence of the veto meant that Congress eventually recognized that it had a keen interest in knowing what the president might veto before bills landed on the chief executive's desk. Members of Congress were soon urging the president to express such opinions; presidents readily recognized that the veto threat, as well as the veto, could be useful in shaping congressional actions; in turn, presidents were soon using this opportunity to broaden executive influence in Congress such that the president's preferences actually became the basis for Congress's legislative agenda.

This process came full circle at the start of President Dwight Eisenhower's term. In his first year, Eisenhower failed to submit to Congress the now-customary laundry list of presidential priorities. His failure to do so prompted a sharp outcry from Congress. One member of the House admonished the president: "Don't expect us to start from scratch on what you people want. That's not the way we do things here–*you* draft the bills and *we* work them over."[9]

My second point is that the veto power, and disputes about related matters, such as the item veto debate and a continuing dispute over proper use of the pocket veto, can be found at the center of the contemporary presidential-congressional relationship. The very fact that the item veto debate occupies such a prominent place in public discourse, and that the two most recent presidents have labored to expand the pocket veto power, reminds us that constitutional disputes are not merely for the academics.

The Veto in the 1990s

The centrality of the veto power to the modern presidency is amply demonstrated by three of the last four presidencies. Gerald Ford found his administration heavily reliant on the veto as the primary and most effective means available to him to shape the actions of a newly assertive Democratic Congress. Indeed, only Harry Truman, Grover Cleveland, and Franklin Roosevelt used the veto more often on a per-year basis. Admittedly, Ford's circumstance was unique, in that he was the first man ever to become president who never ran for national office, and because of the circumstances surrounding the Watergate scandal and Richard Nixon's resignation. Still, Ford's reliance on the veto reflected the fate of other presidencies that possessed few other political resources and little opportunity or desire to develop affirmative programs of their own.

The Ford presidency illustrated the great risk of over reliance on the veto–namely, that greater veto use is accompanied by a rise in political anger and alienation in Congress. As one Ford aide observed, "Each veto crippled future opportunities for success; each veto eroded the President's already limited base of support. No president can afford to veto twenty-five bills a year, not in the 1970s at least. It's too damn much, and Congress won't stand for it."[10] The reason for this reaction is clear: virtually all important legislation is the product of prodigious labor, and one could hardly expect members of Congress to be sanguine when large numbers of bills are struck down at the final stage before passage. Moreover, vetoes of important bills often reflect presidential failure, in that a veto means the president has failed to influence the legislation in question sufficiently to meet his preferences.

Ronald Reagan relied on a different, yet no less significant veto strategy. In comparison with Ford, it is important first to note that Reagan began his presidency with a strong electoral mandate and the Republicans in control of the Senate. Thus, Reagan had far less need to pursue a Ford-like veto strategy. Indeed, Reagan vetoed relatively few bills (about 10 per year, compared to Ford's 26 per year), a fact which aggravated many of his conservative supporters who repeatedly urged him to veto more bills as a way to trim federal spending. Nevertheless, he used veto issues in a variety of symbolic ways to promote his goals that reflected the Gipper's heavy emphasis on style and image over substance that typified his presidency.[11]

First, he issued more public veto threats than any of his recent predecessors, including Ford.[12] Like a bad script from a "B" movie, Reagan taunted Congress with comments like: "If any tax hike ever comes across my desk, my handling of the veto pen will make the way Eliot Ness went after Al Capone look like Child's play"; "if a tax hike makes it to my desk, I'll veto it in less time than it takes Vanna White to turn the letters V-E-T-O"; and most well known, Reagan borrowed a line from a

Clint Eastwood movie, daring Congress to exceed his recommended spending levels: "Go ahead, make my day."[13] While Congress certainly did not take kindly to this public taunting, most in Congress realized that this rhetoric was designed for public consumption, and did not reflect any special animus (or impending avalanche of vetoes) directed at Congress. According to political scientist Larry Berman, "For all his rhetoric, Ronald Reagan proved himself remarkably accommodating when necessary."[14] In point of fact, Reagan's relations with Congress were relatively good, especially in the early part of his administration. This fact, combined with a clear policy agenda (something the Ford administration never had the opportunity to develop) minimized the necessity for many vetoes. Still, Reagan used a *rhetorical veto* to sound, act, and look tough.

Second, Reagan revived calls for a line item veto. Debate over the item veto actually predated not only Reagan, but the twentieth century. Indeed, the first codified form of the item veto appeared in the constitution of the Confederacy of 1861–although Confederate President Jefferson Davis never actually used the power. After the Civil War, most of the states adopted an item veto for their governor, such that 43 of 50 state governors possess some form of the power today. At the federal level, the first president to propose the power was Ulysses S. Grant in 1873. From the end of the nineteenth century to the present, over 150 item veto proposals have been introduced in Congress.

Most experts agree that an item veto would have relatively little impact on overall federal spending.[15] Yet the symbolic political advantages accompanying Reagan's advocacy of the item veto were substantial. By trumpeting the item veto, he could castigate Congress for not cooperating with budget deficit reduction, and offer an idea with wide appeal without taking any real political risks. It also allowed him to sidestep direct responsibility for the deficit mess by arguing that his existing powers, especially the veto, were simply inadequate to the task. Yet if we look at Reagan's record as governor, as well as that of other presidents, I am inclined to reach the opposite conclusion. If one examines Reagan's record as governor (when he possessed an item veto), it is clear that he used his power to little effect. In eight years as governor, Reagan blocked a total of $1.1 billion in spending (all figures controlled for inflation). By comparison, Republican governor George Deukmejian used the same powers to block $2.4 billion in state spending in just his first two years in office. To make a similar comparison at the national level, one finds a similar trend. As president, Reagan blocked an average of $2 billion in spending per year with the veto; but Jimmy Carter blocked $6 billion per year, and Ford $16.4 billion per year.[16] Whatever the merits or limits of the regular veto and the item veto, one is inclined to conclude that faults of the sort described by Reagan and others lie not with the power in question, but with the user. The veto power can be changed by legislation, but the political will to use it cannot.

Third, Reagan attempted to expand the interpretation of pocket veto powers by arguing that he could use the pocket veto during inter- and intra-session adjournments of Congress. In earlier times, presidents indeed used the pocket veto during these times, as such a practice made sense because Congress was in session for only six months of the year. But when Congress began to meet year-round earlier in this century, the necessity for the pocket veto diminished. In the 1970s, presidents Ford and Carter agreed to return vetoed bills to agents of Congress when Congress was not in session, eliminating the need for a pocket veto except at the end of a two-year congress–a practice endorsed by several court decisions.[17] Reagan backtracked on this agreement, however, hoping to reap the advantages of the pocket veto.

The Bush administration advanced this argument even further, arguing that the president could pocket veto a bill even during a three-day congressional recess (as long as the tenth day fell during the break). To further confuse matters, Bush vetoed two bills claiming they were pocket vetoes, despite the fact that he then returned the bills to Congress. While the administration's motive for these actions is not entirely clear, there is no question that the administration was trying to set a broader precedent for pocket veto use, thus hoping to gain political advantage over Congress.[18]

Aside from the pocket veto affair, Bush made the veto a keystone of his dealings with Congress. While his veto average from 1989-1991 was slightly less than that of his predecessor (8.3 vetoes per year), the veto was the pivot point around which he confronted Congress on domestic political matters. The minimum wage, Chinese student immigration, family and medical leave from the workplace, and civil rights are among the most significant policy issues of the Bush years–and all were bills vetoed by Bush. Indeed, Bush's most important domestic political achievement in his term may be the fact that none of his vetoes were overridden. This pattern finds close parallel with the Ford administration, in that it buttresses the observation many have made about the Bush administration–namely, that Bush did not pursue a coherent domestic policy program. Absent such executive policy leadership, Congress takes greater policy initiative, leaving the president to react by veto. In addition, Bush applied prolific veto threats. According to *Congressional Quarterly*, Bush issued no less than 120 veto threats in his first 20 months in office.[19]

Bush also adopted Reagan's call for an item veto, but added a new twist. In 1989, he made it known that the administration was actively considering asserting an item veto unilaterally, and then letting Congress take him to court if they objected. Senate Minority Leader Robert Dole (R-KS), among others, supported Bush's idea.[20] According to the administration, such an action would be justifiable based on the theory that the definition of what constitutes a "bill" has changed in the last two centuries, such that the large, multifarious, rider-laden legislation of today bears no resemblance to what was meant by "bill" in the eighteenth century. Therefore, parts of a bill that deal with different subjects, or that are introduced separately, are in effect separate bills that can be subjected to separate vetoes, even if they fall within a single piece of legislation.[21]

The problems with this novel argument are numerous. First, the evidence that presidents already have such a power based in any reading of the Constitution has managed to escape 39 other presidents. Second, the supposition that legislation in the eighteenth century was limited to single subjects is simply false. The nation's first appropriations bill, passed in 1789, was an omnibus measure that incorporated money for both civilian and military programs.[22]

Third, while the attachment of non-germane riders to legislation accelerated in the nineteenth century, it was a practice well known to the country's founders. As one legal expert noted, "the framers were familiar with detailed and complex appropriations bills, including ones with riders."[23] In fact, the attachment of riders to legislation was a major political issue in the British parliament long before American independence, a practice the British called "tacking."[24]

Fourth, the Constitution does not define the term "bill," but it does give to Congress "All legislative powers herein granted" (Article I, Sec. 1), including the power to "make all laws which shall be necessary and proper for carrying into execution the foregoing powers" (Article I, Sec. 8). In addition, the Presentment clause (Article I, sec. 7) provides no basis for the president to approve or disapprove a bill in anything other than the form in which it is presented. For presidents to in effect alter legislation by vetoing items is in fact the power to re-write legislation after Congress is through with it.

The Bush administration's 1992 effort to acquire item veto powers was described at the start of this essay. The effort to acquire "veto rescission" power through statute follows logically from Bush's other efforts described herein. In these instances, Bush was trying to sidestep the constitutional amendment route; yet most experts agree that an item veto could only be given to the president by constitutional amendment.[25]

Why would President Bush devote time and energy to these rather bizarre theories? Obviously, he hoped to gain some political advantage. But more importantly, he sought advantages attached to the constitutional mantle. If the Constitution mattered so little in 1992, why would a president bother? Obviously, the Constitution matters a great deal.

Conclusion

I do not seek to exaggerate the importance of the veto power, nor belittle the considerable array of informal powers and prerogatives accumulated by presidents in the modern era that are so carefully described in basic textbooks. Rather, I seek to emphasize that the presidency, and Congress, are no less constitutional offices than in earlier eras. More specifically, it is impossible to understand the presidency without understanding its fundamentally constitutional nature. In addition, the informal or "political" powers of the presidency and Congress that the branches have accumulated in the last 200 years are well understood as direct offshoots of the constitutional trunk. To extend the analogy, one cannot understand the branches and leaves of the political system without understanding the trunk and roots.

The great constitutionalist and presidential scholar, Edward Corwin, identified two preeminent roles for the president acquired in this century that extend well beyond original constitutional design : "that of legislative leader and that of recipient of delegated legislative power."[26] Corwin left little doubt that the modern presidency was an institution remade to the preferences of activist presidents, with the complicity of compliant congresses, and an often anxious public. The best way to judge the merit of newly claimed or desired presidential powers is not to simply fall back on strict constructionism, on the one hand, or to settle on what is most expedient politically at the moment on the other hand; it is instead to retain the logic and beauty of the constitutional framework. We would do well to heed Corwin's cautions, but to remind ourselves as well that constitutions are organic, not static, and that the constitutional core of the presidency is not so easily discarded by people who would try to do so for pedestrian political gain.

Notes

1. *Congressional Record*, 102d Cong., 2d sess., 1992, 138, S2279.

2. The vote on this proposal was 44 in favor and 54 against. Sixty votes were required for passage, since the measure required that the normal rules be waived. "Senate Rejects Line-Item Veto," *Washington Post*, 28 February 1992.

3. The nature and consequences of these changes are chronicled in Robert J. Spitzer, *President and Congress: Executive Hegemony at the Crossroads of American Government* (New York: McGraw-Hill, 1993), esp. chapters 1 and 2.

4. The New Jersey Plan, posed as an alternative to the Virginia Plan, gave no veto to the president.

5. Max Farrand, *The Records of the Federal Convention of 1787*, 4 vols. (New Haven, CT: Yale University Press, 1966), 1:101.

6. Max Farrand, *The Framing of the Constitution* (New Haven, CT: Yale University Press, 1913), 119-20.

7. Charles F. Hobson, "The Negative on State Laws: James Madison and the Crisis of Republican Government," *William and Mary Quarterly*, 36 (April 1979): 216.

8. Quoted in Robert J. Spitzer, *The Presidential Veto: Touchstone of the American Presidency* (Albany, NY: SUNY Press, 1988), 32.

9. Quoted in Spitzer, *President and Congress*, 42.

10. Quoted in Paul C. Light, *The President's Agenda* (Baltimore, MD: Johns Hopkins University Press, 1982), 112.

11. See Michael Rogin, *Ronald Reagan, the Movie* (Berkeley, CA: University of California Press, 1987); John Kenneth White, *The New Politics of Old Values* (Hanover, NH: University Press of New England, 1990).

12. This is based on my analysis of veto threats beginning with the Kennedy administration in Spitzer, *The Presidential Veto*, 101-103, and updated in Spitzer, "The Disingenuous Presidency: Reagan's Veto and the 'Make-My-Day' President," *Congress and the Presidency* 21 (Spring 1994): 1-10.

13. Steven V. Roberts, "Reagan and His 'Golden Oldies,'" *New York Times*, 16 July 1987; Gerald M. Boyd, "President Accuses Senate Committee of Retreat in Cuts," *New York Times*, 14 March 1985.

14. Larry Berman, *The New American Presidency* (Boston: Little, Brown, 1987), 323.

15. See Spitzer, *The Presidential Veto*, chapter 5.

16. Spitzer, *The Presidential Veto*, 93, 136. The Reagan data are updated in Spitzer, "The Disingenuous Presidency."

17. *The Pocket Veto Case*, 279 U.S. 644 (1929); *Wright v. U.S.* 302 U.S. 583 (1938); *Kennedy v. Sampson*, 511 F.2d 430 (2d Cir. 1974).

18. See Robert J. Spitzer, "Presidential Prerogative Power: The Case of the Bush Administration and Legislative Powers," *PS: Political Science and Politics*, 24 (March, 1991): 38-42.

19. Janet Hook, "Avalanche of Veto Threats Divides Bush, Congress," CQ Weekly Report (September 1990): 2991-94.

20. Gerald F. Seib, "If Bush Tests Constitutionality of Line-Item Veto, Reverberations Could Transform Government," *Wall Street Journal*, 30 October 1989.

21. See Anthony Haswell, "Partial Veto Power–Does the President Have It Now?," *Federal Bar News and Journal* 36 (March/April, 1989): 142-46.

22. Louis Fisher, "The Item Veto–a Misconception," *Washington Post*, 23 February 1987.

23. Paul R. Wolfson, *Is a Presidential Item Veto Constitutional?* 96 The Yale Law Journal 838, 839 (March, 1987).

24. Spitzer, *The Presidential Veto*, 7, 124.

25. Edward S. Corwin, *The President: Office and Powers* (New York: New York University Press, 1957), 284; Charles J. Zinn, *The Veto Power of the President*, report prepared for the House Committee on the Judiciary, 82nd Cong., 1st sess. , 1951, Committee Print, 34.

26. Corwin, *The President*, 311.

Chapter 11

The Decline of Free Speech in Twentieth-Century America: The View from the Founding

Thomas G. West

It is widely believed that there is more freedom of speech in America today than there was at the time of the founding. Liberals and libertarians celebrate today's freedom. Conservatives worry that there may be too much of it.

The Founders defined freedom of speech and of the press as the right of a citizen or organization to say or publish whatever it wishes without fear of punishment by government, as long as what it says does not injure another individual or the community at large. Against today's conventional wisdom, I will demonstrate that there is substantially *less* freedom of speech in America today than there was at the time of the founding; and that today's liberalism, far from favoring the expansion of free speech (as is commonly believed), is hostile to free speech. (When I use the term "freedom of speech," I generally mean to include "and of the press.")

From the Founders' point of view, we restrict speech where it ought to be free, above all in discussions of candidates for election and of public policy. At the same time, we tolerate abuses of speech that they would have prohibited because they are injurious to individuals or to society. We have precisely reversed the earlier understanding. In the Founders' language: They protected liberty but not licentiousness. We protect licentiousness but not liberty.

Free Speech: The Founders' Approach

For the Founders, freedom is our birthright. The Declaration of Independence calls liberty an inalienable right, meaning that we are born with it ("endowed by our Creator") and can never rightly surrender it to any government or to anyone at all. As we are born free in all respects, we are also born free to speak, write, and publish. When James Madison was preparing his speech introducing the Bill of Rights to the first Congress, he wrote that speech was one of the "*natural rights*, retained," in contrast with government-granted rights such as trial by jury. In this sense, there is an absolute right to freedom of speech, just as there is an absolute or "inalienable" right to liberty in general.[1]

When men live without government, in a state of nature, their lives and liberties are not secure. When government fails to punish evildoers, bad men harm the weak and innocent by robbing, raping, enslaving, and murdering them. Government is established, as the Declaration says, to secure the rights of life, liberty, and the pursuit of happiness. Government therefore has two leading tasks. It must restrain itself from harming the lives and liberties of the citizens. But it must restrain those who would harm their lives and liberties.

The natural right to free speech is the liberty to say whatever does not injure anyone. Government must protect that liberty, as it must protect liberty in general. James Wilson, a leading member of the Constitutional Convention of 1787 and principal draftsman of the Pennsylvania Constitution of 1790, explains: "Every wanton, or causeless, or unnecessary act of authority, exerted or authorized, or encouraged by the legislature over the citizens, is wrong, and unjustifiable, and tyrannical: for every citizen is, of right, entitled to liberty, personal as well as mental, in the highest possible degree which can consist with the safety and welfare of the state."

But a verbal assault may deprive a man of his reputation and honor, or destroy his career. A competent doctor denounced as a quack by a personal enemy will lose patients. The doctor's medical practice can be destroyed more effectively by clever slander than by burning down his office. He deserves the protection of the law against both.

Government must therefore not only restrain itself from infringing the liberty of speech. It must also protect people against the abuse of that liberty.

Libel, says James Wilson, is "a malicious defamation of any person, published by writing, or printing, or signs, or pictures, and tending to expose him to public hatred, contempt, or ridicule." The law therefore views libels, he says, in the same light as physical injury, "as breaches of the peace, and as much resembling challenges to fight." This means there is an inherent limit to free speech: "what is meant by the liberty of the press is that there should be no antecedent restraints upon it; but that every author is responsible when he attacks the security or welfare of the government or the safety, character, and property of the individual."[2]

This understanding was shared by every leading member of the founding generation. All believed that government should protect the right to free speech, and also that government should provide remedies to those harmed by the abuse of that right. There were of course intense disagreements over the *federal* role in limiting abuses of speech. Jefferson and Madison firmly believed that the states alone, not the federal government, ought to police those abuses. But even Madison acknowledged that there is a "proper boundary between the liberty and licentiousness of the press," and that government at some level has a responsibility for curbing its licentiousness. Jefferson's 1789 letter to Madison, in which he suggested language for what later became the First Amendment, reflects this view: "The people shall not be deprived or abridged of their right to speak, to write, or otherwise to publish anything but false facts affecting injuriously the life, liberty, property, or reputation of others or affecting the peace of the confederacy with foreign nations."[3]

There is an obvious danger here. Government might be tempted to punish *noninjurious* speech that it does not happen to approve.

The Founders relied primarily on the rule of law to keep government within bounds when it curbed abuses of speech. "Due process of law" was the means by which all liberty, including liberty of speech, was protected. Abuses of speech had to be defined in law, by general rules. This meant that government could not require printers to get licenses to print. It was well understood that licensing requirements enable government to influence or control the activity licensed. Nor could government punish or limit speech for vague reasons that it never had to explain in court. The Founders followed the great English jurist William Blackstone, who wrote that "freedom of the press" meant above all that government could not "subject the press to the restrictive power of a licenser."[4]

In the absence of controls over the press through licensing, government could correct abuses only by subsequent prosecution or lawsuit. The trial was to be by jury. Private citizens, not government officials, would determine the verdict.

In spite of the almost universal opinion that there is more free speech today than at the time of the founding, all three of the pillars erected by the Founders to protect free speech have suffered serious damage in the twentieth century:

1. For the Founders, *no speech* could be prohibited by government except that which is proved injurious in court. Today, non-injurious speech is routinely prohibited and punished.

2. For the Founders, there could be *no prior restraint* of speech by requiring a publisher to get a government license prior to publishing. Today, the media from which most Americans get their news is subject to a government licensing scheme that is remarkably similar to the system by which England's kings controlled the press in the sixteenth and seventeenth centuries.

3. For the Founders, abuses of speech had to be *defined in law*, and they could be *punished only by juries*–that is, by people who are not government officials. Today, clear legal standards and juries are generally avoided in the many censorship schemes employed by government.

I do not claim to be uncovering some secret plot to take away American liberty. What the Founders would have called today's curbs on free speech have been defended quite openly by numerous scholars and politicians as *expansions* of free speech. The central problem, as these men see it, is the influence of the "privileged." If the press is left free, they fear, the rich will dominate and the poor will be oppressed. Therefore speech rights must be taken away from the rich and privileged and redistributed to the poor and oppressed. University of Maryland political scientist Mark Graber, for example, believes that "Affluent Americans have no First Amendment right that permits them to achieve political success through constant repetition of relatively unwanted ideas." Who is to decide what ideas are "unwanted"? The government, of course. Yale law professor Stephen Carter agrees: "Left unregulated, the modern media could present serious threats to democracy."[5]

Alexander Hamilton sums up the Founders' opposite understanding in these words:

> The liberty of the press consists in publishing, with impunity, truth, with good motives, and for justifiable ends, whether it relates to men or to measures. . . . There is no other way to preserve liberty, and bring down a tyrannical faction. If this right is not permitted to exist in vigor and in exercise, good men will become silent; corruption and tyranny will go on, step by step, in usurpation, until at law, nothing that is worth speaking, or writing, or acting for, will be left in our country.
>
> But I do not mean to be understood as being the advocate of a press wholly without control. I reprobate the novel, the visionary, the pestilential doctrine of an unchecked press. . . . It would encourage vice, compel the virtuous to retire, destroy confidence, and confound the innocent with the guilty. . . .
>
> The check upon the press ought to be deposited, not in a permanent body of magistrates, as the court, but in an occasional and fluctuating body, the jury, who are to be selected by lot. Judges might be tempted to enter into the views of government, and to extend, by arbitrary constructions, the laws of libels. . . . [We have good reason] to cling to the trial by jury, as our greatest safety. . . .[6]

The Federal Election Campaign Act

Let us begin with the first of the Founders' pillars, that no speech may be prohibited except when it is injurious, and that the most important speech to protect is speech discussing, in Hamilton's words, "men or measures"–public officials and issues of public policy.

In 1971, for the first time in American history, the Federal Elections Campaign Act (FECA) made it illegal for a certain category of Americans to publish their opinions about candidates for election. Under the Act as amended, private citizens and organizations who cooperate or consult with a candidate for public office are not permitted to spend more than a set amount of money publishing arguments in support of that candidate or against his opponent. (For a private citizen, the limit is $1,000.) Those who cooperate or consult with a candidate are his friends and supporters. In other words, publication is forbidden to those who have the greatest interest in the campaign and are most likely to want to spend money publishing on behalf of the candidate. The Act does leave them free to publish their views on any other political topic, as long as they do not engage in "express advocacy." However, some courts have held that discussion of public policy issues that are prominent in a campaign are "express advocacy" even when a candidate's name is not mentioned. The "chilling effect" of this vague rule prevents many groups from risking publication because the litigation costs alone are heavy.

Penalties can be severe. In 1990 the FEC attempted to fine the National Rifle Association $416,000 for alleged violations of its regulations.

The law does contain a notable exception. Its restrictions on free speech do not apply to newspaper owners. They may spend any amount of money publishing arguments in support of candidates with whom they consult or cooperate.[7]

The Campaign Act stands in direct opposition to the Founders' understanding of freedom of the press. For a large class of people, it effectively criminalizes the very thing that the right to free speech is supposed to guarantee: open discussion of "men or measures" at election time.

As John Adams wrote, "Our chief magistrates and senators etc. are annually eligible by the people. How are their characters and conduct to be known to their constituents but by the press? If the press is to be stopped and the people kept in ignorance, we had much better have the first magistrate and senators hereditary." Adams would have added, had he been aware of the Campaign Act, that the unconditional right to publish one's sentiments should be a right enjoyed by every citizen, not just newspaper owners.

In *Buckley v. Valeo*, the Supreme Court maintained that the Campaign Act's restrictions are permissible because they are "content-neutral." A leading constitutional law text compares the restrictions to prohibitions of billboards.[8] This is ludicrous. The political character of a supporter's publication is precisely what makes it punishable. By the same logic, it would be "content neutral" to prohibit all citizens, not just a candidate's friends, from publishing their sentiments on public officials running for election. Incumbent politicians would then become completely exempt from criticism by private citizens, instead of being only partially so as they are under current law.

In discussions of freedom of speech today, the massive and unprecedented restrictions on speech in the Federal Elections Campaign Act are generally passed over in silence (as in civil liberties textbooks by David O'Brien and Louis Fisher) or treated as a minor tangential question (as in the 473-page edited volume, *The First Amendment*).[9]

The Supreme Court has piously pronounced, on numerous occasions, that "one of the prerogatives of American citizenship is the right to criticize men and measures," and that it is speech on "matters of public concern that is at the heart of the First Amendment's protection." Textbooks on American government, such as James MacGregor Burns's, dutifully repeat the Court's assurances about the sanctity of political speech. The Court and the scholars are being consciously or unconsciously dishonest when they make such claims. For the Campaign Act prohibits *the* most important kind of political speech–reasoned arguments on candidates and elections. It does so not because these arguments are alleged to injure anyone, not because bribery has taken place, but because publishing by a certain class of citizens (those who cooperate or consult with candidates) might create, in the Court's words, "the appearance of corruption." Their right to publish must therefore be taken away.[10]

Labor and Harassment Law

During attempts to unionize a business, federal labor law prohibits an employer from presenting to his employees certain kinds of arguments against forming unions. The Supreme Court has ruled that the employer is allowed to "make a prediction as to the precise effects he believes unionization will have on his company," but the "prediction must be carefully phrased on the basis of objective fact." When the employer conveys his "belief, even though sincere, that unionization will or may result in the closing of the plant," he is making "a threat of reprisal or force," says the Court, a "threat of retaliation based on misrepresentation and coercion." The Court, however, did not really believe its own incredible equation of coercion with a statement that unionization would probably result in plant closing. The Court admitted that it was "balancing" the employer's free speech rights against "the equal rights of the employees to associate freely." In other words, the right of the workers to be shielded from opinions that would admittedly be perfectly legal to express outside the workplace trumps the First Amendment right to convey an opinion, on the ground that "economically dependent" workers might feel threatened by anything less than a recital of objective facts. The union organizers, it goes without saying, are permitted to say anything they please against the employer.[11]

Civil rights law restrictions on free speech are far more sweeping than labor law. In this area too, most scholarly treatments of freedom of speech seem unaware of the problem. It is not mentioned in Karst's *Freedom of Speech* or Stone's *Constitutional Law*. Yet punishment of noninjurious political and religious speech in the workplace is now required nationwide by federal law.

Title VII of the 1964 Civil Rights Act says that employers may not discriminate on the basis of race, sex, religion, and so on. Courts have ruled that harassment is a form of discrimination, and that "hostile environment" harassment exists, for example, when an employer puts Bible verses on paychecks and religious articles in the company newsletter, or when an employee states his opinion that "women make bad doctors because they are unreliable when they menstruate." A federal appeals court put the matter plainly: "In essence, while Title VII does not require an employer to fire all 'Archie Bunkers' in its employ, the law does require that an employer take prompt action to prevent such bigots from expressing their opinions in a way that abuses or offends their co-workers." In other words, government requires employers to censor themselves and to punish religious believers and conservatives who "express their opinions in a way that offends co-workers." Legal scholar Eugene Volokh comments:

> Said about almost any other variety of opinion, this statement . . . would be a civil libertarian's nightmare. Imagine a law requiring that 'an employer take prompt action to prevent Communists from expressing their opinions in a way that abuses or offends their co-workers.'[12]

In the Founders' approach, employers always had the right to express their political and religious opinions, and they also had the right to fire or refuse to hire an employee for any reason, such as his political views or rudeness to fellow employees. Government could do the same with its own employees. But government could not require private businesses to punish employees for opinions they expressed at work. Nor could government punish the expression of employers' or employees' opinions.

Reflecting the Founders' view of free speech, legal scholar Kingsley Browne writes, "hostile-environment harassment regulation poses a far greater threat to expression than other restrictions that receive far more attention, such as prohibition of flag-burning."[13]

The federal Fair Housing Act also punishes deliberative political speech. A Berkeley couple "argued in newsletters and public petitions that the site chosen for the new homeless shelter–next to two liquor stores and a nightclub–was grossly imprudent." Because of their opposition to the project, the U.S. Department of Housing and Urban Development initiated an investigation against them. They faced "statutory penalties of $50,000 apiece, as well as compensatory and punitive damages." (HUD did offer to drop the charges if they agreed "never to write or speak on housing issues again.") HUD has punished arguments against public housing elsewhere. A favorite tactic is to hold cities liable "for political statements against group homes made by their citizens–a form of indirect censorship." The result: "In every city in which HUD has pursued investigations against individuals and community groups, opposition to planned social-service facilities has been severely chilled–just as intended."[14]

In the Founders' generation, such punishment of private citizens' speech on measures of public policy was completely prohibited. In his study of the Founders' supposed "legacy of suppression," Leonard Levy never found a single case in which government punished a citizen for presenting calm and deliberate arguments against a government policy, or a single Founder whose writings would justify such punishment.[15]

Censorship through Licensing in Old Britain and Modern America

Reading today's scholarship on freedom of speech, one would hardly guess that government control over the content of speech through licensing requirements, supposedly outlawed long ago by the First Amendment and by the Declarations of Rights in state constitutions, is alive and well. It now controls the majority of the media relied upon by the American people for their news.

The sunny naivete with which this matter is usually discussed today may be seen in the words of legal scholar Benno Schmidt, the former president of Yale: "the First Amendment tolerates virtually no prior restraints. This doctrine is one of the central principles of our law of freedom of the press. . . . the doctrine is presumably an absolute bar to any wholesale system of administrative licensing or censorship of the press, which is the most repellent form of government suppression of expression. . . . The message of the prior restraint doctrine is that if you cannot control expression pursuant to general legislative standards, you cannot control it at all."[16] Schmidt forgets that every radio, television, and cable broadcaster in America is subject to a "wholesale system of administrative licensing"–the "most repellent form of government suppression of expression." In America today, government is the legal owner of all broadcast rights, just as the kings of England prior to 1694 owned all printing rights.

Blackstone gave this history of prior restraint on the press in England: "The art of printing, soon after its introduction, was looked upon . . . as merely a matter of state, and subject to the coercion of the crown. It was therefore regulated with us by the king's proclamations, prohibitions, charters of privilege and of license, and finally by the decrees of Star Chamber; which limited the number of printers, and of presses which each should employ, and prohibited new publications unless previously approved by proper licensers." The "demolition of this odious jurisdiction" occurred in 1694.[17]

What Blackstone says of printing in England repeated itself in America with regard to broadcasting in the twentieth century. In both cases, a new communications technology, invented by private persons, was seized by government in the name of the public interest. "Soon after its introduction" around 1900, the art of radio broadcasting "was looked upon as merely a matter of state, and subject to the coercion," not of the crown, but of the federal government. The Radio Act of 1912 asserted the principle that no one could broadcast without a federal license. By the 1920s, not the king, but Secretary of Commerce Herbert Hoover, granted "charters of privilege and of license" to broadcasters. The Radio Act of 1927 established the Federal Radio Commission, later renamed the Federal Communications Commission. This body "limited the number" of broadcasters by deliberately refusing to expand the narrow spectrum available for commercial broadcasting. It "prohibited new [broadcast stations] unless previously approved by proper licensers."[18]

There were two kinds of licenses required under the old English system. First, publishers had to submit items to censors and get a license to publish each particular work. America has never required any such thing. Second, no one in England was allowed to be in the business of printing at all unless he had first obtained a license. This kind of licensing is the means by which broadcasting is controlled in America today. It was also the key to the system of control in old England.

"The most effective single agency for the regulation of the press," writes historian Frederick Siebert, was the Stationers Company, the "corporate and monopoly body of printers." They were expected "to keep a tight rein on member printers in return for the grant of a royal charter," and they did. If anyone was discovered printing without a Company license,

> Having detected and apprehended the unfortunate printer, the Stationers would proceed to the prosecution. . . . A typical entry in the records of the court is the following: 'This day [9 April 1632] a press being erected in Shoredich by John Hammon, contrary to the decree in Star-Chamber, was defaced and made unserviceable the ninth day of this month following in the presence of the wardens and diverse of the assistant.'[19]

In the United States, broadcasters have to obtain a license from the Federal Communications Commission. The FCC is a government agency, while the Stationers Company was a private group authorized by the king. However, the effect in both cases is the same. The right to broadcast in America, like the right to publish in old England, is under the ultimate control of the government, and it is revokable at any time.

Under the Communications Act of 1934, stations receive licenses to broadcast only when the FCC judges it to be "in the public interest, convenience, or necessity." Licenses are granted for a limited period, and the FCC may choose not to renew. The FCC has never defined what the "public interest" means. It prefers an ad hoc, case-by-case approach, which has been called "regulation by raised eyebrow."[20] Occasionally the heavy hand of the FCC becomes public. Usually the knowledge that there could be trouble at license renewal time is enough to compel compliance.

A Brief History of FCC Censorship

The FCC has consistently favored broadcasters that share the views of government officials. Oddball or politically dissident stations were driven off the air from the start.

The first instance was the Radio Commission's refusal to renew the license of Bob Shuler's Los Angeles station. "Fighting Bob's" shows were popular, but California politicians hated him because of his tirades against local corruption. The Commission ordered his station off the air in 1930. John Brinkley's station, on the other hand, broadcast what has been described as "an astute combination of fundamentalist theology and medical information." His medical advice concentrated on such remedies as transplantation of goat gonads to rejuvenate the male sex drive. Organized medicine attacked him, and the Radio Commission took away his broadcast license, also in 1930.[21]

These early cases might be dismissed as comical sidebars. But they set the precedent for the serious and pervasive political censorship initiated by Franklin Roosevelt's FCC in the 1930s. The National Association of Broadcasters, anticipating pressure from the FCC, "announced that paid sponsorship of programs dealing with controversial issues was inappropriate." This seemingly neutral suggestion was in fact directed against stations carrying Father Coughlin, a popular right-wing critic of Roosevelt. This led to cancellation of his program by a number of stations.[22]

The first large-scale censorship occurred in the late 1930s, as Americans were becoming increasingly hostile toward Roosevelt's New Deal. The Yankee Radio network in New England frequently editorialized against Roosevelt. The FCC formally asked Yankee to provide details about its programming. Sensing the drift, Yankee stopped broadcasting editorials in 1938. In order to drive its point home, the FCC found Yankee deficient at license renewal time. Using the sanctimonious tone at which partisan bureaucrats excel, it announced, "Radio can serve as an instrument of democracy only when devoted to the communication of information and exchange of ideas fairly and objectively presented. . . . It cannot be devoted to the support of principles he [the broadcaster] happens to regard most favorably. . . . These requirements are inherent in the conception of the public interest." The FCC renewed the license of the now-repentant network. Yankee's economic self-interest kept it from challenging the federal government's censorship of its conservative programming content, just as it was against the economic interest of England's monopoly printers to challenge their cozy arrangement with the king.

The FCC soon made exclusion of "partisan" content a requirement for all broadcasters. It was understood, of course, that radio stations would continue to carry such supposedly "nonpartisan" fare as presidential speeches attacking Republicans and calling for expansions of the New Deal. In the name of "democracy" and "communication of information and exchange of ideas," the FCC would no longer permit stations to criticize Roosevelt's speeches and programs. Here is a little-known source of the "liberal media" often complained of later by conservatives.[23]

In 1949 the FCC announced its Fairness Doctrine. Broadcasters were required "to provide coverage of vitally important controversial issues . . . and . . . a reasonable opportunity for the presentation of contrasting viewpoints on such issues." But this apparent call for controversy actually continued the policy that the FCC had developed under Roosevelt. To avoid having to provide free air time to those who might disagree with a viewpoint expressed on the air, stations broadcast "balanced" news stories that did not offend the liberalism of the dominant political culture.

From one point of view, it can be said that broadcasting under the Fairness

Doctrine regime was predominantly nonpartisan. Law professor Geoffrey Stone remarks that broadcasting, in contrast with print journalism, is "bland, cautious, and studiously nonpolitical. Broadcasters do not endorse political candidates and they do not stake out controversial positions on issues of public importance."[24] Stone does not add what I believe to be the crucial point: blandness and "nonpartisanship" serve the interest of the governing establishment. Today that establishment is the welfare and administrative state as it has developed since the 1930s and 60s. To the extent that the status quo is not criticized, the public will be less inclined to think there is anything wrong with it. There will be less pressure to change it. If American journalism of the 1760s and 70s had been "bland, cautious, and studiously nonpolitical," there would have been no American Revolution. If Northern newspapers had been studiously nonpolitical in the 1850s, there would have been no effective movement to stop the expansion of slavery.

However, broadcasting has not been quite as bland as Stone and others have claimed. By 1960, as an alternative to the bland liberalism prevailing in mainstream broadcasting, quite a few conservative radio stations had emerged during the Republican Eisenhower years in which the FCC paid little attention to broadcasting content. In the 1960s the Democratic Kennedy and Johnson administrations went on the offensive against these conservatives. Kennedy's Assistant Secretary of Commerce, Bill Ruder, later explained, "Our massive strategy was to use the Fairness Doctrine to challenge and harass right-wing broadcasters and hope that the challenges would be so costly to them that they would be inhibited and decide it was too expensive to continue."

That strategy was highly successful. Hundreds of radio stations canceled conservative shows that they had been broadcasting. The FCC revoked the license of one radio station, WXUR of Media, Pennsylvania, a tiny conservative Christian broadcaster. Judge Bazelon of the D.C. Circuit Court of Appeals noted that by driving WXUR off the air, there was less diversity of viewpoints on the radio, not more. "It is beyond dispute," he wrote, "that the public has *lost* access to information and ideas . . . as a result of this doctrinal sledge-hammer [viz., the Fairness Doctrine]." The Supreme Court refused to review the case on appeal.

The station's former owner made up a "Song of the Fairness Doctrine" to convey his bitter feelings:

> It's designed to protect opposing views
> To prove that speech is free,
> But the song of the Fairness Doctrine
> We regretfully construe
> Is out of tune entirely
> With the Christian point of view. . . .
> It gives full voice to the liberals
> But leaves out you and me.

The government also revoked the owner's license to broadcast on WLTB in

Jackson, Mississippi, a television station that was strongly critical of the civil rights policies of the federal government in the 1960s. Sometimes WLTB would introduce news reports on NBC's *Today* show with this warning: "What you are about to see is an example of biased, managed, Northern news. Be sure to stay tuned at 7:25 to hear your local newscast." After a challenge by liberals, the FCC reluctantly renewed WLTB's license on the condition that "licensee immediately cease discriminatory programming practices" such as not having black children on its children's show. The station immediately complied, introducing an integrated cast into its local programming and ceasing its partisan criticisms of liberals. This was not good enough for the D.C. Circuit Court, which ordered the FCC to revoke WLTB's license. In an extraordinary opinion authored by Warren Burger, soon to be appointed by President Nixon as Chief Justice of the Supreme Court, Burger demanded in indignant tones that WLTB's owner be silenced: "After nearly five decades of operation the broadcast industry does not seem to have grasped the simple fact that a broadcast license is a public trust subject to termination for breach of duty." Again, the Supreme Court had so little interest in this case that it refused to hear the station's appeal.

In a more famous case–because it did reach the Supreme Court–another conservative radio station, Red Lion, was challenged in a Fairness Doctrine complaint secretly financed by the Democratic National Committee. The Supreme Court, by an 8-0 vote, ruled that the Constitution permitted the FCC to order the station to give free air time to liberals who disagreed with conservative broadcast content. The Court, in other words, ruled that the government could dictate the content of a station's broadcasting, as Justice Felix Frankfurter had already affirmed in the 1943 *NBC v. United States* case: The Federal Communications Act "puts upon the commission the burden of determining the composition of that traffic."[25]

These policies and decisions sent an unmistakable message to every radio and television broadcaster in America in the 1960s. If your station advocates conservatism, be prepared for Fairness Doctrine and license renewal challenges from liberals, who will be backed up by all three branches of the federal government.

Conservatives tried to use the Fairness Doctrine to fight back. They failed. Fred Friendly writes, "After virtually every controversial program–'Harvest of Shame,' . . . 'Hunger in America' [1960s programs advocating liberal reforms]–fairness complaints were filed, and the FCC rejected them all. As FCC general counsel Henry Geller put it, 'We just weren't going to get trapped into determining journalistic judgments. . . .'" The FCC adopted rules, as Friendly characterizes them, "with clearly defined protections for the broadcast journalist as opposed to the religious or political crusader." In other words, the FCC interpreted the Fairness Doctrine in such a way as to harass conservatives (demonized by Friendly as "religious or political crusaders"–note the implicit equation of religion, warlike aggressiveness, and conservatism), but it gave liberals ("broadcast journalists" like Walter Cronkite and Eric Sevareid of CBS) the freedom to say whatever they wished.[26]

After 1969 the Nixon administration made a strong effort to change the character of television network news coverage. White House staffers berated network executives on the phone and in meetings. The FCC announced that it was monitoring and analyzing network news programs. Threats of non-renewal of licenses were made against network affiliates.

Although no network became pro-Nixon, all three made accommodations. The networks mostly ignored a huge 1969 antiwar demonstration. The Watergate break-in was barely covered during the 1972 campaign, when it might have made a difference in the election. But the Watergate investigation brought Nixon's campaign against the media to a stop in 1973. Now the networks turned on Nixon with a vengeance and helped to destroy him.

Supreme Court Justice William Douglas once observed, "the regime of federal supervision under the Fairness Doctrine . . . [causes broadcasters to echo] the dominant political voice that emerges after every election." That voice had been largely Democratic and liberal from 1930 to 1969.[27] Nixon was unable to reverse this trend. But what if Nixon had been followed by two or three decades of Republican dominance of the presidency and Congress? There is every reason to think that the electronic media would have become increasingly sympathetic to conservatism. In fact, that is what began to happen in the 1980s and 90s.

In the 1980s President Reagan appointed a majority to the Federal Communications Commission. The Commission abolished the Fairness Doctrine in 1987.[28] The effect was dramatic. Immediately, conservative talk radio blossomed. Rush Limbaugh was the biggest winner. He came along at just the moment, for the first time since the 1950s, when stations could be confident that conservative broadcasting would no longer lead to license renewal problems or Fairness Doctrine complaints and litigation.

The end of the Fairness Doctrine does not mean that broadcast media are now free. In fact, the growing presence of conservatism in the media was a result of the fact that the FCC became more libertarian in the 1980s. The authority of the FCC over broadcasters remains in place. In the 1990s, President Clinton's FCC began once again to dictate programming content. Television stations agreed under pressure to commit to broadcast several hours of weekly educational programs for children. Many expect these programs to be weighted toward environmentalism, multiculturalism, and other "politically correct" themes.

A colleague to whom I was explaining all this asked, "If there is so little free speech in the electronic media today, why aren't people screaming bloody murder?" At present, in the wake of the Reagan-era reforms, government's manipulation of program content is relatively mild. But even when it was more heavy-handed, as in the 1940s, and again in the 1960s through 80s, the profit motive kept most stations quiet. Overt punishment was necessary only for the small number of stubborn broadcasters–like Mississippi station WLTB-TV–who valued their convictions more highly than going along with the government. Otherwise everyone cheerfully towed the line. Of course these examples always remain in the back of broadcasters' minds. As a Nixon administration official once put it, "The value of the sword of Damocles is that it hangs, not falls."[29]

Government Controls on Print Media

Print media have fallen increasingly under the same regime of government control as broadcasters. Government, of course, has never claimed the legal authority to regulate newspaper content. To all appearances the print media are totally free of constraint. Yet there are two major legal devices by which government controls newspapers.

First, many newspapers are owned by companies that also own broadcast stations. Although government's "sword of Damocles"–cancellation of a broadcast license–hangs over the head only of the electronic media, government can always threaten nonrenewal if it does not like what a company prints in its newspapers.

Second, the FCC does in fact issue licenses for some newspapers, namely those whose owners also operate a television station in the same market. The FCC calls this license a "waiver." The Founders would have called it an unconstitutional license of the right to print.

President Nixon made use of the first device. The administration did not limit itself to attempts to correct what it regarded as liberal excesses in television. It tried to go after its biggest enemy, the *Washington Post*, by threatening renewal difficulties for the *Post's* several television stations. As Nixon explained to his White House staff, "The *Post* is going to have damnable, damnable problems out of this one. They have a television station . . . and they're going to have to get it renewed. . . . The point is, when does it come up [for renewal]?" The Watergate scandal became the occasion for a terrible battle between Nixon and the *Post*. Nixon lost. But if he had continued to win the public over to his negative view of the "liberal media," the *Post* might have had to abandon its liberal agenda in order to retain its lucrative television markets.[30]

In the end, just as they failed to stop the television networks, Republicans also failed to stop the *Post*. In contrast, Democrats have managed to silence a major broadcaster (Yankee Radio) and a major newspaper (the *New York Post*), by manipulation of government regulation of "diversity."

The legal basis for this kind of censorship was settled in the 1944 *Associated Press* case. The Supreme Court affirmed, for the first time since the First Amendment was passed, that the federal government may regulate the structure of the print media industry. The government argued that the Associated Press' contracts with newspapers around the country *might* be anticompetitive. AP required its newspapers to send all of their own news stories exclusively to AP, in return for which AP gave them the exclusive right to publish its stories. In the Court's sweeping language, government was given the power to regulate the publishing industry in order to promote "the widest possible dissemination of information from diverse and antagonistic sources." (This is nearly the same ominous language that the FCC used when it forced the Yankee Radio network to stop broadcasting anti-Roosevelt editorials.) A dissenter in the case wrote quite accurately, "It is not protecting a freedom, but confining it, to prescribe where and how and under what conditions one must impart the literary product of his thought and research. This is fettering the press, not striking off its chains." It is worth noting that this 1944 precedent enabled the Nixon administration to pressure the three television networks by suing them for antitrust violations. A Nixon staffer suggested that "Even the possible threat of anti-trust action I think would be effective in changing their views."[31]

Following the *Associated Press* precedent, the FCC has set up a licensing scheme for some newspapers. Companies that own a television station and newspaper in the same market must apply for a "waiver." Democrats used this rule to punish one of their critics, Rupert Murdoch. In 1988 Murdoch had FCC waivers to own television stations and newspapers in New York and Boston. Murdoch's Boston *Herald-American* had frequently criticized liberal Senator Edward Kennedy of Massachusetts. At Kennedy's request, Democratic Senator Ernest Hollings quietly inserted into a larger bill a legislative provision that canceled Murdoch's waiver. He had to sell either his television station or his newspaper in both cities. Hollings later admitted, in Thomas Hazlett's summary, that "it was an attempt to sink the conservative *Herald-American* as a favor to Senator Kennedy." In the event, Murdoch kept his Boston paper; he sold the *New York Post* and his Boston television station. Kennedy managed to harm Murdoch, but the *Herald-American* continued to publish. The *Post* was taken over by an editor who specialized in anti-Jewish and anti-white racism.[32]

As we saw earlier in the case of broadcasting, licensing schemes do not normally lead to overt censorship. The sword hangs without falling. Newspaper publishers and station owners are careful not to arouse the ire of government too much. Companies that own newspapers and broadcast stations have a powerful economic incentive to get along with government, not to make waves.

There is no doubt that the Founders would have regarded these government practices as abridgments of freedom of the press and therefore violations of the First Amendment.

A final note: Using the same diversity rationale, the FCC has forbidden the Bell companies from engaging in electronic publishing (for example, making book texts available on computer disk). Once again, a group of private citizens is singled out by government and told that they are not permitted to publish their views–in this case, on anything. The same argument is used to justify government mandates on the content of cable broadcasting, the newest medium of ideas to be licensed by the federal government. Efforts are underway to bring the Internet under government control.[33]

The Decline of Jury Trials in Freedom of Speech Cases

So much for the first two pillars of the Founders' regime of freedom of speech. First, non-injurious speech is routinely punished through campaign finance law and in other ways, as we have seen. Second, government exercises control over the content of major news media through licensing and other regulatory schemes.

The third pillar of the Founders' scheme was that restraints on the misuse of speech could be imposed only by due process of law. That meant clear legal standards of abuses of speech, and trial by jury.

We repeat here the quotation from Alexander Hamilton explaining the importance of jury trials: "The check upon the press ought to be deposited, not in a permanent body of magistrates, as the court, but in an occasional and fluctuating body, the jury, who are to be selected by lot. Judges might be tempted to enter into the views of government, and to extend, by arbitrary constructions, the laws of libels."[34] What Hamilton says of judges applies even more strongly to bureaucrats, who are appointed precisely because they do "enter into the views of government."

Contrary to the Founders' intent, most of the devices already mentioned in this paper by which government controls the content of speech today avoid jury trials and avoid definitions of abusive speech in laws or clearly stated rules. Government today has decided that it is not in its interest for juries (private citizens who do not necessarily "enter into the views of government") to decide whether a wrong has been done.

Campaign finance law is enforced by a Federal Elections Commission, which is authorized to decide what campaign speech may be forbidden, and to impose fines on those who are deemed to misbehave. Those punished may appeal to the courts. However, the litigation costs of fighting the FEC, and then taking the case to court, are high enough to be de facto punishment for all but the largest organizations.

Labor law restrictions on employers' free speech are determined administratively by the National Labor Relations Board.

The FCC makes its licensing decisions, of course, without recourse to juries.

Perhaps the government's most ingenious avoidance of due process is harassment law. Here the government does not punish the prohibited speech directly. Instead, it threatens employers with liability if they do not punish it. But exactly what speech triggers liability? The government refuses to say. If speech is "sufficiently severe and pervasive so as to create a hostile work environment," then it constitutes harassment. Eugene Volokh writes, "to be safe, an employer must suppress speech that *might* qualify . . . , even though, if litigated, the speech might not meet the legal standard. This gives employers a great incentive to suppress even borderline speech."[35]

The old method of jury trial is still followed in libel proceedings. But here juries have become increasingly superfluous. American juries in free speech cases used to be charged with finding law and fact. Now juries are routinely overruled by judges and appeals courts in their findings of both law and fact. For example, a

Penthouse magazine cartoon showed Miss Wyoming engaging in acts of sexual deviation and perversion that caused her partners to levitate. Did this amount to an injury to the young woman? Under traditional libel law, the answer would have been obvious. Founder James Wilson defined libel as "a malicious defamation . . . published by writing, or printing, or signs or pictures, and tending to expose him to public hatred, contempt, or ridicule." Under today's much narrower definition of libel, the question was whether the portrayal would be understood by a reasonable person to convey statements of fact–that Miss Wyoming actually engaged in these kinds of acts. The jury said yes. The appeals court reversed and threw out the verdict. The woman's exasperated lawyer wrote, "In civil cases, juries are only vestiges of the past. The civil law has been taken over by the judges and is now their exclusive property."[36]

The exclusion of juries from regulation of speech eliminates the single most important device by which the Founders hoped to control government excesses. In today's system, "the views of government" enter into almost every case of speech suppression. Congress does not have to convince a jury that Rupert Murdoch's newspaper should be shut down because of its criticisms of Senator Kennedy. The FCC does not have to convince a jury that a conservative station does not deserve to have its license renewed. Government does not have to convince "an occasional and fluctuating body" of private citizens to punish a traditional Christian who makes an argument that a co-worker finds offensive. Bureaucrats who share "the views of government" are enough to determine what speech deserves correction.

Expansions of Freedom of Speech? Apparent, Not Real

It is true, in spite of all that has been said here, that in some respects publishers have much greater leeway today than they had at any time in the past. But are those respects relevant to freedom of speech? Not from the point of view of the Founders.

Publishers have broad latitude in malicious and inaccurate attacks on the reputations of public officials and private citizens. This is certainly an expansion of what is permitted. But is it an increase of freedom?

The Founders did not believe a person's right to freedom went beyond its noninjurious use. My right to keep and bear arms has not been infringed if I am arrested for shooting my neighbor. Nor is my right to freedom of speech infringed if I am punished for harming the reputation of an innocent person. An anonymous 1788 newspaper article drew the exact parallel: "Every man has a right to the use of the press, so he has to the use of his arms." But if he libels another man, "he abuses his privilege, as unquestionably as if he were to plunge his sword into the bosom of a fellow citizen."[37] The remedy in both cases was not licensing the right to carry a gun or the right to publish a newspaper, but punishment of licentious speech after a trial in a court of law.

Courts today have almost obliterated the law of libel. Does this advance the cause of free speech? When Penthouse magazine mocked Miss Wyoming in the case just mentioned, the woman attacked said she felt "raped" by the cartoon. The jury held that she had been grievously injured. On appeal the courts held that *Penthouse* had done nothing wrong. Meanwhile the supposedly uninjured young woman tried without success to find a job in Wyoming. One prospective employer, leering at her, reported that his wife would not let him hire her, and then said, laughing, "But I'm sure in favor of having a girl around the office who's got talent like you got!" Eventually she tried to escape the sleazy looks and insults by joining the army and going to Europe. But even on the streets of Salzburg, Austria, an American soldier yelled at her, "Hey, Penthouse!"[38]

Hustler magazine published a satire in which Jerry Falwell, a nationally-known television preacher, was made to describe a drunken incestuous relationship with his mother. Falwell said that when he first saw it, "I think I have never been as angry as I was at that moment. I somehow felt that in all of my life I had never believed that human beings could do something like this." *Hustler's* publisher admitted that he was trying "to assassinate Jerry Falwell." But the Supreme Court ruled that no injury, and consequently no libel, had taken place.[39]

Two centuries ago Benjamin Franklin explained why an effective libel law is necessary. If the law refuses to protect people's reputations against injury by the press, people will resort to lawlessness. The "liberty of the cudgel"–the liberty to go to the "impudent writer" who "attacks your reputation" and "break his head"–will be exercised by the injured party, to the detriment of the public peace.[40]

Besides weakening the concept of libel, courts have also redefined free speech as "freedom of expression." "Freedom of speech" now includes nude dancing, pornography, vulgarities in public and on clothing, personal insults, flag-burning, and more. When freedom of expression replaced freedom of speech, the distinction between reason and unreason, which the Founders' view depended on, was abolished. The word "speech" means rational discourse, a series of words arranged grammatically to convey thought. The word "expression" means literally "pushing out," putting outside what is inside. Animals cannot speak, but they can express themselves, by groans, cries, yelps. So can humans, who can use the forms of speech, as well as nonverbal actions, to "push out" into public view their nonrational feelings and attitudes.

The replacement of "speech" with "expression" means two things. First, the distinction between words and action breaks down. Second, the distinction is lost between speech that communicates thought, and speech that expresses mere emotion, such as visceral hatred. The Supreme Court literally cannot see the difference between a jacket with "f--- the draft" lettered on it and a poem by William Shakespeare. The Court explained, "one man's vulgarity is another man's lyric."[41]

The new approach certainly increases the latitude for public indecency, such as the exhibition of sex acts in movies. But protection of nonverbal or irrational expression, whatever one might think of its merits on artistic or other grounds, does not advance freedom of *speech*. There is no spoken or printed argument or course of reasoning that the more inclusive term "expression" protects that was not already protected under the Founders' understanding of speech.

The Founders generally agreed that *seditious libel*–"false, scandalous, and malicious writings against the government, with intent to stir up sedition"–should be punishable. Madison, however, rightly pointed out that "The nature of governments elective, limited, and responsible, in all their branches, may well be supposed to require a greater freedom of animadversion [i.e., criticism] than might be tolerated by . . . Great Britain." From this Madison concluded that speech undermining government should *never* be punishable. No other leading Founder agreed with Madison. Jefferson even praised prosecutions for seditious libel in his Second Inaugural Address: "laws [are] provided by the state against false and defamatory publications. . . . [H]e who has time, renders a service to public morals and public tranquillity, in reforming these abuses by the salutary coercions of the law." Still, the consensus of the founding generation was that attacks on government officials or policies had to be given wider scope than libels of private citizens. They therefore changed the law to allow truth to be admitted as evidence for the defense in prosecutions for anti-government libel, as long it was published with good motives and for justifiable ends.[42]

There was little controversy among the Founders about speech that is destructive to public morality. Washington's Farewell Address stated the consensus: "It is substantially true that virtue or morality is a necessary spring of popular government." For this reason, speech or conduct that tends to injure the public morals was subject to governmental control. Pornography would be treated no differently than shouting obscenities or fornicating in public. In a famous 1824 case, the Pennsylvania Supreme Court wrote: "licentiousness endangering the public peace, when tending to corrupt society, is considered as a breach of the peace, and punishable by indictment. Every immoral act is not indictable, but when it is destructive of morality generally, it is, because it weakens the bonds by which society is held together."[43]

The Founders were not bigots. It was not because they were born in a backward age that they believed libels against free government and public immorality should be punished. They believed so because they knew that the authority of all governments rests on the opinion and minimal decency of the governed. A people that does not respect the rights of others is incapable of being free. Nor can a people be free that cannot control its worst selfish or self-indulgent impulses. Of such a people, James Madison wrote in *Federalist* no. 55, "nothing less than the chains of despotism can restrain them from destroying and devouring one another."

At the foundation of the Founders' way of thinking is the belief that there is such a thing as moral truth, and that, at least for political purposes, we can know what it is. In particular, we can know the principles of justice (for example, "all men are created equal"). We can know what kind of society those principles require (representative democracy). We can know what kinds of habits and convictions are necessary for the survival of such a society (belief in the rights of mankind, and a combination of self-restraint and self-assertion). In his First Inaugural Address,

Jefferson did defend freedom of speech for those who would destroy democracy. But it was not because the law properly "recognizes no such thing as a 'false' idea" (as today's Supreme Court maintains), but because "error of opinion may be tolerated where reason is left free to combat it."[44] Jefferson was not a relativist.

Besides guaranteeing greater scope for licentious speech, government in our time has also supposedly expanded free speech by protecting (selectively) the rights of people to say whatever they wish in government-funded institutions, such as public universities. For example, a school library may not remove books from its shelves that are thought offensive. Courts have held that public university professors have a First Amendment right to complete academic freedom to write and teach whatever they wish.[45]

The courts fail to understand that as long as government funds or licenses student admissions, school libraries, and universities, it will ultimately have its way in what gets placed on the library shelf and said in the classroom. A library does not censor primarily by removing from its shelves books already bought, but in its decisions about what books to buy in the first place. Censorship of professors' ideas usually takes place in hiring and retention decisions (with suitably neutral, "professional" explanations given), not in any obvious act of punishment for something said or written. When government money or control is present, it can call the shots, no matter what sanctimonious claims courts may make about their untiring labors on behalf of free speech.

The point is not that universities should not control what its professors teach and its publications say on campus. Far from it: that is exactly what they should do. As long as most universities are free from government funding and control, they will provide the education they think best for their students. The problem is that in our time almost every university in the land, public as well as private, is subject to considerable federal and state regulation. To the extent they are, they are teaching and publishing what government wants them to teach and publish, which may not be the same as what they would choose to teach and publish on their own.

Free Speech Limited by Pervasive Government Control of Property

Probably the most powerful curb on free speech is the least discussed. Not only is it invisible to the general public. Scholars and courts seem almost completely oblivious to it.

The Founders' understanding of freedom in general, and of freedom of speech in particular, presupposed that most of the wealth of the community would be held in private hands. When government owned substantial resources, as it did in the 1790s in the territories between the Atlantic seaboard and the Mississippi, it was understood that private individuals would eventually acquire ownership of this land through homesteading or purchase. Today, over one-third of the nation's annual income is taken by government in taxes (compared to a tiny fraction of that amount in 1790). Government owns well over half the land in the Western states, and it no longer permits private owners to acquire it. Property that remains privately owned is heavily regulated by all levels of government. Businesses in particular are typically subject to regulation by multiple government agencies. Zoning boards, environmental agencies, state and federal trade commissions, consumer products commissions, and health and safety inspectors are a few of the most noteworthy.

Freedom of speech is effective only to the extent that government cannot punish a person or business who says something it disapproves of in some underhanded way, but only through trial by jury. When the tentacles of government reach so extensively into every variety of business property, government can easily create regulatory difficulties for any number of plausible reasons. Possible devices include permit delays, tax audits, allegations of health and safety violations, and investigations of unfair trade practices. Government never has to explain why a particular business was singled out for an audit, an inspection, or an investigation. To all appearances, it is merely enforcing the laws.

The California Civil Rights Initiative was a proposal to abolish racial and sexual preferences in California law. In 1995, a California businessman who had spoken out in the media in favor of the CCRI was telephoned and threatened with reprisals by a staffer in the office of the Speaker of the California Assembly, Willie Brown.

These kinds of threats seem to be most common at the local level. A businessman in Riverside County, California was threatened with reprisals from local regulatory agencies if he supported a particular candidate in the Republican primary in 1992.[46]

The more government owns, or the more it exercises de facto ownership rights over nominally private property, the less freedom individual property owners have to pay for publications advancing views that government might disapprove of. At what point does government control over private property render free speech in the Founders' sense impossible?

Notes

1. Madison, Notes for Speech in Congress 8 June 1789, *Papers of James Madison*, ed. Charles F. Hobson et al. (Charlottesville: University Press of Virginia, 1979), 12:194.

2. Wilson, Lectures on Law (1790-91), in *Works of James Wilson*, ed. Robert G. McCloskey (Cambridge: Harvard University Press, 1967), 2:649-50. Wilson, speech at Pennsylvania Ratifying Convention, 1 Dec. 1787, in Merrill Jensen, ed., *Documentary History of the Ratification of the Constitution* (Madison, WI: State Historical Society of Wisconsin, 1976-), 2:455.

3. Madison, *Virginia Report* (1799-1800), in Marvin Meyers, ed., *The Mind of the Founder: Sources of the Political Thought of James Madison*, rev. ed. (Hanover: Brandeis University Press, 1981), 258. Jefferson to Madison, 28 Aug. 1789, in Julian P. Boyd, ed., *Papers of Thomas Jefferson* (Princeton: Princeton University Press, 1950-), 15: 367.

4. Blackstone, *Commentaries on the Laws of England* (1765-69; reprint, Chicago:

University of Chicago Press, 1979), 4:152.

5. Quoted in Lucas A. Powe, Jr., *American Broadcasting and the First Amendment* (Berkeley: University of California Press, 1987), 252. Mark A. Graber, *Transforming Free Speech: The Ambiguous Legacy of Civil Libertarianism* (Berkeley: University of California Press, 1991), 233.

6. Hamilton's argument in People *v. Croswell* (New York, 1804), in Philip B. Kurland and Ralph Lerner, eds., *Amendments I-XII* , vol. 5 of *The Founders' Constitution* (Chicago: University of Chicago Press, 1987), 160-61. I have changed the court's summary of Hamilton's words to the present tense and the first person.

7. Allison R. Hayward, "Stalking the Elusive Express Advocacy Standard," *Journal of Law and Politics*, 10 (Fall 1993): 51-72.

8. *Buckley v. Valeo*, 424 U.S. 1 (1976). Geoffrey R. Stone, Louis M. Seidman, Cass R. Sunstein, and Mark V. Tushnet, *Constitutional Law* (Boston: Little, Brown, 1986), 1169.

9. David M. O'Brien, *Civil Rights and Civil Liberties*, vol. 2 of *Constitutional Law and Politics*, 2d ed. (New York: Norton, 1994). Fisher, *Constitutional Rights: Civil Rights and Civil Liberties* (New York: McGraw Hill, 1990). Leonard W. Levy et al., *The First Amendment: Selections From The Encyclopedia of the American Constitution* (New York: Macmillan, 1990), 357-63, but the Act's massive prohibition of speech is never discussed. John Marini, "Money in Politics," in Peter W. Schramm et al., ed., *The 1984 Election and the Future of American Politics* (Durham: Carolina Academic Press, 1987), 183-209, shows the connection between campaign finance regulation and the growth of the administrative state.

10. *Hustler v. Falwell*, 485 U.S. 46 (1988); *Dun & Bradstreet v. Greenmoss*, 472 U.S. 749 (1985). James MacGregor Burns et al., *Government by the People*, 15th ed. (Englewood Cliffs: Prentice Hall, 1993), 93.

11. *NLRB v. Gissel Packing Co.*, 395 U.S. 575 (1969), 617-8. I omit discussion of other New Deal restrictions on speech through the Securities and Exchange Commission and the Food and Drug Administration: Sunstein, *Democracy and the Problem of Free Speech* (New York: Free Press, 1993), 33.

12. Eugene Volokh, *Freedom of Speech and Workplace Harassment*, 39 UCLA Law Review 1793-6, 1804-5 (1992). See also Jules B. Gerard, *The First Amendment in a Hostile Environment: A Primer on Free Speech and Sexual Harassment*, 68 Notre Dame Law Review 1003 (1993).

13. Kingsley R. Browne, *Title VII as Censorship: Hostile-Environment Harassment and the First Amendment*, 52 Ohio State Law Journal 512 (1991).

14. Heather MacDonald, "Free Housing Yes, Free Speech No," *Wall Street Journal*, 8 August 1994, sec. A, p. 10. Probably as a result of this article, HUD dropped the investigation against the Berkeley couple ("HUD's Thought Police," *Wall Street Journal*, 23 August, 1994, sec. A, p. 12). Others have not been as fortunate.

15. Leonard Levy, *Emergence of a Free Press* (New York: Oxford University Press, 1993).

16. Benno C. Schmidt, Jr., "Prior Restraint and Censorship," in Levy, *First Amendment*, 246.

17. Blackstone, *Commentaries*, 4:152.

18. Thomas G. Krattenmaker and Lucas A. Powe, Jr., *Regulating Broadcast Programming* (Cambridge: MIT Press, 1994), 5-32. Jonathan W. Emord, *Freedom,*

Technology, and the First Amendment (San Francisco: Pacific Research Institute, 1991), 25-29, 137-93.

19. Frederick S. Siebert, *Freedom of the Press in England, 1476-1776: The Rise and Decline of Government Controls* (Urbana: University of Illinois Press, 1952), 71, 134, 136, 165.

20. Emord, *Freedom, Technology, and the First Amendment*, 186, quoting E. Barnouw, *The Golden Web* (1968).

21. Emord, *Freedom, Technology*, 177-80; Krattenmaker and Powe, *Regulating*, 24-7.

22. Powe, *American Broadcasting*, 109-10.

23. Powe, *American Broadcasting*, 109-11.

24. Stone, a liberal law professor, is quoted in Krattenmaker and Powe, *Regulating*, 261. Conservative economist Thomas W. Hazlett agrees: "The Fairness Doctrine and the First Amendment," *The Public Interest*, (summer 1989): 103, 109.

25. Hazlett, "Fairness Doctrine," 110-12. Powe, *American Broadcasting*, 112-117. Fred Friendly, *The Good Guys, the Bad Guys, and the First Amendment: Free Speech vs. Fairness in Broadcasting* (New York: Random House, 1976), 80-101, 28, 55, 22.

26. Friendly, *The Good Guys*, 28, 55. S. Robert Lichter et al., *The Media Elite* (Bethesda, MD: Adler & Adler, 1986), 15, 17, 55.

27. Powe, *American Broadcasting*, 121-41. Electronic media bias in the 1970s and 80s is extensively documented in L. Brent Bozell III and Brent H. Baker, ed., *And That's the Way It Isn't* (Alexandria, VA: Media Research Center, 1990), and in Lichter, *The Media Elite*.

28. Krattenmaker and Powe, *Regulating*, 65.

29. Quoted by Powe, *American Broadcasting*, 120.

30. Powe, *American Broadcasting*, 130-2, 137-8; Emord, *Freedom, Technology*, 226.

31. Emord, 222-6, quoting *Associated Press v. United States*.

32. Hazlett, "Fairness Doctrine," 104; "Ted Kennedy Killed the Post," *Wall Street Journal*, unknown date, p. A 14. Emord, *Freedom, Technology*, 227.

33. Emord, *Freedom, Technology*, 222-24.

34. Hamilton, *People v. Croswell* (1804), in Philip B. Kurland and Ralph Lerner, eds., *Amendments I-XII*, vol. 5 of *The Founders' Constitution* (Chicago: University of Chicago Press, 1987), 160.

35. Volokh, "Freedom of Speech and Workplace Harassment," 1811-12.

36. Gerry Spence, *Trial by Fire: The True Story of a Woman's Ordeal at the Hands of the Law* (New York: William Morrow, 1986), 430, 448. See Milo Geyelin, "Libel Defendants Fare Well on Appeal," *Wall Street Journal*, 31 May 1994, sec. B, p. 10: three out of four verdicts against media defendants are thrown out or reduced on appeal; judges knock most libel cases out before they even go to trial.

37. Stephen P. Halbrook, *That Every Man Be Armed: The Evolution of a Constitutional Right* (Oakland: The Independence Institute, 1990), 69, quoting "Philodemos" in Pennsylvania Gazette, May 7, 1788.

38. Spence, *Trial by Fire*, 432-3, 456-7, 476, 403.

39. Rodney A. Smolla, *Jerry Falwell v. Larry Flynt* (New York: St. Martin's, 1988), 3, 54, 62. *Hustler v. Falwell*, 485 U.S. 46 (1988).

40. Franklin, An Account of the Supremest Court of the Judicature in Pennsylvania, viz., The Court of the Press (1789), in *Writings* (New York: Library of America, 1987),

1153-4.

41. *Cohen v. California*, 403 U.S. 15 (1971).

42. House of Representatives, Majority Report on Repeal of the Sedition Act, 1799, in Leonard Levy, ed., *Freedom of the Press from Zenger to Jefferson* (Indianapolis: Bobbs, 1966), 172. Madison, *Virginia Report*, in Meyers, *Mind of the Founder*, 258. Jefferson, *Writings* (New York: Library of America, 1984), 522. Levy, *Emergence*, 340.

43. *Updegraph v. Commonwealth* (Pa. 1824), in Kurland and Lerner, *Founders' Constitution*, 5:174.

44. Jefferson, First Inaugural Address, *Writings*, 493. *Hustler v. Falwell*, 485 U.S. 46 (1988).

45. *Board of Education v. Pico*, 457 U.S. 853 (1985) (removal of books from library). *Sweezy v. New Hampshire*, 354 U.S. 234 (1957) (academic freedom identified with First Amendment).

46. The names of the businessmen referred to here are withheld. This necessity is a further example of the chilling effect of pervasive regulation of property rights on free speech.

This paper was written during my time as Ahmanson Fellow in Religion and Politics at The Claremont Institute. I thank the Institute for its support.

Chapter 12

The First Freedom Today: Church and State in Contemporary America

George Weigel

We cannot begin to think seriously about "Church and State in America today" unless we begin with "America today:" with the country and the culture in which we live. For it is only in that context that we can understand the gravity of the constitutional issues engaged by the first amendment's religion clause, two hundred-odd years after the Bill of Rights was ratified. Those issues are not legal abstractions. They touch the American people "where we live." And that is why they are so explosive.

For our purposes, the most salient fact about the country in which we live is not its diversity, its technological prowess, or its military might, but its "unsecularization." In the 1920s, the British author, G. K. Chesterton, came to the United States and visited among us for several months; coming home to Britain, he wrote of the United States as "a nation with the soul of a church." That was the 1920s, and one telling of the American story has it that Chesterton would have to write something radically different today. But that contemporary secular rendering of the American story is mistaken. The distinctive "unsecularization" of the United States that Chesterton noted continues to our own time.

Indians and Swedes

Peter Berger, our country's most distinguished sociologist of religion, once described the peculiar reality of America in these terms: On any index of intense cultural religiosity, India is the most intensely religious country in the world and Sweden is the least intensely religious; the United States, said Berger, "is a nation of Indians ruled by an elite of Swedes." The secularization hypothesis–the prediction, which often had normative or evaluative overtones, that as humanity becomes more modern, it inevitably becomes more secular or irreligious–has not been borne out in the United States. Which is to say that one of the fixed reference points, not only in much of modern sociology but indeed in much of modern intellectual life, has been, if not completely falsified, then certainly challenged by the American experience.

The basic demographic data is familiar enough. In every general social survey of the population, ninety per cent of the American people declare themselves to be religious believers. Some sixty per cent of our people belong formally to a religious organization. Between forty and fifty per cent of the American people attend a religious service at least once a week and some sixty-five per cent attend a religious service at least once a month. Twenty-five per cent of the American people tell survey researchers that they do voluntary work for a religious organization or institution in the course of the year. And last year alone, the American people gave over ninety *billion* dollars to religious organizations and religious charities.[1]

To be sure, this religiosity of the American people is vastly, even maddeningly, diverse. In some cases, religious conviction and practice are more nominal than real. But anyone who has spent time in Western Europe in the last twenty years will know immediately what I mean by the "unsecularization" of America: think about the dramatic difference in patterns of ordinary life on a Sunday morning in Western Europe and a Sunday morning in the United States. Something is *different* in the United States, in this matter of religion and modernity. And that "something different" bears directly on the way that the American people conduct themselves as a political community.

So much for the "Indians." But then there are Berger's "Swedes"–those elites who do seem to embody the truth of the secularization hypothesis as it has played itself out in the United States. These "Swedes" constitute a particularly influential minority because of their social location. For, in Peter Berger's image, much of the high ground in American culture is very, very "Swedish."

It is now broadly recognized that American higher education has been undergoing a rapid and thoroughgoing secularization over the past fifty, perhaps even eighty, years. There is no elite college or university in the United States today where a knowledge of our nation's religious history, or a passing acquaintance with the great theological traditions of the West, is a requisite for a bachelor's degree. The Congregationalist founders of Harvard and Yale would find this odd; so would the Methodists who launched Syracuse and the University of Southern California.[2]

Then there is the fourth estate. The prestige press, which plays such a large role in American public life, is overwhelmingly secular, not only in its cast of mind, but in the personal practices of its key figures. I have spent considerable time over the past several years trying to help national political reporters, columnists, and editors at the *Washington Post* understand better the relationship between religious conviction and political debate in the United States. And while I find considerable openness there, I also find extraordinary ignorance: an ignorance based not so much on malice as on social location. These highly-educated, competitive, astute, and thoroughly secular professionals just don't know very many intensely religious people–and still less any religious intellectuals. Their's is, if you'll allow me the phrase, an ignorance-based ignorance.

But just think about that a moment: senior reporters, editors, and columnists at the most influential political newspaper in the United States simply don't know religious people. They don't associate with them socially. They don't live in neighborhoods where Saturday and Sunday are days of great churning in religious communities. They live in a kind of secular ghetto, and that fact inevitably frames the way they think and write about public life. Only in recent years, when it has become apparent that no serious professional journalist could ignore the interplay of religion and electoral politics, have *Post* reporters and editors been willing to step gingerly outside their ghetto and have a look at the wider world around them.

The popular entertainment industry in our country is another "Swedish" bunker. Think about (if you can bear to think about!) prime-time situation comedies in the United States over the last twenty years. I think you will find that in only one instance, *The Cosby Show*, did you see a family regularly portrayed as doing what half of America does every weekend–go to church. When was the last time you saw anyone go to church in America–that is, between 8 p.m. and 11 p.m. on network television on Sunday, Monday, Tuesday, Wednesday, Thursday, Friday, or Saturday night? And to note that dramatic lacuna does not even begin to plumb the depths of awfulness by which the film industry regularly mocks the convictions and behavior of orthodox religious believers. When Disney manages to turn "The Hunchback of Notre Dame" into an anti-Christian tract, we may begin to get some idea how widely this particular virus–the virus of militantly anti-religious secularism–has spread.[3]

So in three of the great transmission belts of ideas and values in our societies–in the academy, in the prestige press, and in the popular entertainment industry–there is an inversion or reversal of the situation in the country as a whole: in these social locations, we see the secularization hypothesis confirmed. Which is to say that in these institutions–the institutions charged in some fashion with the responsibility of explaining America to Americans–we see an indifference, and in some instances a hostility, to one of the fundamental characteristics of the American people: the fact that the American people as a whole remain open to, and indeed enthusiastically engaged with, a host of religious practices. Much of the agitation in our culture that is sometimes referred to as the "American culture war" is attributable to this chasm between elite America and the mass of the American people, and to the impact of these secularized cultural institutions on our politics and our public life.

The Supremes

But however much we ought to challenge the indifference of higher education and the press to religious practice, religious conviction, and religious thought, and however much we ought to criticize the entertainment industry for its deprecatory attitudes towards the faiths of the American people, the hard fact remains that the most important secularist bunker in America today is the U.S. Supreme Court. And here we come directly to the question of the First Amendment: the question of Church and State in America today.

That part of the First Amendment relevant to our concerns reads as follows. "Congress shall make no law concerning an establishment of religion or prohibiting the free exercise thereof." Read at face value, that statement would seem to mean two things. First, the Framers of the Constitution and the Congress that passed the Bill of Rights intended that there be no national church; thus the relationship between religious institutions and the national government in the new United States would be different than the relationship that had obtained in Mother England since time immemorial. (Interestingly enough, the Bill of Rights as originally crafted did not proscribe religious "establishments" in the states, and it is a matter of historical record that several of the states maintained established churches well into the nineteenth century. But it does seem clear that the "original intention" of the Framers and the First Amendment was that there be no national church.)

The second thing that seems to have been intended by those sixteen pregnant words–"Congress shall make no law concerning an establishment of religion or prohibiting the free exercise thereof"–is the free, vigorous, and public exercise of religious conviction. Why? Because the Framers believed that free exercise was a good in itself; moreover, they believed that free exercise of religion was good for society and good for democracy. That is why the Framers proscribed a national church: because it was bad for the free exercise of religion, and what was bad for the free exercise of religion was bad for democracy. "No establishment" serves the end of "free exercise."

The logic and language of the First Amendment itself, as well as the original intention of the Framers, tell us that we do not have two "religion clauses"–the language regularly heard in our courts and in the press today. As such distinguished legal scholars as Prof. Mary Ann Glendon of the Harvard Law School and Prof. Michael McConnell of the University of Chicago Law School have argued (from academic redoubts not noted for their piety, I might add) that there is only one "religion clause," containing two provisions. The First Amendment contains a "freedom of religion clause" in which there is a free exercise provision and a no establishment provision. There are not two "religion clauses" whose interests must be "balanced." The constitutional goal is the free exercise of religious conviction, and no establishment is one means ordained to that end. That is the understanding–quite old, but in our circumstances likely to seem new–that I would like to put before you: no establishment in the service of free exercise.[4]

Over the past fifty years, since its *Everson* decision in 1947, a series of Supreme Court decisions has made a hash out of the Framers' intention. The Court first discovered that there were two "religion clauses" in the First Amendment. Then, for some twenty-five years, the Court tried to "balance" these two clauses, not tilting too heavily towards no establishment, not tilting too heavily towards free exercise. Finally, in the past ten to fifteen years, the Supreme Court has inverted the Framers' original intention, such that the constitutional *goal* has become no establishment, with the free exercise of religion understood as something to be tolerated for so long as it doesn't get in the way of no establishment.[5]

In 1978, for example, a widely-used constitutional law textbook authored by Prof. Lawrence Tribe of Harvard described in the First Amendment a "zone of accommodation" that free exercise "carves out" of no establishment. A "zone . . . for [the] permissible accommodation of religious interests:" that is Prof. Tribe's description of the free exercise of religion.[6] To which I have to say, and I think tens of millions of Americans would have to say, "I'm sorry. We're not here to be accommodated. And we refuse to live in some 'zone of permissible accommodation' while being required to check our deepest convictions at the door before we enter the public square of American political life."

The "two religion clauses" model is not only a tendentious reading of the Constitution which makes little historical (or grammatical) sense. Precisely because it is deeply flawed as an idea, it has tied the court up in jurisprudential knots of extraordinary thickness. Perhaps my favorite example is a decision in the early 1970s in which the Court allowed that religious schools could receive some modest federal assistance for the purchase of textbooks, but could not receive federal aid for purchasing "instructional materials," such as maps. To which Daniel Patrick Moynihan acidly replied, at the time, "The court has yet to rule on atlases, which are books of maps."

This is the kind of confusion that is created when you take what was clearly intended to be a single, comprehensive, constitutional provision for religious freedom and turn it on its head: first, by separating free exercise and no establishment; then, by trying to balance the two; and finally, by raising up one "clause" such that the other is relegated to a "zone of permissible accommodation."

The Pathologies of Belief

To grasp the degree to which a virulent form of the secularist virus has infected the Supreme Court's religion clause jurisprudence during the past several decades, we have to look, not simply at what the justices have decided, but what the Supreme Court thinks it is that it is making its decisions about. Which is to say that we have to read these decisions and see how the Court describes religious conviction and practice. And there we find some quite extraordinary statements which illustrate how (to return to Peter Berger's image) an extreme "Swedish" perspective has dominated the Court's thinking about behavior among the "Indians."[7]

According to several justices of the Supreme Court, writing over the past four years, religion has four primary characteristics. In *Lee v. Weisman*, a 1992 decision, Justices Kennedy and Blackmun said that religion is "inherently divisive," and that any public manifestation of religion threatens the civil order. In *Grumet v. Board of Education of Kiryas Joel* in 1994, Justice John Paul Stevens upped the ante by saying that religion is "inherently coercive," "authoritarian," and "vaguely undemocratic" in its public manifestations. Stevens, in the same case, went so far as to find it "disturbing" that parents should be constitutionally enabled to transmit their religious faith to their children. That, in Justice Stevens' considered opinion, constituted a serious constitutional problem.

The Justices are also given to portraying religion as irrational and vaguely crazy, a phenomenon with no intellectual seriousness to it. On this reading of things, religious conviction is something quirky, like rooting for the New York Yankees, that ought to be tolerated for the sake of civil order, but that does not really engage our intelligence. Thus Justice Blackmun in *Lee v. Weisman* contrasted rational debate, on the one hand, and "theological decree," on the other hand–the clear implication being that theology is an irrational exercise and that religious life has no serious intellectual component to it. (Thomas Aquinas and John Calvin, please call the Supreme Court.)

Finally, and in the fourth place, the Justices regularly describe religious conviction as being devoid of any enduring substantive core. Religious conviction, on this reading of it, is fungible in all of its characteristics, a kind of lifestyle preference (much like parakeet-keeping and vegetarianism), but certainly not the life-long and life-forming commitment that most of the American people imagine it to be.

So: a divisive and coercive phenomenon, a bit pathological, devoid of real content and marginal in its impact on individual's lives–that is what the Supreme Court seems to think it is adjudicating when it considers the place of religion in public life.

In February 1995, to bring all of this to a particularly sharp edge, Justice David Souter complained that a student Christian publication at the University of Virginia, a publicly funded institution, had been "proselytizing." To which the students' lawyer, Prof. Michael McConnell, replied, "'Proselytizing' is nothing but an ugly word for persuading." Which is exactly what the free speech clause of the constitution is designed to protect. So we now find ourselves in an even graver situation than we might have imagined: for in dealing with religion, the Justices not only think that they are addressing an inherently divisive, coercive, and irrational phenomenon; in their passion to drive religious conviction and religious practice out of the public square, the Justices are quite prepared to put such other basic constitutional guarantees as freedom of speech in jeopardy.

Now, any serious religious person in America–Christian, Jewish, Muslim, whatever—would admit, and should admit, that some forms of religious expression and practice are coercive, some are divisive, some can be irrational. But to dismiss all religious conviction and its impact on American life today in those deprecatory terms is, to put it bluntly, a grotesque caricature and a serious act of discrimination against the overwhelming majority of the American people.

Why We Can Get Along

Moreover, to indulge in that deprecatory attitude and that discrimination is to ignore a crucial fact of contemporary public life: namely, that, for the overwhelming majority of the American people, religious tolerance is a function of *religious* conviction. As Richard John Neuhaus has put it, the majority of the American people believe it to be the will of God that we not take up arms against each other over our differences as to what constitutes the will of God.[8]

Religious tolerance, *religiously* grounded: what an important thing that is. Imagine what would happen if religious toleration in this vast and diverse society of ours–which will only become more diverse in the foreseeable future–were merely a pragmatic bargain. Imagine what would happen if Americans were to say, "Look, this is simply the arrangement that causes the least hassle; we'll be tolerant of others' religious convictions because it's just easier to live that way." That is a very, very thin foundation on which to build a public culture capable of handling the engagement of genuine religious differences, and the passions attendant on great differences. If, on the other hand, people of religious faith believe that it is the will of God that they be tolerant of others who have different theological convictions, then religious tolerance rests on much more secure ground. Pluralism then becomes a genuine cultural accomplishment, rooted in a people's most deeply-held convictions. In my judgment, the Supreme Court has been wholly ignorant of this crucial fact–the *religious* grounding of religious tolerance, or religion as a *source* of civility in America–in recent years. And its ignorance has caused the Court to attempt the further marginalization of that which, for most Americans, legitimates the tolerance and civility the Justices claim to be defending.

Departments of Trouble-Making

The problems caused by the Court have metastasized far beyond the legal system. For the Court has created a set of assumptions in federal and state bureaucracies, such that any public manifestation of religious conviction is thought to constitute a violation of no establishment (rather than being understood as an expression of free exercise). In Prince William County in the state of Virginia, just south of where I live, a woman recently had to take her daughter out of the public schools after the principal had barred her daughter from reading the Bible on the school bus. This, somehow, was thought to constitute a violation of no establishment.

In the Alaska public schools today, students are prohibited from using the word "Christmas" at school, from exchanging Christmas cards or presents, or from displaying anything with the word "Christmas" on it–because the word "Christ" is contained in the word "Christmas." In California, Internal Revenue Service (IRS) workers were ordered several years ago to keep items "which would be considered intrusive" off their desks and out of sight, so as not to offend fellow workers. What were the examples used of intrusive and offensive items? "Religious symbols and sexually suggestive cartoons or calendars."[9] Which seems to suggest that the IRS thinks a cross or a star of David is as offensive as a Playboy pinup calendar.

But my favorite example of the degree to which the regulators have gotten completely out of control, thanks to the warped religion clause jurisprudence of the Supreme Court, comes from the Roman Catholic archdiocese of Los Angeles. The archdiocese operates a series of shelters for homeless people, including the largest shelter in Los Angeles County. These shelters received a modest amount of money from the U.S. Department of Housing and Urban Development for beds, blankets, and so forth. About ten years ago, the archdiocese received a letter from someone I shall describe as the deputy assistant secretary for troublemaking at the Department of Housing and Urban Development. The letter went on at some length about how gratified the Department was that the archdiocese was doing this great public service, and how pleased the Department was to be able to provide a modest amount of funding for blankets and cots. But in order not to create First Amendment problems, would it be possible for the archdiocese to change the name of the shelter from the St. Vincent de Paul Shelter to the Mr. Vincent de Paul Shelter?[10]

We laugh, but this is madness. And it poses a serious threat to American democracy by rendering suspect the moral legitimacy of the rule of law.

The Integrity of Faith

This attempt to create a secularized public square in America–this determination to enforce secularism as the officially-sanctioned national ideology–is the essential background for understanding the rise of the Religious Right in America today. Whatever else it has or has not done, the Religious Right in America has alerted the entire country to the fact that something is seriously wrong with the courts, with the federal regulatory apparatus, and indeed with the condition of religious freedom in America today. In the name of no establishment of religion, an ideology is in fact being "established" in the United States of America: an aggressively secular ideology which will allow no room for the most deeply-held convictions of the overwhelming majority of the American people in the American public square.[11]

The rise of religious conservatism in America should thus be understood as an "defensive offensive," as Harvard sociologist Nathan Glazer has put it.[12] The Religious Right began as a defensive movement by people long accustomed to living on the fringes of our public life, but forced onto the offensive when it became clear that they were not going to be let alone any longer. Whatever else it has or has not accomplished, then, the Religious Right has started a useful and welcome debate on the relationship between religious conviction and public life in our country today.

That debate has begun to have effects beyond the worlds of religious conservatism where it originated. It has, in fact, made a difference in liberal circles. Concern about officially-sanctioned and officially-enforced secularism is not a phenomenon limited to the conservative world. Yale Law professor Stephen Carter's much-discussed book of several years ago, *The Culture of Disbelief*,[13] was a plea from a self-identified liberal, Democratic, African-American, Ivy-league law professor, who is also a devout Episcopalian, to his fellow political theorists and lawyers to think again about what it means to drive religiously grounded moral argument from public life and to ban all religious symbols and all religious practice from our common life as a political community. I don't happen to think that Prof. Carter's constitutional prescription (which is something on the order of "maximum feasible accommodation" of religion in public life) is adequate. But the fact that he even made the argument against established secularism is a sign that this issue is not limited to a certain fevered section of American conservatism.

President Clinton should also be given credit for having his Department of Education write every school board in the country, instructing them against some of the ridiculous practices I described a moment ago—such as forbidding the reading of a Bible on a school bus as an infringement of no establishment, a *diktat* of which Stalinists would be proud.

Thus there is a sense across the political spectrum that something has gone considerably awry here. Moreover, and to turn the issue on its side for a moment, the rise of the religious right has not been without its shadow dimensions. If the threat posed by the Supreme Court is the attempt to establish secularism as the official national ideology, the problem posed by the religious right is the politicization of religion–turning religious conviction into a partisan program.

This is problematic, not primarily on constitutional or political grounds, but on theological grounds. The constitutional order is not jeopardized when a legislator invokes the Bible in defense of his public policy judgments. But the integrity of religious conviction may be.

I think it demeans Jewish and Christian religious conviction to suggest that the Hebrew Bible or the sayings of Jesus transmit detailed instructions about marginal tax rates, social security funding, welfare reform, or the efficacy of building the superconducting supercollider. It demeans the message of Judaism and Christianity to suggest that Jews and Christians have been given divine instructions on the minutiae of public policy. We haven't. What we have been given is a vision of the human person, an understanding of human community, and a model of human destiny which constitutes the horizon of moral conviction against which we are meant to apply the resources of our reason to the doing of the public business. But there is certainly not a Christian position, as some of my friends at the Christian Coalition suggested there was three years ago, on whether the delegate from Guam should have a vote in the Committee of the Whole in the U.S. House of Representatives. Jesus did not leave us any instructions about Guam in any New Testament text that I'm familiar with.[14]

The Restoration of Democracy

Now: what to do about all of this? What might be suggested by way of a remedy to the judicially-enforced secularization of America and the attendant loss of religious freedom? I should like to suggest two lines of redress, one constitutional, the other, cultural.

We do need a constitutional remedy for the dangerous mess that the Supreme Court has made of the First Amendment religion clause over the past fifty-odd years. I am a conservative by political disposition, which means that I don't like amending the Constitution. But the Court's religion clause jurisprudence has gotten so completely out of control, and the likelihood of the Court repairing its own damage seems so remote, that I think an amendment is in order. The amendment that I would favor is that being offered by Congressman Henry Hyde of Illinois, which is known as the Religious Equality Amendment and reads as follows:

> Neither the United States, nor any state, shall deny benefits to or otherwise discriminate against any private person or group on account of religious expression, belief, or identity. Nor shall the prohibition on laws respecting an establishment of religion be construed to require such discrimination.

That strikes me as a sensible, moderate, and necessary addition to our constitutional structure. It creates a level playing field once again in American public life. It makes it possible to recreate a civil public square rather than a religiously naked public square. It allows us to engage our differences rather than ignore those differences. And it does not require the state, in the form of the United States government or any of the several state governments, to become a theological actor. That, as well as state-sanctioned and state-enforced secularism, is what has to be avoided.

The Religious Equality Amendment carefully avoids the danger of creating a theologically-active state. The state is theologically incompetent: a judgment confirmed by classic American political theory and by American political experience. It is simply not the business of the state of Maryland or the state of Texas to write prayers. It *is* the business of the state of Maryland and the state of Texas and the government of the United States to protect the right of American citizens to freely and non-coercively express their religious conviction through prayer–and in public space, if that is what they so choose to do.

But the constitutional remedy does not completely solve the problem. The necessary complement to constitutional reform is cultural reform: the rededication of religious people to self-discipline in public life. If the goal is to create, not a sacred public square but a civil public square, the Religious Equality Amendment (or something like it) must be complemented by a new self-discipline on the part of religious believers and religious organizations, who must recognize that the civil public square has its own distinctive identity and etiquette.[15] Religious people must commit themselves to developing a genuinely public discourse that allows all

Americans, of whatever religious convictions or of no religious conviction, to share in the public debate over our common life. And religious people must avoid aggressively confrontational approaches to evangelization, because such approaches do damage to the cause of religion itself.

What kind of America would we have if we had a constitutional remedy like the Religious Equality Amendment in place? What kind of America would we have if religious believers acted in the self-disciplined fashion that I have just described? We would have an America that was feisty, loud, pluralist, contentious, sometimes confused, sometimes noble. In a word, we would have, once again, a democratic America.

That is what we have lost. That is what we must regain.

Notes

1. For some of the recent survey data, see Richard John Neuhaus, ed. *Unsecular America* (Grand Rapids, MI: Eerdmans, 1986), 115-26.

2. See George M. Marsden, *The Soul of the American University: From Protestant Establishment to Established Nonbelief* (New York: Oxford University Press, 1994).

3. See James Bowman, "Disney's Mickey-Mouse Religion," *The Weekly Standard,* 1 July 1996, 41.

4. See Mary Ann Glendon and Raul F. Yanas, *Structural Free Exercise*, 90 Michigan Law Review 477 (December 1991).

5. Terry Eastland, ed., *Religious Liberty in the Supreme Court* (Grand Rapids, MI: Eerdmans, 1993), 1-10.

6. Laurence Tribe, *American Constitutional Law* (Mineola, NY: The Foundation Press, 1978), 823.

7. In what follows, I am indebted to the analyses of Russell Hittinger in "The Supreme Court v. Religion," *Crisis*, May 1993, 22-30.

8. See Richard John Neuhaus, "What the Fundamentalists Want," *Commentary*, May 1985, 43.

9. House Committee on the Judiciary, *Incidents of Limitations on Religious Liberties,* report compiled by staff of the Hon. Henry J. Hyde, 104th Cong., 1st sess., November 1995.

10. George Weigel, *Catholicism and the Renewal of American Democracy* (Mahwah, NJ: Paulist Press, 1989), 213 n. 8.

11. Cf. Richard John Neuhaus, *The Naked Public Square: Religion and Democracy in America* (Grand Rapids, MI: Eerdmans, 1984).

12. "Fundamentalism: A Defensive Offensive," in Richard John Neuhaus and Michael Cromartie, eds., *Piety and Politics: Evangelicals and Fundamentalists Confront the World* (Washington, DC: Ethics & Public Policy Center, 1987).

13. Stephen L. Carter, *The Culture of Disbelief* (New York: Basic Books, 1993).

14. Cf. "Christian Conviction and Democratic Etiquette," in George Weigel, *Soul of the World* (Grand Rapids, MI: Eerdmans, 1996), 65-82.

15. Cf. ibid.

Chapter 13

How High The Wall?: American Jews and the Church-State Debate

David G. Dalin

Introduction

Since the 1940s, at least, most American Jews have conceived of religion and public life as being rigidly separate arenas. They have been, for the most part, strict separationists, committed to the proposition that the First Amendment was intended to erect a high and impregnable–an absolute–wall of separation between church and state. According to the prevailing liberal Jewish consensus, its often assumed that Jewish survival and religious freedom are most secure where the wall separating church and state is strongest and least secure where government and religion are intertwined.

For several decades, Leo Pfeffer, one of America's foremost scholars of church-state relations, was the preeminent Jewish spokesman for this strict separationist position. Pfeffer, for many years staff attorney and director of the American Jewish Congress' Commission on Law and Social Action, argued more church-state cases before the United States Supreme Court than any other person in American history, and did more than anyone else to shape and further the legal doctrine of church-state separationism.[1] Indeed, it has been widely recognized that Pfeffer's major books, such as *Church, State, and Freedom* and *God, Caesar and the Constitution,* as well as his numerous articles and legal briefs, constitute the most "polished expression" of the strict separationist constitutional position. Moreover, during his forty-year association with the Commission on Social Action, Pfeffer was instrumental in formulating and planning Jewish communal policy on issues of religion and state, and was the "guiding spirit" of Jewish litigation in this area.

The text at the heart of the church-state debate within the American Jewish community is, of course, found in the first part of the First Amendment to the Constitution, which is traditionally divided into two clauses, the Establishment Clause and the Free Exercise Clause: "Congress shall make no law respecting an establishment of religion, or prohibiting the free exercise thereof."

Instead of embracing the "narrow" interpretation of the Establishment Clause, Pfeffer and most other Jewish leaders consistently embrace the "broad interpretation" of the Establishment Clause espoused by the Supreme Court in its famous *Everson v. Board of Education of Ewing Township* decision of 1947, wherein it claimed, quoting the words of Thomas Jefferson, that the Establishment Clause "was intended to erect a 'wall of separation between church and state.'" Speaking for the majority in the *Everson* case, Justice Hugo Black stated the "broad interpretation" of the Establishment Clause, in a famous–indeed, now classic–statement–that is frequently cited by Jewish proponents of the strict separationist position, and that reads (in part) as follows:

> The "establishment of religion" clause of the First Amendment (said Black) means at least this: Neither a state nor the Federal Government can set up a church. Neither can pass laws which aid one religion, aid all religions, or prefer one religion over another. Neither can force or influence a person to . . . profess a belief or disbelief in any religion . . . No tax in any amount, large or small, can be levied to support any religious activities or institutions, whatever they may be called, or whatever form they may adopt to teach or practice religion. Neither a state nor the Federal Government can, openly or secretly, participate in the affairs of any religious organizations or groups and vice versa. In the words of Thomas Jefferson (concluded Justice Black) the clause against the Establishment of Religion . . . was intended to erect a "wall of separation between Church and State."[2]

Pfeffer and his fellow strict separationists within the Jewish community (as within other religious groups in America), who embrace this "broad interpretation," believe (with Justice Black) that the "intent" of the First Amendment is not merely to prevent the "establishment" of a state church, but preclude government aid to any and all religious groups or dogmas. In addition, as Pfeffer argued in *Church, State and Freedom*, any and all government support for, or involvement with religion, "even on a nonpreferential basis," violates the Establishment Clause and is thus unconstitutional.[3] Reasoning that the establishment clause, broadly interpreted, was the best guarantor of both religious freedom and religious equality, they shared Pfeffer's oft-quoted assumption that the Establishment and Free Exercise clauses of the First Amendment were "two sides of the same," or (as it were) two separate clauses, expressing the principle "that (religious) freedom requires separation," and that the non-establishment of religion is an end unto itself, guaranteed by the First Amendment.

Beginning in 1948 with the landmark Supreme Court case of *McCollum v. Board of Education,*[4] which ruled that released time-programs that used public school classrooms for religious instruction during regular school hours were unconstitutional, Pfeffer led an unrelenting fight against prayer and religious instruction in the public schools, state aid to parochial schools, tax exemptions for churches and synagogues, and the presence of any and all religious symbols in American public life. In the 1948 case, the McCollums challenged the constitutionality of a released-time program that used public-school classrooms for religious instruction during regular school hours. Pfeffer supported their challenge in a "friend of the court" brief on behalf of the Synagogue Council of America (an umbrella organization representing Orthodox, Conservative and Reform rabbinic and congregational groups) and the National Jewish Community Relations Advisory Council (NJCRAC), which represents a wide spectrum of Jewish community relations agencies, including the American Jewish Congress, the American Jewish Committee, and the Anti-Defamation League of B'nai B'rith.

The decision of the court in the *McCollum* case was that such released time programs were unconstitutional. A month after this decision, the Synagogue Council of America and NJCRAC formed a Joint Committee on Religion and the Public School (later the Joint Advisory Committee on Religion and State) which, under Pfeffer's astute guidance, formulated public statements and drafted legal briefs in opposition to released and shared time, government support for private religious schools, prayer, Bible reading and religious observances in the public schools and the teaching of religion under the guise of "moral and spiritual values."

Like other immigrant Jews of his generation, Pfeffer had been taught by both Jewish history and his own experience to embrace strict separationism as the only defense against what they perceived to be a Christian-dominated state. For these strict separationists–and the vast majority of American Jews until the 1980s were strict separationists–it became axiomatic that any religious influence in the public institutions of Christian America impinged upon the full citizenship of Jews. Only strict separation, they believed, could ensure the kind of free society and political climate wherein Jews, and Judaism, could flourish.

Pfeffer's view that "complete separation of church and state is best for the church and best for the state, and secures freedoms for both" seemed to most American Jews to be logically consistent and historically convincing. When the Supreme Court in *Engal v. Vitale* (1962) and *Abington Township School District v. Schempp* (1963), outlawed state-composed prayers and state-sponsored Bible reading in the public schools, the overwhelming majority of American Jews applauded these decisions. Pfeffer proudly asserted in a 1966 address to the Joint Advisory Committee, "our absolutist policy has now become the supreme law of the land through a series of decisions to which our test cases, briefs and other writing contributed substantially."

And yet, it's important to remember, that the separationist position did not go unchallenged, in the Jewish community, even in its heyday. In articles published during the 1950s and 1960s, the Jewish theologian and religious thinker Will Herberg–the author of *Protestant, Catholic, Jew* and other important books–began to call for a reassessment of the prevailing Jewish consensus that religion should play no role in American public life. The authors of the Constitution never intended to erect a "wall of separation," said Herberg. The Establishment Clause of the First Amendment had been profoundly misunderstood: although the Founding Fathers did not want to favor any single religion, they were not against helping all religions, or all religion, equally. In drafting the Establishment Clause, they merely intended to prohibit the designation or establishment of any church as an official state or "national" one, and to prevent "a preference of any one religious sect or denomination" over others. "Neither in the minds of the Founding Fathers nor in the thinking of the American people through the nineteenth and twentieth century," wrote Herberg, "did the doctrine of the First Amendment ever imply an ironclad ban forbidding the government to take account of religion or to support its various activities."[5]

Herberg was especially vocal in his criticism of liberal American Jews and their insistence that religion be rigidly distinct from public life. In several articles published during the 1950s and 1960s, Herberg urged the liberal Jewish "establishment" to reassess their position. "The American Jew must have sufficient confidence in the capacity of democracy to preserve its pluralistic . . . character without any "absolute" wall of separation between religion and public life," he wrote in 1952.[6] Eleven years later, frustrated by liberal Jewish support for the 1963 Supreme Court decision banning Bible reading and recitation of the Lord's Prayer in the public schools, Herberg entered a plea for the restoration of religion to a place of honor in American public life. Writing in *National Review* he said:

> Within the meaning of our political tradition and political practice, the promotion [of religion] has been, and continues to be, a part of the very legitimate "secular" purpose of the state. Whatever the "neutrality" of the state in matters of religion may be, it cannot be a neutrality between religion and no-religion, any more than . . . It could be a neutrality between morality and no-morality, . . . [both religion and morality being] as necessary to "good government" as "national prosperity."[7]

"The traditional symbols of the divine presence in our public life," Herberg warned, "ought not to be tampered with."[8]

During the 1960s and 1970s, other prominent Jewish thinkers, such as Milton Himmelfarb, Irving Kristol, and Rabbi Seymoujr Siegel, began to eschew their earlier liberal faith in separationism, and to develop a strong Jewish conservative argument for the desirability of greater religious involvement in American public life. While supporting state aid to parochial schools and questioning Jewish opposition to some forms of public school prayer, they (like Herberg) called for an abandonment of the Jewish separationist agenda in favor of a more pro-religion stance. Thus, writing in *Commentary* in 1966 on the subject of public aid to parochial schools, Himmelfarb argued:

> It is not true that freedom is most secure where church and state are separated . . . Separationism is potentially tyrannical. . . . It is harsh to those who prefer non-public schools for conscience sake; and it stands in the way of a more important good (and more important safeguard of Jewish security), the best possible education for all . . . It is time that we [American Jews] actually weighed the utility and cost of education against the utility and cost of separationism. All the evidence points to education, more than anything else, influencing adherence to democracy and equalitarianism. All the evidence points to Catholic parochial education having the same influence. . . Something that nurtures a humane, liberal democracy is rather more important to Jews than twenty-four carat separationism.[9]

During the 1970s and 1980s, a Jewish neoconservative consensus began to emerge concerning the proper relationship between religion and politics, and the role of religious and moral values in shaping American public life. Himmelfarb, Siegel, Irving Kristol, and Murray Friedman, among others, all persuasively warned that an American moral and political culture uninformed by religious beliefs and institutions undermined the position of Jews and Judaism, and the health of a democratic society.

One issue that forced a reexamination of the separationist hegemony for many Jews was whether the government should give aid to parochial schools. Prior to the 1950s, the issue of government aid to parochial schools, even when addressed by the U. S. Supreme Court, generated little interest or debate within the Jewish community. Thus, for example, the landmark case of *Pierce v. Society of the Sisters of the Holy Names of Jesus and Mary* (1925), in which the Supreme Court ruled unconstitutional a Ku Klux Klan-sponsored anti-Catholic Oregon law that sought to require all parents to send their children to public schools, did not seem to affect the majority of American Jews directly.[10] Nor did the Supreme Court's ruling in the 1930 case of *Cochran v. Louisiana State Board of Education*, which permitted the State of Louisiana to lend secular textbooks to schoolchildren who attended parochial schools. Yet, Louis Marshall, a renowned constitutional lawyer and one of the leading Jewish communal leaders of the era, who represented the American Jewish Committee in its *amicus curiae* brief opposing Oregon's public-school law, enunciated a basic principle–the right of parents to control the education of their children and to send them to private schools–that, as Jonathan D. Sarna has noted, "made all subsequent debate possible."[11] Attacking as "an invasion of liberty" any effort to make public schools "the only medium of education in this country," Marshall pointed out that private schools could in many cases accomplish what public schools could not – including "religious instruction, the importance of which cannot be minimized."[12]

The growth of parochial schools, Catholic and Jewish alike, during the 1940s and 1950s, coupled with heightened national concern over the quality of primary education, led to renewed pressure on behalf of state and federal measures to grant limited assistance to parochial schools on the basis of the "child benefit theory," the idea, supported by the Supreme Court in its *Chochran v. Louisiana State Board of Education* decision, that state aid could be extended to parochial-school children so long as "the school children and the state alone are the beneficiaries."[13] In the aftermath of the Supreme Court's historic *Everson v. Board of Education of Ewing Township* 1947 ruling, which permitted states to fund the cost of transporting students to parochial schools, leading Jewish organizations and religious denominations, including the Orthodox, united behind the 1948 Synagogue Council of America-NCRAC policy statement broadly opposing all government aid to parochial schools.[14]

Beginning in the 1950s, however, demands for a reassessment of this Jewish communal policy of opposition to government support for parochial schools were increasingly heard within the American Jewish community. In 1962, the *American Jewish Year Book*, reviewing the events of the previous year, pointed out that "unexpectedly strong support for the Catholic position [favoring state aid to parochial schools] appeared within the Jewish community, especially among the Orthodox."[15] As the number of Jewish parochial schools began to proliferate during the 1950s and 1960s, Orthodox Jews abandoned their earlier opposition to state aid to parochial schools in the hope of obtaining funds for their own Jewish religious schools. They began to argue, as Catholics had before them, that education in a religious setting benefited not only members of their own faith, but also the nation as a whole, and that money used to support secular studies at these schools should not be denied because the schools happened to teach religious subjects on the side.[16] As more and more private Jewish parochial schools were established during the 1970s and 1980s, and as the costs of parochial school education continued to escalate, a growing number of Jewish religious leaders and intellectuals, began to recognize the "justice" of the Catholic claim to public support of parochial schools, whether in the form of textbooks, bus transportation and school lunches, or proposals for tax credits and vouchers. "In principle," as Herberg put it, "there is no reason why the religious school should be barred from governmental support because of what is said or implied in the First Amendment." In 1965, when Congress debated the Elementary and Secondary Education Act, which proposed to extend $2.3 billion dollars in federal aid to the nations' elementary and secondary schools, Rabbi Moshe Sherer testified before Congress in support of financial aid to private and parochial schools. Sherer, the executive vice-president of Agudath Israel of America, argued that Jewish day schools faced "extremely difficult financial circumstances," and that denial of tax aid to these schools would constitute "a discrimination which is not in accordance with basic American ideals." He vigorously urged the extension of federal aid to the 251 Orthodox elementary and secondary religious schools he represented.[17] He was soon joined by representatives of other Orthodox religious groups, such as the National Council of Young Israel and the Jewish Day School Organization, Torah Umesorah. Even more surprisingly, aid to parochial schools was "simultaneously endorsed" by a leading Conservative Jewish lay leader, Charles H. Silver, who was also at the time president of the New

York City Board of Education.[18]

Throughout the 1970s, 1980s and early 1990s, the growth of Jewish day schools outside the Orthodox community prompted some Conservative and Reform rabbis and educators also to rethink their earlier opposition to state aid. "The time has come," argued Rabbi Seymour Siegel of the Jewish Theological Seminary in 1970, in an argument that he (and others) would reiterate many times over the following two decades, "for the Jewish community to revise its stand . . . and to support the public officials who are in favor of state aid to all schools, including parochial schools, day schools and yeshivoth":

> There is more and more realization in the Conservative movement that the strengthening of the Day School movement is essential for the maintenance of religious life. Even the Reform movement, once positively antagonistic, seems to be opening such schools, recognizing that they are vital to Jewish survival. So Jewish parents are now more sympathetic to the plight of Catholic parents. They have been complaining that without government aid for their parochial schools they are carrying a double load of taxation and that the special financial burden of supporting children in church-related institutions constitutes, in effect, a threat to their religious freedom.[19]

As Jewish parochial school tuition has increased enormously in recent years, government support for private religious schools, in the form of tax credits and vouchers, has emerged as a public policy alternative that more and more Jewish leaders have begun to support.[20]

Jewish critics of the Jewish strict separationist position have frequently pointed out that the American Jewish community's commitment to separationism has never been absolute. On the contrary: At the beginning of the Civil War, Jews in America, as a community, fought for the right of rabbis to serve with priests and ministers as chaplains in the armed forces.[21] Today, American Jews take it for granted that rabbis can and should serve as military chaplains, whose salaries are paid by the United States government. American Jews also take it for granted that rabbis, together with priests and ministers, are invited to give prayers or benedictions at the opening of both houses of Congress and sessions of our state legislatures, and at our Presidential inaugurations. They would protest vigorously if this tradition were ever abrogated. American Jews, like American Protestants and Catholics, never complained when the words "Under God" were added to the pledge of allegiance during the 1950s, not did they object to the fact that the words "in God We Trust" are on our currency. Moreover, despite their commitment to separationism in other areas, American Jews (with few exceptions) have staunchly opposed legal efforts to challenge the constitutionality of tax exemptions for churches and synagogues. Most American Jewish leaders have, for several decades, consistently favored tax exemptions, some arguing, in fact, that to deny them would infringe upon the religious freedom of all religious groups. Such support for tax exemption is, of course, not surprising. Synagogues and churches, and the religious schools they operate, are dependent upon the exemption of their property from taxes, and the deductibility of contributions made to them, for their very survival.[22] Most congregational rabbis of all denominations, even the more ardently separationist among them, agree that few synagogues could survive in today's economic climate without tax exempt status. As one rather astute commentator has so aptly noted: "A court decision holding tax exemptions for religious institutions unconstitutional under the establishment clause" would do for the churches and synagogues of America "what Henry VIII did for the monasteries of England."[23]

The issues of government support for Jewish day schools and tax exemptions for synagogues and churches are only two of many issues that have forced many liberal Jews to rethink and reassess how high the so-called "wall of separation" should be. Throughout the American Jewish community in recent years, there has been a growing recognition that the triumph of strict separationism as a legal doctrine, with its promise to expunge any and all religious symbols and teachings from the public arena, may actually infringe upon the free exercise of religion so cherished by American Jews. The 1986 U.S. Supreme Court decision in *Goldman v. Winberger* is illustrative of this tendency. For many religiously-devout Orthodox Jews, the wearing of a small cap or head covering, called a yarmulke, is a tenet of Jewish religious faith, and a matter of Jewish religious obligation. Hence, in this much-publicized case,[24] Simcha Goldman, an Orthodox Jew serving as a clinical psychologist in an Air Force hospital who normally wore a yarmulke at all times, contended that an Air Force dress-code regulation that forbade the wearing of headgear indoors, infringed upon his First Amendment right to the free exercise of his religious belief. Despite the fact that every major American Jewish organization filed legal briefs in support of Goldman's right to wear his yarmulke in public, the Supreme Court upheld the Air Force regulation, ruling that the military was not required to accommodate Captain Goldman's religious obligation. Implicit to the doctrine of church-state separation that the Court enforced in this case, is the assumption that religious symbols, such as the yarmulke, while appropriate for private religious devotion in home or synagogue have no legitimate place in any public institution, whether educational or military.

Also implicit to this doctrine of strict church-state separation is the assumption that any and all forms of school prayer, even the most innocuous and nonsectarian, are unconstitutional, a position shared by the vast majority of American Jews for many decades. Indeed, since the mid-nineteenth century, Jews had been united in their opposition to both prayer and Bible reading in the public schools. The development of the free public school system in antebellum America had coincided with the immigration to America of tens of thousands of German Jews, who had embraced the public school ideal, and who's children flocked to them in ever-increasing numbers. By the late nineteenth century, American Jews had become ardent supporters of public school education, enthusiastically embracing the opportunities and promise offered by a free, tax-supported school system open to all children, rich or poor, of all religious faiths.[25] Most, however, were also uncomfortable with the fact that since their inception during the three decades prior to the Civil War, public schools in most parts of the United States had been culturally Protestant, requiring Bible reading, and classroom prayers, as well as other devotional exercises. Jews who attended America's public schools in the late nineteenth and early twentieth century vividly recalled the "Christian ambiance" of the classroom, wherein the school day often began with compulsory morning religious exercises, including reading from the Protestant King James version of the Bible, the recitation of the Lord's Prayer, the singing of hymns and the celebration of Christian holidays such as Christmas and Easter. First Massachusetts, and then several other states, required Bible reading and school prayer by state law, on the principle that the public schools should not be "godless," secular institutions. Believing that religion and religious instruction should remain a private matter, the province of church or synagogue, Jewish leaders opposed these practices, advocating the ideal of "unsectarian," religiously-neutral public school education, while staunchly opposing any and all sectarianism in the schools. "It is our settled opinion here," said the prominent American Rabbi Isaac Mayer Wise in the late nineteenth century, "that the education of the young is the business of the State, and that religious instruction . . . is the duty of religious bodies. Neither ought to interfere with the other."[26] Over the years, as Lloyd P. Gartner has noted, Wise's "settled opinion" became a principle of Jewish communal ideology,[27] and as a result, a Jewish consensus emerged in opposition to prayer and other manifestations of religion in the schools that would last for a century, until the 1980s.

Thus, when the U.S. Supreme Court, in its historic *Engel v. Vitale* decision, outlawed state-composed school prayers in 1962, the vast majority of American Jewish leaders supported the Court's decision.[28] The prayer in question was a nondenominational one composed by the New York Board of Regents and actually approved by several rabbis, including Rabbi Menachem Schneerson, the Lubavitcher Rebbe, who argued that "it is necessary to engrave upon the child's mind the idea that any wrongdoing is an offence against divine authority and order,"[29] and who subsequently stated that it was the duty of all Jews "committed to the Torah" to work for the reversal of *Engel.*[30] Nonetheless, the overwhelming majority of American Jews applauded the Engel decision as "an affirmation of the position they had long espoused." So, too, American Jews, committed as they were to the strict separation of church and state, praised the Supreme Court's ruling prohibiting the recitation of the Lord's Prayer, in the public schools, the following year. And yet, today, the Jewish consensus in opposition to any and all forms of school prayer is not as solid as it once had been. Indeed, another issue that has forced some Jews, to rethink and reassess how high the so-called "wall of separation" should be is the very reasonable argument in favor of voluntary school prayer and, especially, a "moment of silence" for such voluntary prayer, long opposed by the organized Jewish community on strict separationist grounds. This is, of course, an issue that has been at the center of a great deal of public debate and discussion throughout the past decade and, especially, in recent months. In 1984, President Reagan supported a constitutional amendment to overturn the Supreme Court's *Engel v. Vitale* decision and to permit vocal prayer in public institutions, including schools. Although the amendment was supported by fifty six senators, it still fell eleven votes short of the two-thirds Senate majority needed for further consideration. Parenthetically, it's significant to note, the diversity of both the support for and the opposition against this proposed constitutional amendment indicated how such controversial church-state issues have, and continue to, split normal coalitions in American politics. Supporters of the proposed amendment included both liberals and conservatives (e.g. the liberal Senator William Proxmire of Wisconsin and Jesse Helms of North Carolina), Jews and Mormons (such as Senator Edward Zorinsky of Nebraska and the Mormon Orrin Hatch of Utah) and representatives of both the mainline and evangelical wings of Protestantism. In 1984, the forty-four Senate opponents of organized school prayers included some of the most conservative members of that body (such as Barry Goldwater of Arizona), the Senate's only clergyman (John Danforth of Missouri, an ordained Episcopal priest), and one of its most prominent evangelical spokesman (Mark Hatfield of Utah). More recently, the new Speaker of the House of Representatives, Georgia's Congressman, Newt Gingrich, called for a vote by July 4th, 1995 on a constitutional amendment that would restore some form of public school prayer and the previous November, President Bill Clinton stunned many Democrats when he suggested that a properly crafted measure might gain his support. Several states and the District of Columbia are also considering measures to restore some form of voluntary school prayer–especially non-sectarian student led prayer at school activities–and these measures are gaining some unanticipated Jewish support. While a majority of Jews still oppose vocal, organized school prayer, a growing number of American Jews now support voluntary, silent prayer. Many of these Jews find it difficult to understand why so many Jewish leaders and Jewish communal organizations persist in their long-standing position of opposition to any and all forms of school prayer, including voluntary, non-sectarian student-led prayer, silent meditation and "moments of silence" in the classroom. At lease some Jewish communal leaders and political figures have begun to publicly question this position, especially since the 1985 Supreme Court decision, in the case of *Wallace v. Jaffree*, that ruled, on strict separationist grounds, that an Alabama law authorizing one minute of daily silence "for meditation or voluntary prayer" was unconstitutional. Such a statue requires no one to pray, and establishes no official prayer. Many Jews agreed with the dissenting opinion of Justice Sandra Day O'Connor who said that "she could not discern a threat to religious liberty from a room of silent, thoughtful schoolchildren." Nor, contrary to what some Jewish leaders have suggested, does such a statute seem to be a subterfuge for the introduction of sectarian, Christological school prayers that Jewish children would find offensive. Rather, it seems to be an entirely reasonable attempt to accommodate the potential desire of students, Jewish and non-Jewish, for the free exercise of their religion in schools that they are compelled to attend. Many Jews–indeed, many Jewish communal leaders–now feel that "the passage of such a law permitting silent prayers would be an important gesture to affirm freedom of religious expression and to signal that it is okay to be religious if you desire."

One especially recent school prayer case, *Lee v. Weisman*, decided by the Supreme Court in 1992,[31] has forced a vocal minority of American Jews to rethink and reassess the once-traditional liberal Jewish consensus against any and all public school prayer, as well as the more general question of how high or "absolute" the "wall of separation" should be. The case arose in Providence, Rhode Island, where Middle and High School principals regularly invited members of the city's clergy to give invocation and benediction prayers as part of their school's graduation ceremonies. In June, 1989, Leslie Gutterman, the Rabbi of a Providence synagogue, delivered a nonsectarian prayer at the eighth-grade graduation of one of the city's middle schools, "praising God for the legacy of America where diversity is celebrated and the rights of minorities are protected" and for "its court system where all can seek justice." His prayer was challenged by Daniel Weisman and his daughter Deborah, a member of the middle school's graduating class, who sued the Providence School Board, arguing that Rabbi Gutterman's commencement benediction violated the Supreme Court's 1962 *(Engle v. Vitale)* ban on public school prayer. In a 5-4 decision, the Supreme Court agreed stating that graduation ceremony benedictions, such as Gutterman's, however innocuous and nonsectarian, were unconstitutional, and explaining that its ban on graduation prayers and benedictions in this case was a logical extension of three decades of court decisions (since *Engel*) regarding organized prayer in the public schools. Many Jewish leaders found the Supreme Court's decision, as well as the case itself, both ironic and puzzling. After all, Jewish opposition to school prayer had traditionally been predicated upon a concern about overtly Christological prayers, offered by Christian clergy, that Jewish children would be compelled to listen to and recite. It struck many American Jews as highly ironic that a Jewish family, such as the Weisman's, would go to court to stop a rabbi from delivering the most innocuous of nonsectarian prayers that could not possibly have offended any of the Jewish–or, for that matter, Christian–children in attendance. In what possible way, they asked, could such a nonsectarian prayer delivered by a rabbi, pose a threat to the religious freedom of American Jews?

Yet another controversial issue that has forced many Jews to rethink and reassess high how the "wall of separation" should be has revolved around the unbending efforts of liberal Jewish organizations to keep religious symbols, such as the creche and menorah, outside the public arena. Most liberal Jewish organizations had long opposed the public display of creches on government property, arguing that such displays amounted to an impermissible establishment of religion. And yet, while most of these liberal Jewish organizations opposed the Supreme Court's 1984 decision, in the controversial case of *Lynch v. Donnelly*, affirming the constitutional right of local municipalities to erect a creche or nativity scene as part of its annual Christmas celebrations, a vocal minority of Jews did not disapprove of Christmas displays on public property, and applauded this decision. They found nothing wrong or inappropriate about the public display of any religious symbols, Christian or Jewish. Their dissent from the prevailing liberal Jewish consensus opposing such public displays was encouraged, in part, by the vigorous campaign of the Chabad (Lubavitch) organization, an independent Orthodox Hasidic movement, begun in the late 1970s, to construct privately funded Chanukkah menorahs on public property in cities throughout the United States, which had precipitated a heated debate within the American Jewish community over whether it was constitutionally permissible and proper to do so. Recently, moreover, as part of the changing debate generated by the Supreme Court case *Allegheny County, City of Pittsburgh, and Chabad v. ACLU*,[32] the traditional opposition to the public display of religious symbols has been countered by a growing demand for "equal time" for the display of specifically Jewish religious symbols in the public square. This 1989 case, in which the Supreme Court ruled that a Chabad-sponsored menorah standing next to a Christmas tree in front of Pittsburgh's City Hall did not violate the First Amendment, forced many Jews to reexamine their earlier opposition to the placing of Chanukkah menorahs in front of a public building or within a public park. To be sure, many Jewish opponents of these displays continue to argue "the kindling of huge menorahs in public places across America opens a dangerous constitutional can of worms"[33] and that "since there is no religious need to place sacred symbols of any faith on public property" there is no religious need to be accommodated by government.

Other Jews, and a growing number in recent years, have made the argument that a compelling religious need does exist. Where religious symbols of differing faiths–e.g. the Chanukkah menorah and the Christmas tree–are displayed side by side, as in the *Allegheny* case, say these proponents, the government is not favoring one religion but rather is expressing equal respect for all religions. Promoting harmony amongst religious groups, they contend, is profoundly different from the "establishing" of one religion that the First Amendment seeks to protect us from. By giving a Jewish religious display "equal time" with a Christian one, Pittsburgh was showing the very neutrality with regard to all religions that the First Amendment was enacted to guarantee. Moreover, as Nathan Lewin, the attorney for Chabad in the *Allegheny* case, has argued, public displays of a menorah symbolize to all the fact "that America is a country where Jews are welcome and are first class citizens," and "engender emotions of pride and confidence among Jews who see them." Banishing menorahs from public places, he and other proponents of public menorah displays contend, would mean "derogating religion and denying to Jews the equal access to public forums that are available to secular organizations."[34]

Conclusion

No longer can it be said, as it could in the 1940s and 1950s, that American Jewry speaks with one "official" voice on the issues of religion and public life. To be sure, a number of American Jewish leaders remain wedded to a strict separationist position on most, if not all, issues concerning religion and state. But a growing, and increasingly vocal, minority of American Jews seem uncomfortable with at least some aspects of the strict separationist position. And several seem to share the post-separationist faith of Rabbi Walter Wurzberger, first espoused more than a decade ago,[35] and reiterated in a recently published essay, that in place of "excessive preoccupation with the Establishment Clause," greater attention should be given to the free exercise claims of religiously observant Jews and other religious believers within American society. Instead of "clamoring for an impenetrable wall of separation," argues Wurzberger, "we should concentrate upon protecting the Free Exercise Clause, thus insuring that unpopular religious practices, such as accommodating Sabbath observers and serving Kosher food in public institutions, will be safeguarded."[36]

A growing number of American Jews seem to have rejected the secular view that the interests of American Jews, and American Judaism, are best served by what Richard Neuhaus has called "the naked public square," one that is morally neutral and from which religious beliefs and values have been expunged. They think that religion has a legitimate place in American public life, that the Constitution does not embody what Supreme Court Justice Arthur Goldberg once described as " a brooding and pervasive devotion to the secular and a passive, or even active, hostility to the religious." Such views, though they cannot be said to represent a mainstream Jewish consensus, command greater intellectual force and weight than ever before.

Notes

1. On Pfeffer's career, achievements and legacy, see James E. Wood, Jr., ed., *Religion and the State: Essays in Honor of Leo Pfeffer* (Waco, TX: Baylor University Press, 1985); and David G. Dalin, "Leo Pfeffer and the Separationist Faith," *This World* (winter 1989): 136-140.

2. *Everson v. Board of Education of Ewing Township,* 330 U.S. 1, 15 (1947).

3. David G. Dalin, "Leo Pfeffer and the Separationist Faith," *This World* 24 (winter 1989): 136-137.

4. *McCollum v. Board of Education*, 333 U.S. 203 (1948). On the Jewish communal involvement with, and response to, the McCollum case, see Naomi W. Cohen, *Jews in Christian America: The Pursuit of Religious Equality* (New York: Oxford University Press, 1992), 140-147; and Gregg Ivers, *To Build a Wall: American Jews and the Separation of Church and State,* (Charlottesville: The University Press of Virginia, 1995), 70-86.

5. David G. Dalin, "Will Herberg in Retrospect," *Commentary* 86 (July 1988): 42.

6. Will Herberg, "The Sectarian Conflict Over Church and State: A Divisive Threat to Our Democracy?" *Commentary* (November 1952), reprinted in David G. Dalin, ed., *From Marxism to Judaism: The Collected Essays of Will Herberg* (New York: Markus Wiener Publishing, 1989), 209.

7. Dalin, "Will Herberg in Retrospect," 42.

8. Ibid.

9. Milton Himmelfarb, "Church and State: How High a Wall," *Commentary* 42 (July 1966), as reprinted in Milton Himmelfarb, *The Jews of Modernity* (New York: Basic Books, 1973), 169-171.

10. Jonathan D. Sarna, *American Jews and Church-State Relations: The Search for "Equal Footing"* (New York: American Jewish Committee, 1989), 27.

11. Ibid., 28.

12. Marshall's brief is reprinted in Charles Reznikoff, ed., *Louis Marshall: Champion of Liberty: Selected Papers and Addresses* (Philadelphia: The Jewish Publication Society of America, 1957), 2:957-967. The historical context of Marshall's involvement in this historic Supreme Court case is discussed in Morton Rosenstock, *Louis Marshall: Defender of Jewish Rights* (Detroit: Wayne State University Press, 1965), 211-213.

13. *Cochran v. Louisiana State Board of Education*, 281 U.S. 370, 375 (1930).

14. Sarna, *American Jews and Church-State Relations*, 28. On the Jewish organizational response to the *Everson* case, see also Naomi W. Cohen, *Jews in Christian America*, 139-140; and Gregg Ivers, *To Build a Wall*, 17-28.

15. Sarna, *American Jews and Church-State Relations*, 29.

16. Jonathan D. Sarna, "Christian America or Secular America? The Church-State Dilemma of American Jews," in Richard John Neuhaus, ed., *Jews in Unsecular America* (Grand Rapids, MI: William B. Eerdmans Publishing Company, 1987), 17-18.

17. David G. Dalin, ed., *American Jews and the Separationist Faith: The New Debate on Religion in Public Life* (Washington, D.C.: Ethics and Public Policy Center, 1992), 5.

18. Jonathan D. Sarna. *American Jews and Church-State Relations*, 29-30.

19. Seymour Siegel, "Church and State: A Reassessment," *Sh'ma* 1/3 (December 11, 1970).

20. On this point, see, for example Jacob Sullum, "Educational Choice for Parents: Vouchers Will Make More Jews," *Moment* (February 1994): 38-41; and the comments by Murray Friedman, a senior official of the American Jewish Committee, in his essay in David G. Dalin, ed., *American Jews and the Separationist Faith*, 51.

21. Bertram W. Korn, *American Jewry and the Civil War* (Philadelphia: The Jewish Publication Society of American, 1951), 56-97.

22. These points are developed in greater detail in my review essay, "Leo Pfeffer and the Separationist Faith," 136-140; On the issue of tax exemptions for churches and synagogues, and their clergy, generally, see also: Leo Pfeffer, "Religious Exemptions," in Thomas Robbins and Roland Robertson, eds., *Church-State Relations: Tensions and Transitions* (New Brunswick, NJ: Transaction Publishers, 1987), 103-108; Dean M. Kelly, *Why Churches Should Not Pay Taxes* (New York: Harper & Row, 1977); and Ronald B. Flowers, "Tax Exemptions and the Clergy: On Vows of Poverty and Parsonage Allowances," in James E. Wood, Jr., Religion and the State, 359-376.

23. George Goldbert, *Church, State and the Constitution: The Religion Clauses Upside Down* (Washington D.C.: Regnery Gateway, 1987), 79.

24. *Goldman v. Weinberger*, 106 S.Ct. 1310 (1986); for discussions of this celebrated case, see: Daniel D. Chazin, *Goldman v. Secretary of Defense: A New Standard for Free Exercise Claims in the Military*, 1 National Jewish Law Review 13-40 (1986); Martin Edelman, *Goldman v. Weinberger: Yarmulkes, The Supreme Court and the Free Exercise of Religion*, 8 The Jewish Law Annual 210-220; Michael W. McConnell, "Taking Religious Freedom Seriously," in Terry Eastland, ed., *Religious Liberty in the Supreme*

Court: The Cases That Define the Debate Over Church and State (Washington, D.C.: Ethics and Public Policy Center, 1993), 503-504; and Michael J. Sandel, *Democracy's Discontent: America in Search of a Public Philosophy* (Cambridge: Harvard University Press, 1996), 69.

25. On this general topic, see Lloyd P. Gartner, "Temples of Liberty Unpolluted: American Jews and Public Schools, 1840-1875," in Bertram W. Korn, ed., *A Bicentennial Festschrift for Jacob Rader Marcus* (New York: KTAV Publishing House, Inc., 1976), 157-189.

26. Sarna, *American Jews and Church-State Relations*, 19.

27. Gartner, "Temples of Liberty Unpolluted," 177.

28. *Engel v. Vitale* 370 U.S. 421 (1962). Leo Pfeffer's detailed discussion of the case can be found in Leo Pfeffer, "The New York Regents' Prayer Case," *Journal of Church and State* 4 (November 1962): 150-159; a thorough discussion and analysis of the Jewish reaction to, and communal debate over, the Supreme Court's decision in this case can be found in Naomi W. Cohen, *Jews in Christian America*, 171-186.

29. "Letter from the Lubavitcher Rabbi (1964)," quoted in Naomi W. Cohen, "Schools, Religion and Government–Recent American Jewish Opinions," *Michael* 3 (1975): 364.

30. Naomi W. Cohen, *Jews in Christian America*, 178.

31. *Lee v. Weisman*, 112 Sup. Ct. 2649 (1992); see, also Terry Eastland, ed., *Religious Liberty in the Supreme Court*, 439-467; Leonard W. Levy, *The Establishment Clause: Religion and the First Amendment*, 2d ed., rev. (Chapel Hill: The University of North Carolina Press, 1994), 200-204; and Samuel Rabinove, "Weisman's Complaint," *Reform Judaism* (fall 1991), reprinted by (and available from) the American Jewish Committee, of which Samuel Rabinove is the legal director.

32. *Allegheny County, City of Pittsburgh and Chabad v. ACLU*, 492 U.S. 573 (1989). The *Allegheny* case, and the general public debate it precipitated, are discussed in Leonard W. Levy, *The Establishment Clause*, 207-212; and Michael McGough, "Menorah Wars," *The New Republic*, 5 February 1990, 12-14.

33. Allan Nadler, "Lubavitchers Setting Fire to Wall of Separation," *The Jewish Week*, November 29-December 5, 1991, 28 and 47.

34. Nathan Lewin, "Making A Case For Menorahs on Public Property, *The Jewish Press*, 22 November 1991, 92.

35. Walter S. Wurzberger, "Separation of Church and State Revisited," *Face to Face* 8 (fall 1981): 8.

36. Walter S. Qurzberger essay in David G. Dalin, ed., *American Jews and the Separationist Faith*, 149.

Chapter 14

Affirmative Action and American Equality: A Constitutionalist Perspective

Herman Belz

Affirmative action is a method of enforcing legislation enacted in the 1960s to secure the goals of the twentieth century civil rights movement. Dealing with education, employment, voting rights, pubic accommodations, and government sponsored programs, the civil rights laws in general declared it unlawful to deny individuals equal access or opportunity or otherwise to discriminate against them because of race, color, national origin, religion, and sex. Thirty years after it was begun as a temporary expedient in civil rights enforcement, affirmative action has become a seemingly permanent feature of the American polity and a continuing source of public controversy. There are many factors involved in this public policy dispute, but the principal reason why affirmative action is controversial is that it requires employers, school officials and the countless organizations subject to the civil rights laws to base their policies and practices in decisive respects on racial, ethnic and sex considerations.

Affirmative action can be defined as government policies which, through compliance pressure on public and private employers and social organizations, directly or indirectly award jobs, admission to educational institutions, and a variety of social goods and resources to individuals on the basis of membership in designated protected groups. Several rationales are offered to justify preferential treatment for members of protected groups, including the need to remedy past discrimination against the designated groups, to correct their under representation in occupations, professions and social institutions, and to utilize their diverse talents and abilities to increase economic productivity.

The term "affirmative action" is of course rich with rhetorical potential and is used to mean different things by different people. Some critics of the policy assume that civil rights enforcement has categorically been subjected to the thrall of protected class quotas and proportional representation. Although it may be a slight exaggeration, Assistant Attorney General for Civil Rights Deval Patrick has a point when he complains that "Society's collective thinking on the meaning of opportunity seems to begin and end with the topic of affirmative action."[1] It is important to remember that a major focus of civil rights policy, particularly in the fields of fair housing and public accommodations, continues to be the guarantee of equal opportunity for individuals irrespective of race, sex, and ethnicity and other proscribed factors. At the same time, on the other side of the debate some defenders of affirmative action, while conceding that the policy may appear to give preference to protected groups, insist that in reality it is nothing more than a means of enforcing equal opportunity for individuals. This description is as misleading as the reductionist attack which equates civil rights policy with affirmative action.

The purpose of this essay is to offer an historical account of the origin and development of affirmative action as the basis for an evaluation of it from a constitutionalist perspective. There is need to do so in part because affirmative action has proved curiously resistant to constitutional analysis. Developed almost wholly by administrative agencies and courts, as public policy it has a substantially legislative basis that places it in the area of statutory interpretation and enforcement, in contrast to that of constitutional interpretation. Even after the revolutionary expansion of judicial review in the twentieth century, it is still the case today that most legislation is presumed to be constitutional. This is especially true of legislation based on the commerce, taxing and spending powers of Congress, which since the New Deal have been broadly applied for social regulatory purposes. Many of the civil rights laws that are used to sustain affirmative action are based on these federal police powers, far more than on what might appear to be more logical sources of authority such as the equal protection clause of the Fourteenth Amendment. Accordingly there are valid considerations in constitutional law, apart from the politically controversial nature of the subject, which explain why the Supreme Court has on relatively few occasions considered affirmative action in a constitutional context.

I believe this reticence is misplaced and that affirmative action warrants closer examination from the perspective of constitutionalism. In the first place, affirmative action has a direct bearing on the meaning of equality, a fundamental constitutional principle. If equality was not implicit in the original Constitution, in the sense that the new national government was intended to embody and apply the principles of the Declaration of Independence, it was expressly written into the Constitution in the

Reconstruction amendments. In order to apply the Constitution, therefore, it is necessary to know what the equality principle requires. If equality as defined in affirmative action programs is found to be consistent with constitutional equality, the legitimacy as well as legality of the policy are confirmed. If affirmative action contradicts or is inconsistent with the requirements of constitutional equality, the policy requires revision and reform, if the Constitution is to be an effective restraint and source of legitimate authority in political life.

It is furthermore important to consider affirmative action in constitutional perspective because, as a major element in civil rights policy, it has the potential to define the nature and tendency of the American polity in the foreseeable future. Many issues converge in the affirmative action controversy, but the most critical in my view is whether the United States as a political community will preserve–or should we say restore–limited government and guarantees of individual liberty and property rights as essential features of American constitutionalism. The alternative development, which affirmative action encourages, is to proceed further toward the establishment of a centralized state dedicated to the redistribution of wealth and the regulation of individual liberty and property rights in the name of social welfare, justice and security.

The history of affirmative action suggests a distinct tendency in the direction of statist centralization. The logic of the welfare state requires a legal theory and public policy rationale under which persons can be dealt with categorically, as members of legally defined classes in which they are considered fungible for purposes of advancing the interests of class, rather than individually according to their distinctive attributes and abilities. The theory of the regulatory welfare state rejects the idea that property and wealth can and should be continually distributed by recognizing the right of individuals to make contracts and pursue their interests in the free market. Either through deliberate design or as the result of contingent historical events, affirmative action has redefined the meaning of equality to serve the ends of the egalitarian-redistributivist project.

Constitutionalism

The horizon of constitutionalism on which our analysis proceeds can be briefly described. Constitutionalism is a way of political life in which a people constitute themselves as a community, conducting their affairs in accordance with fundamental principles and through prescribed forms, procedures and primary rules of obligation, in order to achieve the ends and purposes that define their corporate existence. In the western political tradition, constitutionalism both ancient and modern has generally aimed at securing the goods of virtue, reason, justice, liberty, property, equality and order, through a process of constituting government power that also defines and limits that power. Although the act of making or constituting a thing logically requires and is unintelligible without definition and limitation, in the contingent world of historical experience the theoretical unity or integrity of this action becomes problematic, appearing as a practical dichotomy. There is an inevitable tension between making a government and imposing limits on a government. It is difficult to balance these requirements, and the attempt to do so is always subject to political judgment and criticism. Accordingly, the practice of governments in the western political tradition can be described as tending either toward an energetic, activist type of constitutionalism that emphasizes the positive exercise of power to achieve the ends of the polity, or toward a limited and constrained constitutionalism that permits greater scope for decision making by individuals, local communities and private associations.

The American regime was founded as a liberal republican confederation in which communities of virtuous and acquisitive individuals govern themselves under the natural rights principles expressed in the Declaration of Independence. Properly speaking the end of the regime is civil liberty, consisting of the rights to liberty, equality, consent, and the pursuit of happiness to which individuals are entitled by their human nature. From the Revolution until well into the twentieth century the Declaration, the Articles of Confederation, the Constitution, and the Bill of Rights were viewed as constituting a normative civil rights tradition against which social and political institutions and practices could be measured. This idea was central to both the nineteenth century antislavery movement and the twentieth century civil rights movement. It provided the theoretical framework for Gunnar Myrdal's famous study of race relations, *An American Dilemma* (1944), which signaled the emergence of civil rights as a political issue in the postwar period. In this epochal work, Myrdal criticized white Americans for their failure to apply the American creed of liberty and equality to the country's Negro population.

Whether a morally authoritative civil rights tradition based on the nation's constitutional foundations can still be relied on is a central issue in the affirmative action controversy. Those who question the founders' moral authority view their assertion of universal natural rights as a hypocritical exercise contradicted by their tolerance of racist, sexist and elitist institutions. Justice Thurgood Marshall spoke to this point in his 1987 Bicentennial speech cautioning against uncritical acceptance of the framers' ideas of liberty and equality. Justice Marshall appealed to the Civil War and Reconstruction amendments as the source of more timely conceptions of civil rights and equal opportunity relevant to the needs of twentieth century Americans.

Justice Marshall, who as a civil rights lawyer argued for a color-blind Constitution in the school desegregation case of 1954, made the transition to the race-conscious Constitution of affirmative action. In the *Bakke* case, in which the Supreme Court first considered an explicit quota policy on constitutional grounds, he claimed that the constitutional settlement arrived at in the Fourteenth Amendment permitted race-based preferential programs, as in the Freedmen's Bureau Act. Weighing against this conclusion is the fact that the authors of the Freedmen's Bureau Act were careful to include "refugees"–that is, dislocated white southerners–as beneficiaries of the temporary relief that the statute provided for, along with the emancipated slaves.

The equal rights policy of the Reconstruction amendments and civil rights statutes was not an empty and automatic gesture designed to achieve token conformity with national ideals while obscuring entrenched patterns of racial discrimination. Alternative measures were considered and rejected. The policy proposed by the Democratic party would have established a system of legal restrictions and qualifications based on color that consigned blacks to an intermediate status between slavery and freedom. Another approach, recommended by abolitionists and radical Republicans, was to define blacks as a dependent class requiring supervision and tutelage before being integrated into the community as equal citizens. Benign paternalism, however, was no more acceptable to mainstream Republican opinion than the invidious racial classification desired by southerners and their Democratic allies. Congress therefore rejected both of these race-conscious schemes. And it was supported by the black leaders of the day, who demanded that the freed people be recognized as American citizens entitled to equal civil and political rights, and the chance to earn their way in society on the basis of their own initiative and self-reliance.

Employing the typology used by political scientist Richard Ellis, we may say that postemancipation civil rights policy was based on a competitive individualist conception of equality, in contrast to the egalitarian communitarian conception proposed by abolitionists and radical Republicans, referred to above as "benign paternalism."[2] These rival theories of equality are pertinent to an understanding of twentieth century American constitutionalism and the ideological context in which affirmative action developed in the 1960s.

In the American regime individuals, not social groups or classes, have constitutional and legal rights. Individuals are members of communities that can have either a legal-territorial existence under the federal principle, or a socio-cultural identity as private voluntary associations organized for religious, philanthropic, commercial or other purposes. In the increasingly pluralistic society of nineteenth century America, an individualistic interpretation of equality emphasized equal opportunity in a procedural sense, while an egalitarian communitarian interpretation stressed substantive equality of socio-economic condition. Despite the seemingly obvious theoretical contradiction presented in this typology, fundamental political and ideological conflict could be avoided because both individualists and egalitarians believed that process-based equality of opportunity, in the forms and institutions of common law liberty and property rights, was the best way to achieve substantive equality of condition. Across what to a twentieth century observer appears a deep ideological divide, both points of view accepted the market as a liberating and equalizing system of social regulation and opposed government interference in its operation.

This consensus, which Richard Ellis terms "the exceptionalist alliance of individualism and egalitarianism, equal process and equal results," broke down in the twentieth century.[3] It was first rejected by Populist and Progressive reformers who concluded that the free market of laissez faire constitutionalism no longer served the ends of republican liberty, social equality and economic justice. Subsequent liberal reform movements in the twentieth century demanded government intervention either to restore self-regulating market mechanisms (the liberal interpretation of progressive reform), or to replace those mechanisms and establish a bureaucratic regime based on administrative discretion in which the government would determine standards of social and economic justice (the conservative interpretation of progressive reform).

The central rationale of New Deal constitutionalism was to restrict property rights and redistribute wealth in order to equalize the material conditions on which liberty and equality were thought to depend in industrial society. This redefinition of liberal ideals rested on four propositions: property rights are subordinate to civil rights; private property is a public resource; people are the victims of the organizational structures and institutional processes of industrial society; and individuals are not responsible for themselves, but society is.[4] Liberty, reconceived in terms of social security and welfare, commanded more attention in New Deal liberalism than equality of civil rights. Indeed, as long as the New Deal coalition was beholden to the southern wing of the Democratic party it could make no general appeal to the color-blind conception of equality intended by the authors of the Reconstruction amendments. In the two decades following World War II, however, as the result of a continuing process of social change, partisan political competition, and civil rights litigation by black organizations, civil rights gradually became a national issue. A decade after the Supreme Court declared school segregation unconstitutional in *Brown v. Board of Education* in 1954, these liberalizing forces culminated in the adoption of the Civil Rights Act of 1964. With the end of legal racism, resolution of the American dilemma seemed imminent.

Equality Transformed

Paradoxically and ironically, race-conscious affirmative action began immediately after the enactment of this historic law establishing the nondiscrimination principle as the basis of national civil rights policy. Although a full account of this remarkable development is beyond the scope of the present inquiry, the decisive steps in the transformation of equality that occurred can be described.

In the context of the regulatory interventionism that characterized the liberal reformism of the 1960s, the Civil Rights Act of 1964 was an anomaly. To be sure, the statute was an exercise of federal legislative authority under the commerce clause aimed at bringing the private labor market under government regulation. The purpose of the regulation, however, according to the supporters of the act, was to stimulate economic productivity and market forces by removing barriers that denied blacks and members of other minority groups equality of opportunity to compete. It was as though race relations, so long sidetracked in a kind of historical time warp as a result of racial prejudice and the structure of American politics, could only be dealt with by recurring to legal postulates from the constitutionalism of an earlier era. The Civil Rights Act thus embodied a conception of civil rights and a theory of limited government and the rule of law that harked back to the otherwise discredited public philosophy of laissez faire constitutionalism.

The Act conferred a private, individual right not to be discriminated against in private employment, public accommodations, and federally funded activities because of race, color, national origin, religion, or sex. Directed against both state action and private conduct, the act sought to remove formal barriers to social and economic freedom, guaranteeing equality of opportunity in a procedural sense. In legal terms it prohibited disparate treatment of individuals. Departing from the New Deal model of government regulation by administrative enforcement of an abstract public right, the Civil Rights Act identified a limited legal objective–application of the rule of nondiscrimination–and conferred limited enforcement authority on the federal judiciary. The administrative agency created by the act, the Equal Employment Opportunity Commission, was given no law enforcement authority, but simply the power to conciliate disputes between employer and employee over discrimination charges. From a constitutionalist perspective, the act was consistent with the rule of law defined as general, abstract, and prospective rules that fix the indivisible border line within which each individual may obtain a secure and free sphere.[5]

The Civil Rights Act was interpreted, however, according to an entirely different constitutional calculus, under the command theory of law and the ideological vision of equality of condition or result. The command theory of law, known also as legal instrumentalism, provides the legal sinews of the modern administrative state. It holds that law is a command or order that singles out and confers on particular persons or groups special rights and duties. The rational basis of law in this view is presumed to be scientific knowledge possessed by the lawmaker (in the regulatory state typically a judge or administrator) concerning the requirements of social justice and equality for particular persons or groups. In the interventionist state, command-based policies resting on class legislation are by definition designed to discriminate or differentiate between social groups. Under the egalitarian imperative the government is not content to treat people with different interests and abilities equally, as the rule of procedural equal opportunity requires, for to do so leads to inequality of results. It is necessary therefore to determine the material position of particular groups in order to enforce what is perceived to be a just–and politically desirable–distribution of goods and resources.

Title VII of the Civil Rights Act of 1964, the legal matrix of affirmative action, was transformed into a statute aimed at equality of condition for designated protected groups. This development occurred through a complex process of litigation and administrative rule making that was effectively insulated from public scrutiny. In legal terms, the Civil Rights Act was applied retrospectively for the benefit of particular groups, rather than prospectively to protect the rights of all individuals without regard to race, ethnicity and sex. Title VII employment benefits were initially conferred as a remedy for identifiable acts of past discrimination against individuals. The purpose of the relief was to make the individual plaintiff "whole," placing him in the position he would have occupied but for the discriminatory treatment. Subsequently the type of injury claimed as justification of race-conscious remedial awards was broadened to cover societal and institutional discrimination. Affirmative action became a policy of preferential treatment for members of protected classes who had not themselves been discriminated against, at the expense of persons who themselves were not guilty of discriminatory practices but were members of a group to which past discrimination was attributed in categorical terms.

In order to provide a legal rationale for this new approach to civil rights enforcement, as well as a compliance instrument to force changes in employer practices, a new concept of discrimination was devised. Previously, from the time of the Reconstruction amendments, unlawful discrimination because of race referred to intentional unequal treatment of an individual, or injury or denial of an individual's rights motivated by racial bias and prejudice. Now, however, unlawful discrimination was conceived to mean business or organizational practices, intended to promote productivity, efficiency, safety or other organizational ends, that had a statistically disproportionate or disparate impact on designated protected classes. In this legal scenario, if the practices used by an employer to select and promote a qualified work force had the effect of excluding members of protected groups disproportionately to their percentage of the relevant labor market or local community population, those practices were held to be prima facie unlawful. The burden of proof was then placed on the employer to show that the practices in question were necessary for business purposes.

In disparate treatment discrimination law suits, the person charging discrimination had to prove that the defendant-employer acted unlawfully with discriminatory intent. In disparate impact litigation statistical disparity or racial imbalance was in effect held to be wrong per se, irrespective of intent, and the employer had to prove it had not discriminated "because of race." Predictably enough, employers' rational response to the possibility of discrimination charges based on racial and ethnic group imbalance was to hire and promote people on the basis of race and ethnicity, in order to have a satisfactory numerical balance and avoid legal liability under the civil rights laws.

The development of affirmative action group remedies under the disparate impact theory of discrimination obscured, but did not render legally irrelevant, the older disparate treatment concept of discrimination. In many fact situations either concept of discrimination could be used, depending on which offered greater tactical advantage to the complaining party. Moreover in housing, public accommodations, and commercial relations governed by the rules for making and enforcing contracts, the disparate treatment concept was more appropriate. In these areas intentional discrimination motivated by racial and ethnic animus is still an obstacle to the equal enjoyment of individual rights. Nevertheless, from the standpoint of creating a "civil rights society" conforming to the egalitarian vision of distributive justice, the disparate impact theory of discrimination is more significant.[6] Its practical importance is evident in the fact that, after the Supreme Court in a series of decisions in the late 1980s tried to restore the disparate treatment concept as a unified theoretical framework for civil rights enforcement, Congress wrote the disparate impact concept into the Civil Rights Act of 1991.[7]

A decade ago Harvey C. Mansfield wrote that "affirmative action is settling down in our constitutional polity like a determined guest seeking squatter's rights."[8] Because civil rights advocates had so long appealed to the ideal of a color-blind Constitution, the policy of race-conscious affirmative action seemed anomalous and had to be justified as a remedial measure of temporary duration. Courts insisted that affirmative action plans be "narrowly tailored" to avoid "undue trammeling" of the rights of innocent individuals belonging to unprotected groups. This was reason enough, apart from the perception of disingenuous bureaucratic coercion that required companies to adopt "voluntary" quotas and preferences, why, in Mansfield's image, affirmative action has not been welcomed with open arms into the constitutional community.

In recent years affirmative action has been justified under rationales that reflect a more benign and optimistic view of race, ethnicity and sex as reasonable standards of public policy classification. Race-conscious measures have been upheld as a means of correcting for the underrepresentation of protected groups. This justification defines equality in statistically proportional terms based on the group's percentage of the relevant population universe. It assumes that in the absence of discrimination, every protected class will be represented in every occupational category and sector of society in proportion to its percentage of the population.

Another rationale for affirmative action is "diversity." This idea was introduced into the affirmative action debate by Justice Lewis Powell in the *Bakke* case in 1978. Powell was concerned to justify and put a better face on race-conscious decision making than was possible through the use of absolute racial and ethnic quotas. The assumption underlying the diversity rationale is that each racial or ethnic group has distinctive skills, attitudes and traits to contribute to the productivity of public and private organizations. Diversity considerations were controlling in the Supreme Court's approval, in *Metro Broadcasting Inc. v. F.C.C.* (1990), of government regulations awarding a type of radio license exclusively to minority firms. This approach to civil rights enforcement is starkly illustrated in the recent New Jersey teacher lay-off case (*Taxman v. Piscataway*), in which a white teacher was fired–without regard to experience, qualifications or any nonracial standard of selection including a flip of the coin–in order to retain a black teacher for the sake of diversity. Explaining the federal government's support of this approach to equal employment opportunity, a Department of Justice official said: "We don't see the law as limiting affirmative action to remedial contexts."

Affirmative Action in Constitutional Perspective

In concluding this review of affirmative action in constitutional perspective, it is important to recognize that affirmative action is only one of several policies in the area of civil rights that attempt to improve the quality of life of socially disadvantaged individuals and groups. The nondiscrimination principle continues to be an effective enforcement tool in guaranteeing equal access to housing and public accommodations. Programs to assist the economically disadvantaged also form part of civil rights strategy broadly conceived in relation to issues of economic redistribution. Although government assistance programs do not operate on an explicitly racial or ethnic basis, they acquire such a dimension to the extent that they disproportionately serve the needs of minority groups. Affirmative action is nevertheless the most controversial and constitutionally significant branch of civil rights policy.

In the perspective of American constitutionalism, affirmative action veers off in a sharply different direction from the course marked out by the Reconstruction amendments. While addressing the situation of the emancipated slaves, those amendments maintained the racially impartial individual rights outlook of the original Constitution. In contrast, the logic of affirmative action defines equality as a status assigned to individuals as members of a group. Identification with the group qualifies and conditions the rights and opportunities available to individuals. This approach to civil rights denies the ideal of a common republican citizenship consisting of the natural rights of individuals.

Far from resolving the old American dilemma of a gap between the promise of American ideals and the performance of American institutions, the theory of affirmation action identifies a new American dilemma. In this view the basic American values of individualism, self-reliance, and majoritarian democracy are seen to be inherently and irredeemably racist.[9] Proponents of this interpretation contend that the basic American value system, if it is permitted to continue, will categorically preclude the redistribution of wealth and power that is necessary to give protected classes "background equality of opportunity" in a socio-economic sense. Affirmative action therefore requires what can euphemistically be described as the transcending of liberal democratic constitutionalism. In practical terms, it means looking to judicial and administrative elites who can make the tough decisions needed to rectify economic and cultural inequalities and bring about real equality.[10]

The significant role played by judges and administrators in adopting race-conscious measures outside the forum of democratic deliberation in the 1960s provides ground for questioning the constitutional legitimacy of affirmative action. This conclusion emerges as a plausible interpretation of the political and legal events which gave rise to affirmative action in the critical period 1965 to 1972.[11] In my own research, testimony supporting this critical judgement came from a Justice Department civil rights lawyer, active in employment litigation at the time, who told me that affirmative action could never have won majority approval in Congress if it had been presented in the form of a positive proposal for racial and ethnic group preferences.[12]

In support of affirmative action, it is argued that the refusal of Congress to reverse or modify judicial orders and administrative regulations establishing the policy over a twenty year period is tantamount to positive legislative approval signifying constitutional legitimacy. Eventually Congress passed statutes requiring a certain percentage of public contracts in highway construction and other specific areas to be awarded to minority group enterprises. And in the Civil Rights Act of 1991 Congress adopted the disparate impact concept of discrimination, finally giving statutory sanction to the legal rationale on which group preferential employment practices are based. The 1991 law can thus be seen as reflecting a political and constitutional consensus confirming the legitimacy of the group-rights concept of equality.[13]

The Civil Rights Act of 1991 may in time become the organic statute of the civil rights society that its proponents intended, consolidating and reforming affirmative action policy for the long haul. It is possible, however, that the politics of civil rights in the 1990s will be less receptive to the egalitarian vision of regulatory interventionism in which affirmative action has been nurtured in the past thirty years.[14] In any event, as things now stand the enforcement of the civil rights laws rests on two fundamentally conflicting concepts of discrimination, the disparate treatment and disparate impact models. Each of these strategic models in turn is derived from a basic conception of equality, procedural equality of opportunity and substantive equality of result. If it is reasonable to assume that a well ordered polity rests on consensus about fundamental values, it would seem essential for Americans to arrive at a more unified understanding of equality, one of the fundamental principles on which the regime was founded.

Over the long course of its development Anglo-American constitutionalism has emphasized the need for strong and effective government under the discipline of the rule of law. The purpose of our constitutionalism, broadly conceived, has been to protect the civil liberty of individuals within a general framework of concern for the common good. In American constitutional history the balance between individual liberty and government regulation has fluctuated. Even in the era of the interventionist regulatory state, however, the basic distinction between public and private action has been maintained. It is still the case today that legal regulation by government generally takes the form of general prohibitions on harmful or injurious conduct, leaving individuals otherwise free to pursue their interests. This is the sense in which the restraints of the rule of law establish "negative liberty" as a sphere of personal autonomy and an essential criterion of constitutional government.

The political ethos of affirmative action challenges this conception of limited constitutional government. In employment relations, the area where it has been carried farthest, affirmative action goes beyond the requirements of the nondiscrimination principle and places an affirmative duty on business organizations to conform their practices to government mandates. Private employment becomes a public utility, and ostensibly private conduct an extension of the state's affirmative responsibility to guarantee the social welfare and material security of its citizens. This development is the consequence of the erosion in the past thirty years of the distinction between state action and private conduct, a constitutional principle which from the end of Reconstruction to the mid-twentieth century was a major obstacle to national protection of civil rights.

When the barrier between state and private action is removed, the national government is free to assume responsibility for the private actions of its citizens. In principle this vast expansion of authority and responsibility is signified by the decision, in all aspects of social and public life, to prohibit or permit the actions and activities that individuals wish to engage in. The next logical step, after the government imposes affirmative duties on business organizations and other associations formerly regarded as private, is for the government itself to assume an affirmative duty to enforce affirmative rights directly rather than indirectly.[15] All across the policy spectrum, in health care, employment, environmental protection, housing, social services, and in yet to be discovered problem areas, the government would assume the responsibility of conferring on individuals the positive capacity to exercise their rights. In the theory of the regulatory welfare state, this is referred to as "positive liberty." Affirmative action is a theoretical and practical experiment in applying this method of governance in the far-reaching sphere of equality.

Can such an ambitious and total project in affirmative government possibly succeed? Does not human nature, not to speak of contingency and necessity in the world in which human beings act, impose limits on government? Philosophical considerations aside, politics in the United States and the western industrialized world in the twenty-first century will provide practical answers to these questions. The collapse of collectivist egalitarian regimes in Europe and Asia in the past decade is perhaps an indication of future political and governmental trends.

In the American context it is nevertheless likely that further efforts will be made to extend the egalitarian project of social redistribution and human reconstruction. If the attempt is successful, it will end constitutional government as we have known it. If the egalitarian project fails, it will be the task of a responsible constitutionalism to apply the principles of limited government to the changing environment of postindustrial society. In that case the experience of affirmative action will perhaps be seen as evidence that equality is not an utterly protean and socially constructed concept. Rather, the principle of equality has objective limits established by reason and nature, and a meaning and significance in American constitutionalism that requires recognition of the rights which individuals possess by reason of their common human nature.

Notes

1. Remarks by Deval L. Patrick, Assistant Attorney General, Civil Rights Division, United States Department of Justice, Before the Town Hall, Los Angeles, California, October 4, 1994, 5.

2. Richard J. Ellis, *American Political Cultures* (New York: Oxford University Press, 1993), 1-27.

3. Ibid., 52.

4. Theodore J. Lowi, "The Welfare State: Ethical Foundations and Constitutional Remedies," *Political Science Quarterly* 100 (1985): 197-220.

5. F. A. Hayek, *The Constitution of Liberty* (Chicago: University of Chicago Press, 1960), 148.

6. Karen Bumiller, *The Civil Rights Society: The Social Construction of Victims* (Baltimore: Johns Hopkins University Press, 1988).

7. Herman Belz, *Civil Rights: Forcing Congress to Clarify the Law*, The Public Interest Law Review 59 (1993).

8. Harvey C. Mansfield, Jr., "The Underhandedness of Affirmative Action," *National Review*, 4 May 1984, 30.

9. Jennifer Hochschild, *The New American Dilemma: Liberal Democracy and School Segregation* (New Haven: Yale University Press, 1984).

10. Cheryl I. Harris, *Whiteness As Property*, 106 Harvard Law Review 1709 (1993).

11. Hugh Davis Graham, *The Civil Rights Ear* (New York: Oxford University Press, 1990); Herman Belz, *Equality Transformed: A Quarter Century of Affirmative Action* (New Brunswick, NJ: Transaction Publishers, 1991).

12. David Rose, U. S. Department of Justice interviewed by author, July 1983.

13. Robert A. Sedler, *Employment Equality, Affirmative Action, and the Constitutional Political Consensus*, 90 Michigan Law Review 1315 (1992).

14. Paul M. Sniderman and Thomas Piazza, *The Scar of Race* (Cambridge: Belknap Press, 1993). The election of a Republican majority in Congress in 1994 proved the occasion for legislative proposals to reform affirmative action in government contracting, federal employment, and federally conducted programs and activities. Several judicial decisions meanwhile restricted the scope of affirmative action. In *Adarand Contractors v. Pena* (1995) the Supreme Court required federal affirmative action programs to be subjected to strict scrutiny judicial review, making it harder to justify preferential measures. In *Hopwood v. Texas* (1996) the Fifth Circuit Court of Appeals invalidated a state law school's affirmative action admission policy as a violation of the equal protection clause of the Fourteenth Amendment. In *Podberesky v. Kirwan* (1994) the Fourth Circuit Court of Appeals struck down a University of Maryland program that awarded scholarships exclusively to African-American students.

15. Richard S. Kay, "The State Action Doctrine, the Public-Private Distinction, and the Independence of Constitutional Law," *Constitutional Commentary* 10 (1993): 329-360.

About the Editors

Kenneth L. Grasso is Associate Professor of Political Science at Southwest Texas State University. He is the co-editor of *John Courtney Murray and the American Civil Conversation* (1992) and *Catholicism, Liberalism and Communitarianism: The Catholic Intellectual Tradition and the Moral Foundations of Democracy* (1995).

Cecilia Rodriguez Castillo is Assistant Professor of Political Science at Southwest Texas State University. She is the author of articles and reviews appearing in *Minerva*, *The Journal of Politics*, and *The Journal of Texas Catholic History and Culture*.

About the Contributors

Herman Belz is Professor of History at the University of Maryland at College Park. A past recipient of the Albert J. Beveridge Prize of the American Historical Association, his books include *The American Constitution: Its Origin and Development* (7th ed., 1991), *Equality Transformed: A Quarter Century of Affirmative Action* (1991), and *Emancipation and Equal Rights: Politics and Constitutionalism in the Civil War Era* (1978).

Randall W. Bland is Professor Emeritus of Political Science at Southwest Texas State University. His books include *Private Pressure On Public Law: The Legal Career of Justice Thurgood Marshall* (2d revised ed., 1993) and *Constitutional Law in the United States* (1992).

Gerard V. Bradley is Professor of Law at Notre Dame Law School. The co-editor of *The American Journal of Jurisprudence*, he is the author of *Church-State Relationships in America (1982).*

Francis Canavan, S. J., is Professor Emeritus of Political Science at Fordham University. His books include *Freedom of Expression: Purpose As Limit* (1984), *The Political Economy of Edmund Burke* (1995) and *The Pluralist Game: Religion, Liberalism and the Moral Conscience* (1995).

David G. Dalin, an ordained rabbi and Associate Professor of American Jewish History at the University of Hartford, is currently a Bradley Fellow at the Heritage Foundation. The editor of *American Jews and the Separationist Faith: The New Debate on Religion in Public Life* (1992), his *Religion and State in the American*

Jewish Experience (co-authored with Jonathan Sarna) will be published by the University of Notre Dame Press in 1997.

Jean Bethke Elshtain is currently Laura Spelman Rockefeller Professor of Social and Political Ethics at the University of Chicago. The author of the widely acclaimed *Public Man, Private Woman* (1981), her most recent books are *Democracy on Trial* (1994) and *Augustine and the Limits of Politics* (1995).

Robert Booth Fowler is Professor of Political Science at the University of Wisconsin at Madison. His books include *Unconventional Partners: Religion and Liberal Culture in the United States* (1989), *The Dance With Community: The Contemporary Debate in American Political Thought* (1994) and *Religion and Politics in America: Faith, Culture and Strategic Choices* (1996).

William Gangi is Professor of Government and Politics at St. John's University (Jamaica, New York). A widely published scholar in the field of constitutional law, he is the author of *Saving the Constitution From the Courts* (1995).

Sanford Levinson holds the W. St. John Garwood and W. St. John Garwood, Jr., Centennial Chair in Law at the University of Texas School of Law. The author of *Constitutional Faith* (1988), he is the co-editor of *Responding to Imperfection: The Theory and Practice of Constitutional Amendment* (1995).

Thomas L. Pangle is Professor of Political Science and Fellow of St. Michael's College at the University of Toronto. His books include *The Ennobling of Democracy: The Challenge of the Postmodern Era* (1992) and *The Spirit of Modern Republicanism: The Moral Vision of the American Founders and the Philosophy of John Locke* (1988).

Robert Scigliano is Professor of Political Science at Boston College. His books include *The Supreme Court and the Presidency* (1970).

Robert J. Spitzer is Professor of Political Science at the State University of New York, College at Cortland. His books include *The Presidential Veto* (1988) and *President and Congress* (1993).

George Weigel is currently senior fellow at the Ethics and Public Policy Center. One of America's most respected public intellectuals, his recent books include *Freedom and Its Discontents* (1991) and *Idealism Without Illusions: U.S. Foreign Policy in the 1990s* (1994).

Thomas G. West is a senior fellow at the Claremont Institute and Professor of Politics at the University of Dallas. His book *Vindicating the Founders: Race, Sex, Poverty and Justice in the Origins of America* is forthcoming from Rowman and Littlefield.

Christopher Wolfe is Professor of Political Science at Marquette University and President of the American Public Philosophy Institute. The author of the widely acclaimed *The Rise of Modern Judicial Review*, his most recent book is *How to Read the Constitution* (1996).